*Praise for this title:*

Patricia Meyer Spacks's *Reading Eighteenth-Century Poetry* will be of great help to both beginning and advanced students of the subject. Spacks clarifies without oversimplifying, deftly supplies background when needed, but consistently keeps the poetry in the foreground.

Her strategy of dividing the century into thirds allows selective close-ups and revealing comparisons, as in chapters on Pope and Lady Mary and, surprisingly, William Cowper and Mary Robinson. Concentrating on the shifting ethics of "how to live," the varying ranges of feeling, and the evolving poetic diction of the early, middle, and late century, Spacks persuasively demonstrates just "how far from univocal" eighteenth-century poetry is.

Spacks has been guiding us through eighteenth-century novels and poems for more than forty years. Twenty-first-century readers of *Reading Eighteenth-Century Poetry* will benefit from the erudition of a lifetime everywhere alert to the full life of its subject.

**John Sitter, University of Notre Dame**

## Reading Poetry

The books in this series include close readings of well known and less familiar poems, many of which can be found in the Blackwell Annotated Anthologies. Each volume provides students and interested faculty with the opportunity to discover and explore the poetry of a given period, through the eyes of an expert scholar in the field.

The series is motivated by an increasing reluctance to study poetry amongst undergraduate students, born out of feelings of alienation from the genre, and even intimidation. By enlisting the pedagogical expertise of the most esteemed critics in the field, the volumes in the *Reading Poetry* series aim to make poetry accessible to a diversity of readers.

**Published:**

| | |
|---|---|
| *Reading Eighteenth-Century Poetry* | Patricia Meyer Spacks, Boston University |

**Forthcoming:**

| | |
|---|---|
| *Reading Sixteenth-Century Poetry* | Patrick Cheney, Penn State University |
| *Reading Romantic Poetry* | Fiona Stafford, Oxford University |
| *Reading Victorian Poetry* | Richard Cronin, Glasgow University |
| *Reading Modernist Poetry* | Michael Whitworth, Oxford University |

# Reading eighteenth-century poetry

Patricia Meyer Spacks

**WILEY-BLACKWELL**

A John Wiley & Sons, Ltd., Publication

This edition first published 2009
© 2009 Patricia Meyer Spacks

Blackwell Publishing was acquired by John Wiley & Sons in February 2007.
Blackwell's publishing program has been merged with Wiley's global Scientific,
Technical, and Medical business to form Wiley-Blackwell.

*Registered Office*
John Wiley & Sons Ltd, The Atrium, Southern Gate, Chichester, West Sussex,
PO19 8SQ, United Kingdom

*Editorial Offices*
350 Main Street, Malden, MA 02148-5020, USA
9600 Garsington Road, Oxford, OX4 2DQ, UK
The Atrium, Southern Gate, Chichester, West Sussex, PO19 8SQ, UK

For details of our global editorial offices, for customer services, and for information
about how to apply for permission to reuse the copyright material in this book
please see our website at www.wiley.com/wiley-blackwell.

The right of Patricia Meyer Spacks to be identified as the author of this work has
been asserted in accordance with the Copyright, Designs and Patents Act 1988.

Wiley also publishes its books in a variety of electronic formats. Some content that
appears in print may not be available in electronic books.

Designations used by companies to distinguish their products are often claimed as
trademarks. All brand names and product names used in this book are trade names,
service marks, trademarks or registered trademarks of their respective owners. The
publisher is not associated with any product or vendor mentioned in this book. This
publication is designed to provide accurate and authoritative information in regard
to the subject matter covered. It is sold on the understanding that the publisher is
not engaged in rendering professional services. If professional advice or other expert
assistance is required, the services of a competent professional should be sought.

*Library of Congress Cataloging-in-Publication Data*
Spacks, Patricia Ann Meyer.
  Reading eighteenth-century poetry / Patricia Meyer Spacks.
      p. cm.
  Includes bibliographical references and index.
  ISBN 978-1-4051-5361-4 (hardcover : alk. paper) — ISBN 978-1-4051-5362-1
(pbk. : alk. paper)  1. English poetry—18th century—History and criticism.
2. English poetry—Appreciation.  I. Title.  II. Title: Reading 18th-century
poetry.
  PR551.S66 2009
  821'.509—dc22
                                                                    2008033217

A catalogue record for this book is available from the British Library.

Set in 10/13pt Palatino by Graphicraft Limited, Hong Kong
Printed and bound in Malaysia by Vivar Printing Sdn Bhd

1  2009

# Contents

# Preamble

For the purposes of this book, the eighteenth century begins in 1700 and ends in 1799. That may sound like an uncontroversial definition, but it is not: historians, both literary and political, have often described the eighteenth century – the "long eighteenth century" – as extending from 1660 to 1819, say, or even 1832. A friend recently explained to me that the "1890s" take in the years 1750 to 1914. Literary periods – like centuries, arbitrary designations – shift according to their designators' purposes. The various spans assigned to a given period may all prove plausible, given that modes of writing remain always in flux, with varying degrees of continuity and change; different definitions suit different purposes. I prefer a definition that announces its own arbitrariness. Starting in 1700, ending in 1799, we may see a century's poetic richness and see how trends grow and wane in every span of years.

Equally arbitrary is the division of the century roughly into thirds that organizes the chapters. Dominant literary practices changed in the course of a hundred years, and segmenting the century makes it easier to focus on the changes, just as dividing the eighteenth century from the seventeenth and the nineteenth helps to illuminate how distinct time spans differ from one another. They differ, and they remain the same. To call attention to this constant paradoxical pattern of literary development, the five chapters focused on each third of the century follow a common scheme. In each section, the first chapter examines the vision of the good life promulgated or suggested by the period's poetry. The second chapter looks at the place of feeling in verse and the kinds of feeling that attract poetic interest; the third investigates a structural question; and the fourth examines issues of diction. The fifth chapter of each section focuses attention on a pair of the period's poets, providing an opportunity for more detailed investigation of individual poems than that possible in chapters concerned with general issues. The opportunity for comparison, implicit and explicit, created by the patterns of recurrence emphasizes complicated relations among the productions of different poets.

The tripartite division of the century and the chapter organization by topic rather than author guarantee that individual poets will make their appearance in more than one chapter – sometimes in several chapters. Alexander Pope, for instance, does not neatly confine himself to the first third of the century. Moreover, he concerns himself with the nature of the good life; he writes poetry of passionate feeling; his work exemplifies the power of the couplet; he varies his diction in provocative ways. He might plausibly appear in seven or eight chapters – and he actually figures prominently in six. This structural fact underlines a point that the book makes repeatedly in verbal terms: the poets treated here do not fit neatly into separate boxes. On the contrary, their conjunction demonstrates over and over how intricately their achievements comment on one another. I have deliberately tried to place at least some of them in diverse contexts in order to emphasize this fact.

The authors – although not necessarily the specific poems – discussed in this volume for the most part coincide with those included in *Eighteenth-Century Poetry: An Annotated Anthology*, eds. David Fairer and Christine Gerrard (Blackwell, 1999), and the texts for the poems included in that anthology are taken from it. For individual poems not printed in the anthology, the sources for texts are indicated in the bibliography (pp. 276–8).

Many of the texts reproduce the poems' original orthography, which may in some respects seem unfamiliar. Through much of the eighteenth century, capital letters began all nouns, common and proper alike. Proper nouns sometimes received the differentiation of italics, which might elsewhere serve the purpose of emphasis. Moreover, printers on occasion used italics rather than quotation marks to set off quotations. As the century went on, orthographic practices gradually moved closer to those of our own time. The relatively unfamiliar appearance of some earlier poetry, however, may provide a salutary reminder that this verse, from a different era, has necessary aspects of strangeness that should not be elided. Although much eighteenth-century poetry explores issues still pressingly important, it does so with a perspective inevitably different from our own. We learn by acknowledging difference as well as by recognizing similarity.

As its title indicates, this volume concerns itself above all with *reading*. Poetry, like prose, lends itself to many purposes. It may reveal political and social attitudes or reflect biographical facts or speak of an immediate or past national situation. Such matters receive glancing attention in the present study, but the book will concentrate primarily on the individual encounter with a text. From ancient times, writers and readers alike have believed that the written word provides both pleasure and instruction: enlightenment about particulars and about large and lasting truths. Pleasure, however, matters as much as instruction, and the pleasure provided by works from the past may remain inaccessible without help.

By sketching ways of reading individual texts, this book aspires to provide such help. To encounter multiple and varied examples of how eighteenth-century poetry works familiarizes readers with a range of possibilities and makes new encounters less startling than they might otherwise feel. To pay close attention to the workings of words exposes meanings and enriches perceptions. To think about poems in conjunction with one another reveals connections and clarifies nuances. Thus readers may come to see more in unfamiliar poems – and thus find new inlets for pleasure.

# 1

# How to Live: The Moral and the Social

In 1700, the first year of a new century, John Dryden, not long before his death, composed *The Secular Masque*. At its conclusion, a group of mythological figures occupies the stage, reflecting in derogatory terms on the historical period immediately past. The final chorus ends,

> 'Tis well an Old Age is out,
> And time to begin a New.

New ages do not necessarily coincide with new centuries, yet years ending in double zeroes carry special imaginative weight. We want to believe that something important will happen as a century changes, although, inevitably, much remains the same. Let us begin our story, then, at the arbitrary starting point of 1700, a year that saw the publication not only of Dryden's *Masque*, with its skepticism about the past ("Thy Wars brought nothing about; / Thy Lovers were all untrue") and its implicit optimism about the future, but also of John Pomfret's enormously popular poem, *The Choice*, a work that holds in some respects to the distant past, although its large readership endured through much of the century to come.

Pomfret's subject, a favorite one in the eighteenth century, is the choice of life: how an individual man might determine the best circumstances and the best conduct available to him. The topic would have had particular urgency in 1700, less than sixty years after the English had executed their king, Charles I, in the immediate aftermath of a cataclysmic civil war. It would be hard to exaggerate this event's traumatic repercussions. To kill a king, a figure whose divine right to govern had long been a matter of general conviction, and to do so as a result of purportedly legal judicial determination: such an act not only overturned centuries of tradition; it also created new uncertainties. Who could be trusted, if not the king? What could be counted on, if not the monarchy's continuity? Was the execution of Charles I justice or sacrilege? Such questions lingered long after the deed itself.

The 1642 execution did not produce a stable government. England became for a time a commonwealth, governed by Oliver Cromwell under the title of Lord Protector. By 1660, however, Charles II, son of the executed monarch, returned to the throne, to be succeeded in 1687 by his Catholic son, James II. Two years later, the so-called Glorious Revolution deposed James in favor of his sister Mary and her husband, William of Orange, Protestants both, who remained on the throne as the new century began. James, however, was still alive and well in France, and some believed him the rightful king. If the English felt uncertain of the monarchy's stability, they had reason.

The political forces that generated this confused sequence of rulers had religious and moral aspects as well. Antagonism between Protestants and Catholics shaped the rebellion against James II. Catholics had become a small minority in England; the decision to expel a Catholic king reflected a strong majority view. More deeply disturbing, because more widely divisive, was the split that had produced the civil war. On one side, the so-called Puritans represented Protestants who dissented from the doctrine of the Church of England, following stricter moral and more rigid doctrinal principles. The Cavaliers, who supported the monarchy of Charles I, espoused more moral permissiveness and laxer theological discipline than did their opponents. Aristocrats predominantly, although not invariably, supported the Cavaliers and the king; the Puritans attracted wide advocacy among commoners. Thus class interests as well as theological ones worked to generate conflict.

The Puritans won the war, but eighteen years later the Cavaliers triumphed, with the return of Charles II. A long, painful struggle had in a sense resolved nothing. The conflicts at issue in the mid-seventeenth century, between different forms of belief, different modes of conduct, and different class allegiances, remained alive at the beginning of the eighteenth century. A personal choice of life could thus be understood as a political commitment. Many, however, might hope for a kind of choice that could separate them from politics. The proliferation of poetry about the subject, although it seemed to concern individuals, in fact had large social implications.

*The Choice* sets forth details of what purports to be Pomfret's personal choice. No practical restrictions limit his imagining. He conjures up an ideal situation, in which friends remain ever faithful and agreeable, a mistress both intelligent and attractive is at his disposal, no wife or children impede his pleasures, the natural environment abounds in delights, and he possesses as much money as he desires.

With the fierce civil war just behind them, the English would have found a vision of gratifying and peaceful noninvolvement especially appealing. More to the point, they would find poetry articulating such a vision attractive. The poetry of the Restoration (the period beginning in 1660, when Charles II ascended the throne; the term loosely designates the last forty years of the seventeenth century) had included much political verse, often fiercely partisan about religious and national matters, and much bawdiness. Cynicism often controlled poetic utterance. Thus Samuel Butler, at the beginning of his popular *Hudibras* (1663), could write of England's agonizing civil war, not long past:

> When *Civil Dudgeon* first grew high
> And men fell out they knew not why;
> When hard words, *Jealousies*, and *Fears*
> Set Folks together by the ears,
> And made them fight, like mad, or drunk,
> For Dame *Religion*, as for Punk [prostitute],
> Whose honesty they all durst swear for,
> Though not a man of them knew wherefore . . .
>                                        (1–8)

Religion had been a matter of life and death, yet the poet felt free to suggest that men who killed and were killed did not even know why they fought.

Pomfret's tone of reflective seriousness, his respectful claims of piety, and his insistent modesty differentiate him sharply from poets like Butler, or the often obscene Rochester, or even the poet laureate Dryden in his characteristic rhetorical dignity. Unlike such important Restoration figures, he appears to make few claims on his readers, demanding neither cynicism nor large tolerance. *The Choice* provides easy reading.

Like many poems that followed it, though, it is less simple than it seems. For one thing, it bears a complicated relation to literary tradition. As classically educated eighteenth-century readers would notice, Pomfret drew on the verse of the great Latin poet, Horace, as a model. An ideal of rural retirement informs many of Horace's epistles, which may turn, implicitly or explicitly, on a contrast between the corruption of the court and the innocence of the country. Inasmuch as Pomfret could be seen as alluding to Horace, he might be seen also as commenting on the relative corruption of public men – not only courtiers, but also politicians. *The Choice* advocates opting out.

Closer to Pomfret's historical moment were the many country-house poems of the seventeenth century that celebrated a luxurious version of the rural retreat. A poet writing in 1700 could plausibly expect his readers to notice both his allusions to and his differences from such models. The differences help to locate Pomfret's achievement. Ben Jonson, writing *To Penshurst* in 1616, praised the estate as a place of plenty, rich in provisions for hospitality. Here he describes the catching of fish and game to supply the table:

> The painted partrich lyes in every field,
> And, for thy messe [meal] is willing to be kill'd.
> And if the high-swolne *Medwaye* fail thy dish,
> Thou hast thy ponds, that pay thee tribute fish,
> Fat, aged carps, that runne into thy net,
> And pikes, now weary their own kinde to eat,
> As loth, the second draught, or cast to stay,
> Officiously [dutifully], at first, themselves betray.
> Bright eeles, that emulate them, and leape on land,
> Before the fisher, or into his hand.
>
> (29–38)

The fanciful notion that birds and fish alike demonstrate eagerness to be killed for the master's table animates the verse, creating a bizarre vision of coordinated activity, the animal world unified in happy self-sacrifice, as fish from the Medway River or from the estate's ponds rush into the net and eels leap into the fisherman's hand. Jonson offers this not as literal description, but as a metaphor of abundance, one of many such images in the poem.

Pomfret traffics in no such exaggeration. Avoiding the extravagance of much seventeenth-century poetry, he stresses the modesty of his desires, in this respect resembling Horace: he wants a house "Built Uniform, not little, nor too great" (6), containing only things "Useful, Necessary, Plain" (10), the capacity to live "Genteelly, but not Great" (34), and so on. Frequent invocations of "Heaven" remind us that the speaker seeks to govern himself by Christian imperatives. The poem ends by imagining a death as peaceful and harmonious as the life that has been evoked. "Then," it concludes, "wou'd my Exit so propitious be, / All men wou'd wish to live and dye like me" (166–67).

This final couplet consolidates abundant earlier suggestions that, despite the speaker's proclaimed moderation, his fantasy has its own extravagance. Everyone, everywhere would realize it if they could, once they perceived its perfection. Above all, the vision Pomfret offers speaks of human harmony. Not only the nation as a whole but also, frequently, individual families had found themselves divided by opposed political views that became causes for bloodshed during the civil war. *The Choice* imagines male friends "Not prone to Lust, Revenge, or envious Hate; / Nor busy Medlers with Intrigues of State" (90–91); a female companion "Civil to Strangers, to her Neighbours kind, / Averse to Vanity, Revenge, and Pride" (121–22); and a self "concern'd in no litigious Jarr, / Belov'd by all, not vainly popular" (140–41). It provides a detailed alternative to division.

The harmonious verse of *The Choice* reiterates the ideal of harmony and thus emphasizes the poem's import. Like most of his contemporaries, Pomfret wrote in heroic couplets: ten-syllable lines rhymed successively and patterned by iambic meter, a sequence of unstressed followed by stressed syllables. "'Most Women have no Characters at all'": this, the second line of Alexander Pope's *An Epistle to a Lady*, exemplifies the regularity and easy emphasis of iambic verse. Even within such regularity, though, much variation flourished. In Pomfret's hands, the couplet became a soothing form. *The Choice* moves smoothly. Its rhymes (lend–spend, contain–Plain, Row–grow) seldom surprise and never shock. Each couplet typically encapsulates a complete thought, yet the larger sense proceeds through several couplets, following readily recognizable logical patterns. Although the poem generates little urgency – nothing is obviously at stake – the verse draws the reader along, placing few obstacles in the way. The rhythm never slows us down; the meaning develops so clearly that we rarely need pause to ponder. The poem feels inevitable, an effect achieved both metrically and logically.

It comes as no surprise, given the emphasis on straightforwardness in all its devices, that Pomfret's poem offers little opportunity and makes no demand for profound exegesis. It does not depend heavily on symbolism; its meanings appear to lie all on the surface. Yet the pressure of the counterfactual suggests a level of complexity in addition to that of the poem's relation to classic and vernacular tradition. *The Choice* begins with the word "If," which locates all that follows it in the realm of conceptual possibility rather than that of actuality. Everything depends on "Heav'n," which may grant – or, more probably, refuse to grant – individuals a choice of life. Typically, human beings have little choice about their economic circumstances. The vision of ideal existence that the poem constructs therefore accretes poignancy: it has not been realized, and its conceivable realization hinges on an act of divine benevolence.

The poem, then, knows itself to be fantasy. In this context, the tension between the declarations of moderation and the desire for perfection assumes special meaning. The speaker often formulates his wishes in terms of negatives: "not little, nor too great"; "no other Things . . . But what are Useful"; "Genteelly, but not Great"; "healthy, not luxurious"; "no such rude Disorders"; "not Uneasy," and so on. He thus calls attention to the fact that he's not requesting too much. In the context of his knowledge of that portentous "If" at the beginning, his awareness that free choice is a stupendous gift, he must be careful – he knows, after all, that he is asking for an enviable mortal condition.

In the company of his chosen friends, the speaker writes, he "cou'd not miss, / A permanent, sincere, substantial Bliss" (ll. 95–96). The word *Bliss* carries powerful overtones. It suggests the divinely ordained happiness of heaven as well as, conceivably, the transcendent satisfactions of erotic love. Pomfret's envisioned life promises delights more enduring than those of love, more immediate than those of heaven. *The Choice* articulates the precise nature of the happiness it promises: "substantial" in its accumulation of particulars; permanent because its endurance is essential to the vision; sincerely imagined and sincerely longed for. Yet the longing remains poignant in its historical context, not only because of the vision's counterfactual nature but also because of the national circumstances that would have made it seem especially difficult to realize. It is not surprising that readers avidly purchased and perused a poem that fully specified a happy ideal, one that might provide material for dreams if not for realization.

*The Choice* articulates a model of a good life. It has little autobiographical bearing, except as fantasy: the poet was married when he wrote his encomium of an existence without human encumbrances. It participates, though, in a lively eighteenth-century tradition. If it seems escapist in its emphatic rejection of public life, it chooses escapism as a deliberate alternative to internecine strife. The good life, at Pomfret's historical moment, might plausibly seem the life of opting out.

In the twenty-first century, poetry would seem a peculiar genre for advice about life. We turn, rather, to self-help books, or to biographies and autobiographies for possible models of conduct, or conceivably to novels for delineations of imagined life choices. In the first third of the eighteenth century, though, novels had not developed into an important genre, nor had biography and autobiography, beyond narratives of conversion. Conduct books flourished, recommending proper behavior for specific situations, but they did not deal significantly with fundamental choices beyond, say, a young woman's decision about what man to marry.

Readers turned to poetry for investigation of such matters as how one should live not primarily because of the absence of other resources, but rather because they believed poetry a particularly authoritative literary mode. The assumption that verse dealt with important concerns permeated literate society. Moralists would soon complain that novels dwelt only on love; no one could say that about verse. Poetry aspired to educate, even to reform, both individuals and society at large. It considered philosophical issues, politics, and morality, but also how to shear sheep or grow cucumbers. It criticized governments and inveighed against such social habits as tea-drinking and gambling. And it dared to claim authority even about such fundamental matters as how a man should live in order to go to heaven.

The convention that allowed poets to hold forth on such subjects permitted them on occasion to say unexpected things. For an extreme example, we might consider Sarah Fyge Egerton (1670–1723), whose assertive utterances about the female situation ring with outrage about the limited choices open to women. Her implicit prescriptions about the proper conduct of female life emerge indirectly, almost entirely through her expressed indignation at things as they are.

> Shall I be one of those obsequious Fools,
> That square their lives by Customs scanty Rules;
> Condemn'd for ever to the puny Curse,
> Of Precepts taught at Boarding-school, or Nurse,
> That all the business of my Life must be,
> Foolish, dull Trifling, Formality.
> Confin'd to a strict Magick complaisance,

And round a Circle of nice visits Dance,
Nor for my Life beyond the Chalk advance.
                              (*The Liberty*, 1–9)

Shall I be one of those fools, she asks, going on to specify the nature of the fools in such a way that the noun becomes synonymous with "respectable young women." *The Liberty* answers the question most eloquently by asking it in those terms. Its speaker finally specifies, with some bravado, how she proposes to differ from others of her sex, but she holds forth no hope that her kind of behavior will be imitated.

Unpredictable adjectives fill urgent needs in the opening lines of *The Liberty*. *Obsequious* establishes the outrage that permeates the poem. Women's folly perhaps consists in their obsequiousness, their servile compliance; or perhaps women are fools because they are forced to be compliant. In any case, the poem's speaker loathes folly and obsequiousness, whether or not they are identical. But the targets of her anger, as conveyed by the adjectives, become less predictable as she continues her discourse. "Customs scanty Rules": *scanty* meaning "deficient in extent, compass, or size." From a woman's point of view, the deficiency of the rules intended to govern her inheres in their limitation. Inadequate in their imagining, they limit her possibilities in ways echoing their own limitations.

Yet more unexpected is "strict Magick complaisance." As a glance at any conduct book will reveal, "complaisance," or willingness to please, was insistently recommended to eighteenth-century women, whose capacity to please others would largely determine their fates. The only kind of power legitimate for women, complaisance might have the metaphorically magic capacity to transform their destiny – but a capacity that, Egerton's phrasing emphasizes, can operate only within strict bounds. The poem's speaker, therefore, resents even the resources she has: too scanty, too strictly regulated, all part of what she tellingly alludes to as "the puny Curse": trivial in conception and in articulation, yet as potent as any prophet's imprecation in deforming women's lives.

I hardly know whether to admire more the energy or the economy of the phrasing through which Egerton conveys her sense of the female plight and of a female response to it. The poem's resolution is equally striking. *The Liberty* continues specifying restraints on women, with the speaker increasingly articulate about her own defiance of them:

> Some boast their Fetters of Formality
> Fancy they ornamental Bracelets be,
> I'm sure they're Gyves and Manacles to me.
>                                    (26–28)

Then she concludes by forthrightly stating her intentions:

> I'll blush at Sin, and not what some call Shame,
> Secure my Virtue, slight precarious Fame.
> This Courage speaks me Brave, 'tis surely worse,
> To keep those Rules, which privately we Curse:
> And I'll appeal to all the formal Saints,
> With what reluctance they indure restraints.
>                                    (47–52)

   The firm separation of sin and shame and the scorn for mere reputation give way to a conclusion marked by increasing self-assertion and
defiance. The speaker declares her own courage, suggesting it as self-
justification. Distinguishing between sin, which conscience detects,
and the shame responsive to pressure from without, she insists on her
virtue, even though she implicitly rejects concern for the reputation
of virtue. In the final couplet, she appeals ironically for support from
"all the formal Saints." The noun *formality* has appeared twice earlier,
both times with a negative weight: we have encountered the "Trifling
[and] Formality" that define the business of a good girl's life and the
"Fetters of Formality" that bind her. The formality of the "Saints" now
alluded to presumably refers to the precision and rigorous observance
that marked many Puritan sects of the period – some of which, as the
*Oxford English Dictionary* reminds us, referred to their own members
as saints. If such "saints" responded to the speaker's appeal, they would
have to throw off the hypocrisy that, to her mind, characterizes them:
enduring restraint without complaining, they hide in practice the
reluctance they actually feel. The voice of the poem, celebrating its own
courage, declares integrity by self-revelation instead of concealment,
and the poem glorifies its speaking out, even while tacitly acknowledging the isolation implicit in such defiance of social norms.
   Like Pomfret, Egerton offers no direct advice about the proper way
to lead one's life. She speaks only of how she herself would want to
live, implying the meretriciousness of female lives conducted purely
by social standards. Although *The Liberty* presents itself as intensely

personal, it too is inflected by immediate political actualities. Religious politics, which had played a large role in the civil war, colors the poem's choice of reference. More inclusively, gender politics – a concept that, of course, had not yet been formulated – shapes the entire work. Egerton's dissatisfaction focuses on the impossibility of living a personal life apart from social constraints. The individual life, virtually all eighteenth-century poems on the subject acknowledge, necessarily takes place within society, and society implies the pressures of a specific time and place. Few before her had articulated the same perception, but Egerton points out that those pressures impinge with special force on women.

The loudest poetic voice offering recommendations about conduct was that of Alexander Pope, who even in his early *Essay on Criticism* (written about 1709, when the poet was 21 years old) constructed an ideal figure to model the way a good man would behave.

> But where's the man, who counsel can bestow,
> Still pleas'd to teach, and yet not proud to know?
> Unbiass'd, or by favour, or by spite;
> Not dully preposses'd, or blindly right;
> Tho' Learn'd, well-bred; and tho' well-bred, sincere;
> Modestly bold, and humanly severe?
>
> (631–36)

Meaning infuses form here, and form shapes meaning. The six lines exemplify how flexible and powerful an instrument the heroic couplet provided for eighteenth-century poets. The lines comprise a single interrogative sentence (the question mark at the end of the first couplet does not in fact mark a sentence's end) that establishes a set of crucial characteristics and defines relationships among them.

Those relationships depend centrally on balance and antithesis, enacted by as well as stated in the verse. Different conjunctions (*or . . . or*, *Not . . . nor*, *Tho' . . . and*) together with the adverbial pairing *Still* (here meaning *always*) and *yet*, enforce a single point: the good man harmoniously incorporates a series of paradoxically related qualities. The shifting rhythms and pace possible within the iambic pentameter couplet emphasize meanings. Thus in the first line, the iambic structure underlines *can*, the line's most important word. The fact that the hypothetical good man has the capacity to give wise counsel differentiates him immediately from all those capable of no such thing. Alone among the six lines, this one evokes no contrast. It moves, therefore, more deliberately than the others. The monosyllable that inaugurates the next line, *Still*, unlike the other monosyllabic first words, has sonorous weight lending it so much emphasis that "Still pleas'd" sounds like a spondee, a metrical foot in which both words carry equal emphasis. The final line echoes, with a difference, the same device, placing the initial accent on the first syllable, this time to create a trochaic foot, a stressed syllable followed by an unstressed one. Line 635 sounds longer than line 636, though it contains the same number of syllables. The variations in word length and number of words (e.g., line 632 contains only one-syllable words, ten words altogether; line 636, with two three-syllable words, comprises only five words) contribute to the variety in sound among couplets all written in a single form.

Variety is the message as well as the medium: the good man incorporates a great deal. His boldness is modest, his severity humane. He gives instruction gladly, without taking pride in all he knows. His learning does not interfere with his courtesy, and his courtesy derives from genuine impulse rather than from hypocrisy. Such ideas demand pondering, and so does the verse that contains them. Heroic couplets can seem deceptively simple, and one might assume their monotony. The assumption would be wrong. Although they insistently proclaim their harmony, although their structure emphasizes their balance, they demand close attention to the range of possibilities they can incorporate and to the ways those possibilities contribute to meaning.

Pope's characterization of his hero continues, but these few lines suffice to suggest its tone of authority (despite its rhetoric of questions), its moral vocabulary, its skillful manipulation of form, and its insistence on the compatibility of manners and morals. The three couplets begin the poem's description of the ideal critic, but nothing separates the good critic from the good man.

The fact that Pope could plausibly advance such an argument, claiming identity between the propriety and virtue necessary for the critic and that suitable for a good human being, suggests the status of both poetry and literary criticism. The *Essay on Criticism* can plausibly assume the high seriousness of poetry and criticism as human endeavors. In the face of unsettling political possibility, it recommends the life of the mind. Although Pope's subsequent moral criticism did not necessarily equate literary activity with other modes of behavior, the expertise of his verse always implicitly attested his moral authority: the precision and grace of couplets can hint of the discipline and integrity of a life.

Like all satirists, Pope works most often by means of negative examples. Multiplied instances of lives badly lived, often violating moral imperatives behind a façade of social compliance, gradually shadow forth a complex counter-image of virtuous existence marked by both the resistance Egerton advocates for herself and a more elevated version of the ease for which Pomfret yearns. In his *Essay on Man* (1733–34), Pope considered humankind ("man") in the context of the entire created universe, mocking the presumption that enables a human being to consider self in all respects more important and more percipient than the rest of the animal creation and that allows "man" to forget his own insignificance in comparison to the God Who created him. As part of what was originally a large philosophic project linked with the *Essay*, the poet also produced four "moral epistles" about specific human characteristics. Epistle IV, addressed to Richard Boyle, Earl of Burlington, subtitled "Of the Use of Riches," exemplifies the force and pointedness with which Pope denounces deviations from proper behavior and argues for a strenuous version of the good life.

"Strength of mind is Exercise, not Rest," Pope wrote in the *Essay on Man* (2: 104). The life he both implicitly and explicitly recommends demands constant exercise of moral intelligence. Such intelligence can and should operate in every realm of human endeavor. Landscape design and architecture provide the nominal subject for much of *Epistle to Burlington*. Description of an estate referred to as "Timon's Villa" occupies many lines.

> Greatness, with Timon, dwells in such a draught [plan or scheme]
> As brings all Brobdignag before your thought.
> To compass this, his building is a Town,
> His pond an Ocean, his parterre a Down:
> Who but must laugh, the Master when he sees,
> A puny insect, shiv'ring at a breeze!
> Lo, what huge heaps of littleness around!
> The whole, a labour'd Quarry above ground.
>
> (103–10)

*What huge heaps of littleness*: the line conveys a moral judgment rather than a physical description. The ocean-sized pond and the town-sized house are literally huge but metaphorically tiny, even as Timon himself, "Smit with the mighty pleasure, to be seen" (128), remains despite his imagining of his own importance nothing but a puny insect. All the appearances he has created fail to provide the fundamental aesthetic satisfactions of order and appropriateness. Schemes substitute for achievement: the grand conceptions rather than the aesthetic effects of his landscapes and buildings matter to Timon. Therefore what has been calculated as awe-inspiring only creates the chaotic impression of a quarry where workers have accumulated random heaps of rocks.

Brobdignag, to which Pope refers in the second line quoted, is the land of giants where Gulliver finds himself in the second book of *Gulliver's Travels* (1726). To Gulliver's eyes, the physical appearances of this country seem grotesque. The scale is wrong, to normal human perception. Just so with Timon's villa – but the scale by which Pope measures is not only physical. Poor design becomes a metaphor for the meretricious life. One explicit standard for design and life alike is what Pope calls "Sense" – a quality assigned to the model woman at the end of *An Epistle to A Lady*, one recommended in *The Rape of the Lock*, an attribute that *Epistle to Burlington* declares only "the gift of Heav'n, / And tho' no science, fairly worth the sev'n" (43–44). Good sense prevents excessive display. It insures that riches are employed productively rather than wastefully. It extends a man's awareness of responsibility from the private to the public realm: this poem that appears to concern individual architectural choices ends with a vision of the virtuous man becoming advisor and enabler for kings, helping to create a harmonious empire. Here too, in other words, a poet finds that a person's choice of life bears on politics as well as personal contentment. More consistently than Pomfret or Egerton, however, Pope advocates a kind of personal responsibility that always extends outward. The good critic of the *Essay on Criticism* acts and is judged in relation to others, and the pattern continues: Pope's poetry assesses its subjects in their social functioning.

The examples provided by these three poets suggest sharply different ways of imagining the good life: as retreat, as defiance, as responsibility. But three such imaginings hardly exhaust the moral doctrines poetically recommended in the first thirty-five years of the eighteenth century. Poets might also, for instance (as they would throughout the century), recommend understanding life under the aspect of eternity.

Isaac Watts's hymns, many of them still sung in Protestant churches, remind their readers that human beings exist not only for their own immediate satisfaction and not only in relation to other humans, but also in relation to God. Indeed, Pope and Pomfret offer the same reminder, despite their stress on the social. Pope's notes to *Burlington* call attention to the importance of Providence as a force in the poem, and his account of Timon's villa lingers on the chapel, effectively desecrated both by lush ceiling paintings and by a dean who "never mentions Hell to ears polite" (150). Pomfret acknowledges at the outset of *The Choice* his dependence on Providence. Neither poet, though, dwells on the human relation to God as fundamentally important to the conduct of life, and neither allows himself potentially controversial specificity.

Even poets whose repertoire included social verse on occasion wrote about the urgency of Christian responsibility, often under the guise of discussing their own experience. Anne Finch (1661–1720) provides an especially compelling case in point, with poems purporting to narrate her own history. One called *Fragment*, which indeed displays a fragmentary form, begins *in medias res*, with a "So," never elucidated. It announces its subject as the soul:

> So here confin'd, and but to female Clay,
> ARDELIA's Soul mistook the rightful Way.
>                                    (1–2)

It reports, however, Finch's worldly career (in several other poems as well she refers to herself as "Ardelia"): her youthful desire for "vain Amusements" (5), giving way to "Ambition" (6), which leads her to life at the court of James II. When James is deposed, she shares in his "Ruin" (14) and subsequently turns her thoughts toward heaven, aspiring, as she writes, "Tow'rds a more certain Station" (18). All her efforts – prayers, ecstatic thoughts, meditation on her faults, retirement – prove vain, though:

> These, but at distance, towards that purpose tend,
> The lowly Means to an exalted End;
> Which He must perfect who allots her Stay,
> And That, accomplish'd, will direct the way.
>                                    (24–27)

The poem then dwells at some length on the glories of heaven, concluding,

> Rest then content, my too impatient Soul;
> Observe but here the easie Precepts given,
> Then wait with chearful hope, till Heaven be known in Heaven.
>
> (37–39)

The poem's speaker divides herself into "Soul" – *impatient*, therefore a less than perfect soul – and other-than-soul. Like the speaker of Egerton's passionate outpouring, she offers no overt advice or criticism to others. For most of *Fragment* – indeed, until those final three lines – she refers to herself in the third person, but not until she uses a first person pronoun ("my") does she provide any injunction. Yet the advice she offers herself is, from a Christian perspective, universal, and the career she narrates in many respects typifies that of the upper class young woman. (The unusual aspect of the speaker's trajectory is only her connection with a deposed monarch.) As long as her desire for heaven resembles the "Ambition" that made her aspire to a place at court (as "Tow'rds a more certain Station she aspires"; 18), it too only declares its own futility. She has been "instructed by that Fall" (16) – a king's fall and her own, faintly corresponding to the original Fall – but the lesson fails to impart the crucial knowledge of her own insufficiency.

When she achieves that knowledge, it becomes the most important lesson she can teach. By using herself as a case history, emphasizing the vanity of her attempts to find earthly satisfaction, evoking the "restless Cares, and weary Strife" (28) of worldly existence, and dwelling on the joys of heaven, "that wond'rous City" (36), she constructs a vivid argument for trust in and submission to God and disarms potential opposition. By using theological language ("Paradice," "the flaming Sword") for her attachment to the royal court, she emphasizes the terrible error of misplacing value. The frequent jerkiness of her couplets (in striking contrast to Pope's smoothness) dramatizes her agitation, implicitly contradicting her simple assertions of faith. In contrast, the alexandrine (a six-stress iambic line) that concludes the poem, the line about waiting in cheerful hope, slows into an achieved, appropriate, and persuasive serenity. The poem demonstrates unworthy and worthy ways to live and dramatizes the difficulty of making the proper choice between them.

Yet it gains much of its power from the poignancy of the personal. The movement from the image of confinement "but to female Clay" to the "chearful hope" of the concluding line, with its restrained evocations of disappointments along the way, conveys a triumphant progress, but one attended by painful experience. Individual, personal tribulations mark the effort to lead a good life. The reward, *Fragment* insists, justifies those tribulations but does not eliminate their pain.

In a poem called *On Affliction*, which also dwells on tribulation, Finch begins with the personal and moves to the general, reversing the development of *Fragment*. The poem contains three five-line stanzas, with alternating rhymes of iambic pentameter and a final drawn-out line in each stanza that adds two more syllables. Those hexameter lines mark significant pause and emphasis. Each of them, like the concluding alexandrine in *Fragment*, evokes the glory of God, in contrast to the emphasis on earthly pain elsewhere in the poem.

Finch contrasts the power of reason, here enlisted in the service of faith, with the weakness of flesh, an inlet to suffering. Reason assures her that affliction constitutes a test and measure of faith. The final stanza summarizes the poem's argument, although it alone cannot convey the complexity of its tone:

> Affliction is the line, which every Saint
>   Is measur'd by, his stature taken right;
> So much itt shrinks, as they repine or faint,
>   But if their faith and Courage stand upright,
>   By that is made the Crown, and the full robe of light.
> (11–15)

This confident assertion develops only as a result of the speaker's embrace of suffering. At the poem's opening, her position seems tentative, as her "tender flesh" (1) wars with her reason. She stresses the hardness of the rock on which she lies and mentions the rod that chastises her, the bitter cup she must drink. The two first stanzas dramatize a process of reinterpretation that allows the forceful concluding generalization – which, in effect, allies the suffering speaker with "every Saint."

Again, the poem provides no overt advice. It illustrates, however, a struggle that must feel familiar to many if not all Christians, that between experience and faith. In this lyric the experience of pain wars with the unverifiable conviction that suffering leads to heavenly glory. The poem's effect depends upon its evocation of both "affliction" and the will to transcend it. It not only preaches a doctrine of submission and belief; it also shows the effort demanded by adherence to such a doctrine, illustrating psychological processes of faith. Once more, Finch offers herself as test case. Far from insisting on the uniqueness of her suffering, as we might expect in a lyric poem, she resolutely generalizes from her pain, achieving the assertiveness of the final stanza by virtue of her realization that hers is not a special case. Finch teaches others how to live by dramatizing the process of her own learning.

When she adopts Pomfret's tactic of evoking an ideal existence (*The Petition for an Absolute Retreat*), her imaginings focus on the inner life and on a complex relation with the natural world. "Give me," she begins, in the imperative mode –

> Give me O indulgent Fate!
> Give me yet, before I Dye,
> A sweet, but absolute Retreat . . .

She stresses the lack of difficulty she will enjoy, there "Where the world may ne'er invade" (20). Her table will be spread with food from nature; she will "covet" only fruit; she will dress in harmony with nature; she will share her life with a loving partner; she will draw morals from nature; she will have a single friend. Her reflections lead her to meditate on the human position in the universe. The final section begins,

> Let me then, indulgent Fate!
> Let me still, in my Retreat,
> From all roving Thoughts be freed,
> Or Aims, that may Contention breed;
> Nor be my Endeavours led
> By Goods, that perish with the Dead!
> (258–63)

The absence of the kinds of thought and aim that belong to the world of earthly striving allows room for better thoughts, better aspirations.

Here are the poem's final lines:

> Give me, O indulgent Fate!
> For all Pleasures left behind,

> Contemplations of the Mind.
> Let the Fair, the Gay, the Vain
> Courtship and Applause obtain;
> Let th' Ambitious rule the Earth;
> Let the giddy Fool have Mirth;
> Give the Epicure his Dish,
> Ev'ry one their sev'ral Wish;
> Whilst my Transports I employ
> On that more extensive Joy,
> When all Heaven shall be survey'd
> From those Windings, and that Shade.
>
> (280–93)

The poet's subject, she insists, continues to be pleasure. If she has given up many conventional sources of delight, she claims for herself the prospect of "more extensive joy" in the contemplation of heaven. As my earlier quotations from the poem indicate, the imaginative movement of this final sequence duplicates and intensifies that of earlier passages that begin with the invocation of "indulgent Fate." Thought and feeling repeatedly move from the worldly to the heavenly: first, only a retreat from the world; later, contemplation of the unsatisfactory nature of "aims" and "endeavours" focused on earthly matters; finally, scornful dismissal of lesser goals like courtship, applause, and mirth in favor of heaven's lasting satisfactions. The poem, in other words, systematically assesses the nature of available pleasures in order to settle on the most gratifying. It concentrates on the divine not as a matter of duty but as the highest form of indulgence.

By choosing to write in four-stress lines rather than the iambic pentameter couplets characteristic of much momentous poetry in her time, Finch suggests a kind of self-deprecation, hinting that her verse will not make serious claims on the reader. She uses her tetrameter lines to considerable effect, demonstrating how she can slow them down or speed them up at will. The briskness of "Give the epicure his dish" – which lacks the unstressed syllable that would ordinarily begin an iambic line – contrasts sharply with the leisurely, almost voluptuous movement of "that more extensive joy" as the poem achieves certainty, the assurance that heaven can indeed be "surveyed" from the absolute retreat the speaker desires.

In the poems about life choices that we have considered, physical circumstances and "practical" choices provide starting points or emblems for psychological or spiritual states and determinations. Twenty-first-century advice, direct or indirect, about life decisions might involve pondering vocational objectives or promising financial rewards. Pope, in contrast, considers an affluent life cause for contempt, if affluence is not properly employed; Pomfret and Finch alike imagine a life of limited occupation as providing a more certain medium of happiness than busier existences could do. Egerton's speaker wants to transcend her society rather than to fit into it. Imagining ease (physical, spiritual, or both) or meditating resistance, valuing ideal community while retaining a certain skepticism about the nature of actual human relations, cogitating about heavenly as well as earthly responsibilities, these poets find varied ways to represent the possibilities of how one should or can or might live. In their variety and in their high seriousness, they suggest the scope of a concern that preoccupied many of their contemporaries and that would also engage their poetic successors.

A consistent preoccupation with the vexed dynamic of the social and the personal, however, underlies the variety of these poets' production. Whether or not they engage directly with social problems, they convey their awareness of being embedded in a social matrix. At one extreme, Egerton struggles with the restrictiveness of social expectation and convention. At the other, Pope sets himself apart as social critic. Pomfret and Finch imagine ideal circumstances outside of society, but such imagining depends on awareness of precisely what they wish to exclude. Only individual solutions, all four suggest, can resolve social ills. Living within the so-called "peace of the Augustans," a time of relatively little national and international tumult, they lived still in the shadow of tumult recently past and in awareness of dire potential within existing social structures. Directly or indirectly, they acknowledged the dilemmas created by the operations of self-interest as opposed to the public good.

# 2

# Matters of Feeling: Poetry of Emotion

The early eighteenth century produced a body of passionate poetry. Men and women wrote of and from fear, rage, hope, faith, and despair. They wrote of social inequity and of personal unhappiness, of their relation to God, to one another, and to death. They even wrote, on occasion, about their love of nature or their amorous attachments – topics that post-Romantic readers perhaps more readily connect with the idea of poetic passion.

Strangely, though, much of the period's poetry of intense feeling disguises itself, placing its emotion not in the foreground but in the background of its representation. Perhaps the prevalent high valuation of reason, thought to differentiate human beings from other animals, contributed to this tendency. Awareness of poetry's significant public role may also partially explain such reticence. Given the notion that poetry speaks to the community about momentous matters, merely personal feeling hardly constitutes a sufficiently compelling subject to justify its centrality in a poetic structure. Thus Isaac Watts, for instance, in the best known of his many hymns, speaks of the human situation in large and general terms. The force of his evocation depends on personal emotion just beneath the surface, but he does not claim that anything special marks his own situation.

*Man Frail, and God Eternal* is better known by its opening line: "Our God, our Help in Ages past." Based on Psalm 90, it takes up the subject of time as an essential element of the human condition. Here are its last three stanzas:

> Time like an ever-rolling Stream
> Bears all its Sons away;
> They fly forgotten as a Dream
> Dies at the opening Day.

> Like flow'ry Fields the Nations stand
>   Pleas'd with the Morning-light;
> The Flowers beneath the Mower's Hand
>   Lie withering ere 'tis Night.
>
> Our God, our Help in Ages past,
>   Our Hope for Years to come,
> Be thou our Guard while Troubles last,
>   And our eternal Home.
>
> (25–36)

The first two stanzas quoted above contain only third-person pronouns – a fact that makes more striking the fivefold repetition of *our* in the final stanza. The situation Watts describes is and is not a personal matter. He can assume a cosmic perspective, figuring nations as fields of flowers and humankind as dreamlike in the evanescence and forgettability of its individual members, but the concluding plea to God reminds us that we cannot always remain at the distance of metaphor from the reality of what the poem sums up as *troubles*. *Troubles*, that mundane word, includes the daily losses that time brings, and it encompasses fear of that death so cheerfully metaphorized in the preceding stanzas. Against such fear, only God, "*our* God," implicitly conceived as concerned for His people, provides a resource: the promise of an "eternal Home."

In the Psalm that supplies Watts's inspiration, God figures as a principle of destruction as well as of salvation:

> Thou turnest man to destruction; and sayest, Return, ye
>   children of men.
> For a thousand years in thy sight are but as yesterday when it
>   is past, and as a watch in the night.
> Thou carriest them away as with a flood; they are as a sleep: in the
>   morning they are like grass which groweth up; in the evening
>   it is cut down, and withereth.
> For we are consumed by thine anger, and by thy wrath are
>   we troubled.
>
> (Ps. 90: 3–7)

The evanescence of humankind, in Watts a product of time alone, in the Biblical source conveys mortals' vulnerability to God's power. The hymn, evoking both hope and fear, locates the source and goal of hope in the divine and makes fear essentially a product of human ignorance. The extreme simplicity of diction and sentence structure, the common references of the metaphors, and the centrality of the Christian doctrine invoked not only make the poetry accessible; such qualities also summon immediate feeling.

But *whose* feeling, exactly? The poem's speaker does not directly assert it as his own. His perceptions tell him and us that trouble and death will inevitably come to mortals; his faith informs the concept of an eternal home. His language directly declares neither what he as an individual person feels nor what we, as his readers, should feel. In a sense, though, our emotion, the immediate response of each reader, as well as the speaker's feelings, informs the hymn. Experiencing the poignancy of a field of flowers unexpectedly mown and dying, perceiving the analogy between flowers and mortals, we thus experience also the need for respite and rescue that the poem's final stanza answers. The poet has created or adopted the images that generate such response, and the poem exists for the response: not to convey the speaker's feeling for its own sake, but to entice the reader toward emotions that will lead to the faith that resolves the hymn. The power of feeling energizes the poem.

Watts wrote more than 500 hymns in the course of his poetic career. Many of them, like the one we have been considering, adapted the language and sentiments of Psalms; some, while remaining close to Biblical messages, sought new language for them. As a Dissenter, one unwilling to conform to all the regulations and doctrines of the Church of England, Watts belonged to a relatively small but close-knit religious community. Speaking for and to that community, he articulated not only its convictions but also its feelings.

Thinkers in early eighteenth-century England held complicated attitudes toward emotion. The passions, they thought, carried danger for their possessors. Nonetheless, as Pope put it in the *Essay on Man*, "Passions are the elements of Life" (1: 170), vital forces that impel achievement of all kinds. Pope shared with his contemporaries the view that reason must control (but not eliminate) passion to support meaningful and pleasurable existence. Appropriately disciplined, passion enabled poetry. The critic John Dennis in 1701 argued that poetry differentiates itself from prose specifically by being more passionate and sensual. He compares passion in poetry to the spirit in the human body: both provide energy.

When the passions ran amok, however, they were thought to threaten the coherence of individuals and of society. They endangered both their possessors and those who might become their targets. The energy they fueled might as easily destroy as create. Built into human nature, the passions required constant attention lest they rush out of control.

Eighteenth-century ambivalence toward the idea of intense emotion expresses itself economically in allusions to "the spleen." Until late in the seventeenth century, the gland still known in our time as the spleen was thought to be the seat both of melancholy and of mirth. Gradually the word's meaning enlarged to take in emotions as well as their physical source. By the early eighteenth century, "the spleen" referred especially to melancholia and gloom, but also to a range of feelings lacking, from the point of view of observers, adequate cause – feelings of the sort that later commentators might call neurotic in origin. Pope sketches a spectrum of possibility, entirely on the gloomy side, in his imagining of a Cave of Spleen, visited by a gnome in Canto 4 of *The Rape of the Lock*. There the gnome encounters bodies that have been changed to various shapes – teapots, jars, goose pies – by the operations of spleen, and the cave's presiding deity is said to rule the female sex. Indeed, just as depression in our own time is said to prevail especially among women, in the eighteenth century women were thought particularly susceptible to the spleen.

In a remarkable early eighteenth-century poem, *The Spleen*, Anne Finch investigates, communicates, and personalizes a broader reach of emotions than Pope had associated with the ailment. She subtitles her work, "A Pindaric Poem," thus justifying its irregular pattern of rhymes and associating it with odes of intense feeling by the Greek poet Pindar (see Chapter 8). *The Spleen* opens with a fundamental question: "What art thou, Spleen, which everything dost ape?" Connecting this mysterious power with the mythological figure of Proteus, who rapidly changed shape from one kind of animal to another in order to avoid capture, the poem alludes to its subject as "perplexing" (5) and evokes a range of appearances that spleen can create. Although "delusions" (15), the images provoked by spleen have imaginative power: the poem's first stanza concludes by evoking Brutus just before the battle he would lose to Octavius. Implicitly, the force of spleen accounts for Brutus's subsequent defeat and suicide.

With the treatment of Brutus, a historical figure from the distant past, Finch retreats from any hint of personal involvement with her subject.

The next stanza, however, immediately alludes to "we": "Falsely, the mortal part we blame / Of our depressed and ponderous frame" (25–26). The blaming "we" gives way to a suffering "we" by the stanza's end. Fallen mortals all endure spleen's depredations.

Even this perception, however, seems fairly impersonal. Although emotion heightens as the poem proceeds, not until the fourth stanza does the poem's speaker specifically implicate herself:

> O'er me, alas! thou dost too much prevail:
> I feel thy force whilst I against thee rail:
> I feel my verse decay, and my cramped numbers fail.
> Through thy black jaundice I all objects see
>     As dark, as terrible as thee,
> My lines decried, and my employment thought
> An useless folly or presumptuous fault.
>
>                                 (72–79)

Finch's verse frequently conveys irritation, rage, or despair at the widespread denigration of poetry writing as a female activity. In the immediate context, her feelings about the familiar subject of how she finds her "lines decried" become ambiguous. Her sense of others' negative response to her poetry may be delusional, a product of spleen's force, as may her conviction of her verse's decay and failure. Alternately, the "black jaundice" of spleen may result from her inability to meet her own literary standards. Spleen always creates the problem of assessing its visions' reality.

Only this stanza employs the first-person singular pronoun. In the succeeding eighty lines, Finch on occasion returns to the first-person plural, but much of her account of spleen's effects depends on imagined characters: coquette, fop, "son of Bacchus" (93), and others. Yet the atmosphere of personal involvement remains, conveyed largely by the verse's agitation as it rapidly changes subjects and tones. The poem allots only a few lines to each individual topic. Dramatizing spleen's Proteus nature, it moves restlessly from one concern to another. Then suddenly it slows down, repeating the same phrase three times:

> In vain to chase thee every art we try,
> In vain all remedies apply,
> In vain the Indian leaf infuse,
> Or the parched Eastern berry bruise . . .
>                                 (128–31)

The effort to defeat the emotional instability that spleen engenders guarantees its own collapse: head-on confrontation must fail. The reiterated phrase emphasizes that knowledge of this fact constitutes the only sure thing about spleen.

The poem ends in an elaborated and disturbing image of defeat: nine lines concerned with the career of Richard Lower, a late seventeenth-century London surgeon who attempted to study "The secret, the mysterious ways, / By which thou [personified Spleen] dost surprise and prey upon the mind" (143–44). According to Finch's account, he pursued the search

> Till, thinking thee to have catched, himself by thee was caught,
>     Retained thy prisoner, thy acknowledged slave,
> And sunk beneath thy chain to a lamented grave.
>
> (147–49)

As a resolution for a poem centrally concerned with unpredictable change, this strikes a grim note. The fact, alluded to in an earlier stanza, that coffee and tea do not dependably alleviate spleen is trivial in comparison to the revelation that disciplined mental activity provides no defense. The "chain" of spleen carries a weight not only heavy, but also irrestible.

Yet the poem's energy, the very energy of its agitation, suggests the speaker's resistance and calls attention to the sense in which the stanzas' irresolute movement communicates that speaker's psychological situation. Lower's intellectual efforts bring him no ultimate success. Finch's efforts arguably work better. The account of Brutus declares her classical learning; the story of Lower tells us of her contemporary awareness; the poem's intricate rhyme and structure reveal her poetic sophistication. The act of writing this poem defies spleen's inherent disorder. If the speaker cannot openly declare her triumph, and even if that triumph remains precarious and temporary, she has yet asserted an intellectual mastery that briefly counters emotional chaos.

Only close attention to *The Spleen* enables one to discern, much less experience, its emotional force. At first glance, the poem may appear remote, mannered, and dispassionate. Eighteenth-century poets, however, did not customarily write to be read "at first glance." Finch's verse, like that of her contemporaries, rewards attention with evidence of strong feeling, strongly controlled.

What, exactly, is the nature of the feeling that dominates *The Spleen*? The question does not allow easy answers, since changeability virtually defines the poem's subject, and its action duplicates the posited pattern of changeability. Beneath that pattern, however, directing the apparently erratic movement of ideas, lie consistent bafflement and frustration, in one sense the poem's dominant emotions. Yet the shifts of tone and subject also convey poetic excitement, a feeling never openly acknowledged. The poem presents the problem of dealing with the incomprehensible – not, it suggests, by insistence on comprehending, but by more devious strategies – as a problem of feeling rather than of reason. Spleen elicits the speaker's reproachfulness, fear, and confusion. The poem exhibits a consistently negative attitude toward the phenomenon it describes, positioning itself clearly against the dangers and terrors of unpredictable emotion. Yet *The Spleen* itself operates almost entirely by means of a series of shifting emotional responses, emotion thus providing its weapon against emotion. It organizes itself around an unstated paradox, on the one hand deploring disordered emotion; on the other, generating lyric intensity out of just such feeling.

Other verse of the period expresses more immediately transparent feeling – by no means necessarily pleasant. Satiric poetry flourished in the early eighteenth century, fueled by and calculated to arouse intense feeling. Inasmuch as satirists aspired "To cure the Vices of Mankind" (Jonathan Swift, *Verses on the Death of Dr Swift, D.S.P.D.* [Dean of St. Patrick's, Dublin], 313), they used contempt and outrage to make those vices appear intolerable. Pope on Timon's villa, in passages we encountered in the last chapter, employs contempt as what we might call a didactic emotion. Elsewhere in *Epistle to Burlington*, Pope provides equally compelling instances of outrage.

Finch reveals and discusses personal feeling in the guise of considering a social problem; Pope, too, disclaims the merely personal. He writes often of individuals he knows or knows about, converting them into representatives of species. Here is a rather terrifying example, an attack against a specific, living, named person:

> Cutler saw Tenants break, and houses fall,
> For very want; he could not build a wall.
> His only Daughter in a Stranger's Pow'r,
> For very want; he could not pay a Dow'r.
> A few grey hairs his rev'rend temples crown'd,

'Twas very want that sold them for two pound.
What ev'n deny'd a cordial at his end,
Banish'd the Doctor, and expell'd the friend?
What but a want, which you perhaps think mad,
Yet numbers feel, the want of what he had.
                              (*An Epistle to Bathurst*, 323–32)

The repetition of "want," the poetic device that most clearly organizes this sequence, takes on the resonance of a refrain; like other refrains, it accretes meaning with repetition. At first, the nature of Cutler's "want" remains obscure, and it is not clear why he cannot build a wall. The suggestion of his daughter's sexual vulnerability makes his inability to pay a dowry horrifying, but the repeated *could not*, denoting impossibility, appears to remove guilt. Yet the irony of *rev'rend* as a characterizing adjective even for this man's physical appearance has already become apparent, as has the fact that it is money that he wants.

At any rate, he *thinks* he wants money, acting on the basis of an imaginary lack. The real lack, as the repeated noun *want* in its diverse exemplary contexts makes clear, is moral rather than economic: lack of the sympathetic feeling for others that numerous eighteenth-century thinkers considered the basis for morality.

The word *want* can and could mean desire as well as lack or need. Cutler's want masquerades to him as need, while actually comprising perverse desire. Its importance as satiric subject emerges clearly in the final couplet ("What but a want, which you perhaps think mad, / Yet numbers feel, the want of what he had."). The invocation of *you*, the reader as well as Bathurst, to whom the verse epistle is addressed, and the insistence that "numbers" share Cutler's psychic malady broaden the relevance of the individual situation. The reader must judge, and the verdict of madness is perhaps the most charitable judgment available to an upright human being. The reader must also remember that despite the bizarre details, Cutler is not an isolated instance: yearning to amass, commitment to Mammon rather than God, tempt many.

The speaker's outrage emerges vividly through the tolling repetition of *want*, with its accumulating meaning, and through the withholding of explicit judgment: the possibility of thinking Cutler's want "mad" offers the only clear hint of how one might respond to the narration. Yet the verse in fact leaves little choice about how to respond. Its absolute tonal assurance conveys the speaker's conviction that the man he has described can win the approval of no sane person. "Numbers" may participate with him in delusions of monetary want, yet everyone must know the wrongness of basing action on such "want." The poem's invocation of "you" calls attention to the public purpose of the speaker's outrage and of the feeling he wishes to create. An imagined audience of Burlington and of like-minded readers supports Pope's clear emotional and moral responses. If we are brought to feel about Cutler (and about the "numbers" like him) as the poem's speaker feels, we have effectively made a moral judgment, a judgment both created and enforced by emotion. Through such judgments, we participate in a fundamental action of community, that of discriminating about conduct.

The intense feeling of early eighteenth-century poetry, however, does not always serve clear moral purposes. When Sarah Fyge Egerton, whose outrage we have already encountered, writes, "So Love and I essentially are one" (*To One who said I must not Love*, 6), she composes a line of naked feeling – though also of deliberate self-display. Her argument in this poem is altogether personal. She sketches her own situation as that of a woman who has married a man she does not love in order to distract herself from the pain of loving one who fails to love her. Now her continuing love for the unresponsive man feels like sin as well as anguish, but she can't eliminate it simply by an act of will.

The line quoted above condenses her argument. Its power comes partly from its diction: entirely one-syllable words, except for the lingering *essentially* that bears so much meaning. The word carries literal force, signifying that Love and "I" share a single essence: the fundamental fabrics of their being duplicate one another. Their separation thus becomes impossible: if the speaker gave up love, she would lose her self. She describes love as "the inherent Pain" (8). Her history of her torments – the attempt to flirt with others producing no relief, the loveless marriage making her previous "guiltless Torture Criminal" (18), the effort at repression producing physical illness – concludes dramatically:

> Distorted Nature shakes at the Controul,
> With strong Convulsions rends my struggling Soul;
> Each vital String cracks with th'unequal Strife,

Departing Love racks like departing Life;
Yet there the Sorrow ceases with the Breath,
But Love each day renews th'torturing scene of Death.

(37–43)

The final alexandrine enacts the prolongation it describes. In the melo-drama Egerton evokes, her personal nature becomes analogous to the great natural fabric of the universe, her soul's convulsions compar-able to those of an earthquake, her attempt to banish love comparable to an agonizing death daily repeated. One could hardly find more extreme metaphors. The extremity insists on the emotional intensity of a private experience.

The poem makes no effort to universalize the suffering it claims. On the contrary, the speaker implicitly maintains her uniqueness. The "One" who urges her not to love stands in for society at large, the mass of others who do not and cannot understand the female anguish here nar-rated. The extravagant statements of that anguish seem designed less to communicate than simply to assert – for this poem is above all an act of self-assertion, permeated by emotion that conveys both the pain of unrequited love and the urgency of proclaiming that pain. The pro-clamation can make no difference to the suffering that supplies the poem's announced subject, but it perhaps alleviates the related pain of invisibility.

Emotion plays so conspicuous a part in *To One who said I must not Love* that no reader could readily ignore it. Although the couplet form supplies discipline to the verse, the entire poem reads like the kind of outpouring one hardly expects from an early eighteenth-century writer (and a woman at that: although women were often associated with emotion, they were not expected to make their feelings public). Unlike the other writers touched on in this chapter, Egerton makes no attempt to suggest public meaning in private experience, despite the fact that she offers her poem to an audience. Atypical, to be sure, she yet calls attention to the close association that eighteenth-century critics often posited between poetry and feeling.

Reading poems such as hers can perhaps alert us to the value of seeking emotional subtexts in less exclamatory works. The status of the self, literal or imagined, is often at issue in evaluating the emotional force of the period's poetry. Watts's hymn represents one extreme. Written for the use of religious communities, hymns by definition seek common emotion and subordinate the speaker, who nonetheless, as we have seen, may communicate his feeling as not only shared but also personal. Egerton's verse marks the opposite pole, making its intense claims for the importance of the individual situation and individual emotional response to it. The territory between these extremes allows for complex and varied possibilities.

A single poem exemplifying both complexity and variety, Jonathan Swift's *Verses on the Death of Dr Swift, D.S.P.D.*, suggests how the idea of the self can lend itself to powerful manipulation in the service of poetic effect. Written in rapid four-stress couplets, a form often associated with comic verse and effective in constructing the numerous shifts of tone that marks Swift's poem, the *Verses* purport to describe social and individual responses to the poet's imagined death. Opening with praise of a familiar maxim by François de la Rouchefoucauld suggesting that everyone finds pleasure in the misfortune of friends, the speaker employs first- and second-person pronouns to striking effect. He starts forthrightly by announcing his own belief in the truth of la Rochefoucauld's maxims, then challenges the reader ("you") to let Reason and Experience test that truth. "I" returns as a kind of test case:

> I love my Friend as well as you,
> But would not have him stop my View;
> Then let him have the higher Post;
> I ask but for an Inch at most.
>
> (17–20)

Not only does this "I" wish always an inch of superiority over his beloved friend; he specifically envies the accomplishments of fellow poets, his friends, whom he names, whose skills he specifies, and with whom he declares his rivalry.

But the case he wishes to make is general as well as specific.

> Vain human Kind! Fantastic Race!
> Thy various Follies, who can trace?
> Self-love, Ambition, Envy, Pride,
> Their Empire in our Hearts divide:
> Give others Riches, Power, and Station,
> 'Tis all on me an Usurpation.
>
> (39–44)

The progression of pronouns calls attention to the fact that, as the poem repeatedly attests, all generalization leads finally back to the self. The human kind, or species, addressed first formally and distantly with "Thy," two lines later becomes "our" domain. The speaker proves by his own emotions the truth of what he avers. Self-love, Ambition, Envy, Pride operate not only in "our" hearts but in his, as he experiences envy and indignation at the good fortune of others.

All these observations, he explains at line 70, constitute only the "Proem": now the poem itself can begin. The reflections about how the good fortune of friends provokes malignance, however, stand powerfully behind the imagined scenario of the Dean's approaching death. It's hard to see how my death can do anyone any good, he reflects, but then he envisions, with sharp human awareness and a keen ear for idiom, the possible reactions of a group of unnamed persons, who deprecate his accomplishment, exaggerate his physical decay, add to his age, feel pleased to hear he's getting worse, and delight in the fact that they have prophesied this death. The matter of fact tone sometimes approaches the comic:

> Yet shou'd some Neighbour feel a Pain,
> Just in the Parts, where I complain;
> How many a Message would he send?
> What hearty Prayers that I should mend?
>
> (135–38)

The poem reiterates its message of universal self-interest as the dominant human emotion, variously hinting contempt, outrage, amusement, and realistic acceptance. Only through these delicately conveyed attitudes does the speaker insert himself into the pattern of his verses until almost the midpoint of the poem.

Yet, after all, he is confronting the subject of his own death, a subject calculated to arouse emotion. For 142 lines he keeps the topic at a distance with his imaginary scenarios. Then comes what sounds like a moment of realization:

> My good Companions, never fear,
> For though you may mistake a Year;
> Though your Prognosticks run too fast,
> They must be verify'd at last.
>
> (143–46)

The irony of "My good Companions" – these are the men and women who have been cheerfully prognosticating his death – cuts only mildly; the energy of the lines comes from sudden awareness that this game the poet has been playing, this imagined mini-drama, will after all turn into fact, and no amount of wit can protect against it.

But the inevitability of Swift's death, as of all our deaths, does not make it real at the moment of writing the poem. The reminder of that inevitability precedes a new bout of imagining, as the speaker assigns derogatory, self-serving, or malicious comments to both anonymous and named observers. Then he turns to the "real" mourners, his true friends: Pope, he allows, will grieve a month; John Gay, a week; Dr. Arbuthnot, a day. Others will mourn out of self-interest: they grieve because they fear their own deaths. The speaker's woman friends, "whose tender Hearts / Have better learn'd to act their Parts" (224–25), can hardly keep their minds on their loss, so absorbed are they in their card game. Finally, the speaker imagines the scene a year after his death: no one misses him any longer, and new books have taken the place of his old ones.

The extended exercise in self-chastening imagination that has composed the poem's first 300 lines concludes at this point. In evoking responses to his prospective and his actual death, the poet has proclaimed his own insignificance in the political, social, and literary world. He avoids explicit judgment of those who demonstrate their superficiality or malignance or selfishness in their reactions to another's death, assuming for himself the stance of disinterested observer. Yet the poem has not lacked emotional clues. The satirist's eye exposes the relentless self-concern that operates in every social situation. Swift has used the fiction of his own death to express a kind of bemused outrage at the consistency with which human beings demonstrate their inability to achieve sustained concern for others.

The poem, however, does not end here. Changing course, it continues for almost 200 lines more, with yet another account of the Dean by a club member who "My Character impartial draws" (306). This new characterization differs sharply from anything previously suggested. Now we encounter a heroic figure, uninterested in power or prestige, not dependent on others, choosing for friends only "the Wise and Good" (332), helping virtue in distress, tireless in fighting for the right. In short, the figure now evoked bears little resemblance to the version of humanity suggested by the reactions of earlier characters to Swift's imagined death.

What are we to make of this? Perhaps we resort to biographical data to confirm, for example, that Swift indeed fought heroically for liberty – with pen rather than sword:

> Fair LIBERTY was all his cry;
> For her he stood prepar'd to die;
> For her he oft expos'd his own.
> Two Kingdoms, just as Faction led,
> Had set a Price upon his Head;
> But, not a Traytor cou'd be found,
> To sell him for Six Hundred Pound.
>
> (346–54)

Investigating, we discover that it's all true: political pamphlets Swift published anonymously in England and in Ireland caused the government to offer, twice, a reward of £300 to anyone who identified the author. Although many knew of Swift's authorship, no one claimed the reward.

Knowing such facts, however, does not solve the reader's problem. Even if the central claims correspond to literal data about Swift's life, isn't there something unseemly about his portraying himself in such exalted terms? Does he really wish us to believe that the rest of the world, including his closest friends, lacks all capacity for commitment, while he alone possesses it? Are we intended to forget everything the satirist has shown us in the first 300 lines? Do the unflattering characterizations of the Dean exist only for the sake of contrast with the final portrait of heroic virtue?

The earlier imaginings of varied responses to the Dean's death range through diverse social contexts: the literary scene, the world of politics, the royal court, all of which Swift literally inhabited in the course of his career. The "impartial observer," who appears set apart from social circumstance, at least glancingly surveys them all in assessing his subject's accomplishment. At the outset, he speaks of Swift's literary works, noting that he cannot

> tell what Criticks thought 'em;
> But, this I know, all People bought 'em;

As with a moral View design'd
To cure the Vices of Mankind:
His Vein, ironically grave,
Expos'd the Fool, and lash'd the Knave.
(311–16)

This description of satire's purpose – morally motivated, designed to reform vice, to expose fools, and to punish knaves – belongs to a long tradition of satiric self-justification. The poem that contains it, however, raises questions about even this claim. In its satiric exposure of pettiness, inattention, malice, and self-interest, through the scenes in which people respond to Swift's death, the *Verses* appear to solicit amusement at the ramifications of human folly rather than aspire to reformative effect. Despite its intimate subject, the poem develops a series of voices predominantly removed from the kind of emotion one might anticipate. The final, allegedly impartial speaker provides moments of emotional intensity (I'll say more about them shortly), but the octosyllabic couplets move rapidly along without developing any single ground for feeling. The poem's satire does not seem reformative, nor does its praise for its subject linger sufficiently to enforce its details.

To be sure, the cumulative effect of the final speaker's panegyric is impressive. Although individual points (Swift didn't care about power or wealth; he pitied those who responded with ingratitude to his generosity; he tried to reconcile rather than to divide, and so on) emerge and are dismissed with great rapidity, they add up to a portrait of a man compelled by selfless moral principle, who acts in many spheres, but always with the same attention to justice and probity. Twentieth- and twenty-first-century admirers of Swift often appear to accept some such characterization of the man.

In the context of this poem, though, it is, as I have already suggested, difficult to believe in such an account of *any* man. After all, the poem has opened by explicitly involving its first speaker, the Dean himself, in the common human failing of competitiveness. He has acknowledged his desire always to be on top and has accepted the maxim that we find something pleasing in the misfortunes of our friends, fully implicating himself in that "we." Must we forget this in order to read the poem's last long section successfully?

On the contrary: the first section arguably offers the richest clue for how to read the last. The Dean who constitutes the subject of the *Verses* and who appears in the first person in the poem's initial passages positions himself as the imaginer of the rest, introducing the sequence of derogatory comments by his so-called friends with "thus, methinks, I hear 'em speak" (77). He reminds the reader of the fanciful status of the poem's speeches and speakers just before the final observer draws his character; "Suppose me dead; and then suppose / A Club assembled at the *Rose*" (299–300). Like everything narrated earlier, the subsequent speech derives not from observation or memory but from supposition. As the imaginer of the man who depicts his "Character impartial" (306) and of that "Character" itself, the Dean remains the same person who earlier acknowledged specific operations of his self-interest. Self-interest, we may posit, underlies his imagining of what an impartial characterization would sound like. To put it otherwise: this is the characterization he would like to have spoken of him.

To say so, however, is not to contradict that characterization altogether. *Verses on the Death of Dr Swift, D.S.P.D.* instructs us not only that all men are mortal – we all die – but that all share mortal natures, natures that partake of Original Sin, natures necessarily mixed, composed of good and evil together. The initial self-characterization of the Dean as motivated by competitive self-interest, the subsequent gibes of false friends, the final "Character impartial": none encompasses the full truth of his being. The positive characterization, however, is the most persuasive: it rings with certitude, its verse itself carrying conviction. Unlike the comments of observers quoted earlier (e.g., "The rest will give a Shrug and cry, / I'm sorry; but we all must dye"; 211–12), the assessment that concludes the poem has moments, as I mentioned earlier, of powerful feeling, sometimes attributed to Swift himself, sometimes implied by the speaker.

> With Horror, Grief, Despair the Dean
> Beheld the dire destructive Scene:
> His Friends in Exile, or the Tower,
> Himself within the Frown of Power;
> Pursu'd by base envenom'd Pens,
> Far to the Land of Slaves and Fens.
> (391–96)

Here a series of nouns labels the Dean's emotions, and the speed of the verse has the effect of deliberate understatement: the speaker

refuses to dwell on these strong feelings, although he provides evidence
of their justification. Elsewhere, as in the poem's concluding lines, we
can sense the force of the speaker's emotion, not articulated, deliberately held back, yet almost bursting the discipline of verse:

> He gave the little Wealth he had,
> To build a House for Fools and Mad:
> And shew'd by one satiric Touch,
> No Nation wanted it so much:
> That Kingdom he hath left his Debtor,
> I wish it soon may have a Better.
>
> (478–83)

The bitter restraint of the final line condenses the import of these concluding passages. The Dean celebrated in them was not perfect, nor
does the speaker think him so. But he was a good man, a man who
worked to stand for the right and oppose the wrong. He did much for
the kingdom he inhabited (Ireland), despite its inadequacies. It is hard
to imagine that a better man will come along.

The point, then, is not that the concluding characterization contains
the whole truth of Swift's nature and career. The poem itself has educated us to understand that no human being remains high-minded
always: the satirist who claims his high moral purpose is quite capable of indulging malice and resentment. Yet the verse has also
impelled us to feel the difference between the casual pettiness of
unconsidered speech and the meditated evaluation that the final
speaker offers. The man here celebrated was morally insufficient, as
all human beings are, but he recognized his insufficiencies and tried
to combat them. He loved his country; he did good; he suffered; he
died. The poem that purports to sum up his life and death evokes our
emotions in order to persuade us, in order perhaps to persuade the
writer himself, that this life and this imagined death carry meaning,
despite the inadequacies and failures inherent in the human condition.

Only by paying attention to the poem's emotional designs on us can
we experience its power and understand its import. Yet the verse itself
makes it difficult to pay such attention, sweeping us along in a confusion of speakers and messages, sounding often not quite serious, then
suddenly very serious indeed. Once more, the casual reader will be
baffled; once more, the poem is not intended for such a reader.

Among the five poets treated in this chapter, only Egerton makes a parade of emotion. Her claim of intense feeling lies at the center of her argument. By recognizing and fully acknowledging the power and permanence of her emotion, and only by doing so, she maintains, the reader may grasp her nature. Conversely, to avoid or deny such recognition amounts to a kind of abuse, or so she would have it. Her insistence about how she suffers comprises, she implies, her only weapon in the unequal struggle she wages against other people's prohibitions and rebukes. Watts, Finch, Pope, and Swift, in contrast, exemplify a common strategy of demanding emotional response even as they appear to disdain it. Their poetry at once invites and makes difficult our realization of its expressive power.

Pope, Finch, and Egerton figured in the preceding chapter as writers who implicitly or explicitly offered recommendations about how to live and who in the process explored links and tensions between individuals and the society they inhabit. Surveyed in the new context of where and how emotion reveals itself in early eighteenth-century verse, further examples of their work bear on the same issue. Egerton makes more dramatic her rebellion against social strictures. Pope demonstrates yet more clearly the degree to which he makes society his subject, while understanding always that "society" consists of a collection of individuals whose individual weaknesses create fault lines in the larger body. Finch places herself in the context of her social setting, defining the members of her society as widely afflicted by the same unaccountable malady that she herself suffers.

Societies as commonly understood exist within a historical context. When Pope attacks Cutler, he implicitly criticizes an evolving capitalistic system in which preoccupation with money came increasingly to seem a source of individual moral weakness – although also of increasing national power. When Egerton inveighs against those who criticize her, she complains about a system of conventions belonging to her moment. Even Finch, describing the operations of spleen, describes also assumptions and behaviors of her place and time. Swift most fully acknowledges the historical, both in his fantasies about how the passing of time will affect attitudes toward him and in his evocations of and suggestions about past political struggles. Only Watts imagines a form of community outside of time, a non-secular society of the saved.

Strikingly, four out of five of these writers aware of their participation – willing or unwilling, happy or unhappy – in community understand themselves in one way or another as outsiders. Egerton, self-described as a malcontent, feels discontent because of her nonconformity. Swift, identified with Ireland, opposed to English policies, in effect exiled from England, uses his position as a vantage point for criticism. Finch expresses a sense of alienation as a woman who presumes to write, thus violating her society's convention. Pope, as satirist, necessarily claims the position of judicious or outraged observer. Watts alone, unconcerned with existing social organizations, fails to consider his own position within them.

These are not, of course, the only early eighteenth-century poets whose work reveals and solicits powerful feeling. Yet their conjunction of the outsider position with the capacity to express intense emotion suggests a new possibility about the relation between individual and society. Emotion belongs only to individuals. Perhaps the feeling of being set apart, which may force outsiders to realize their individual uniqueness, intensifies their ability to wield the power of the emotion they experience.

In any case, as the poems discussed here make apparent, the claim of separation forces poetic attention to the nature and function of the self. Along with contemplating and expressing a wide range of emotions – erotic love to social outrage, religious fervor to neurotic self-castigation – these poems convey different attitudes toward the imagined self. *Verses on the Death of Dr Swift, D.S.P.D.* begins by evoking greed, competitiveness, and aggression as inherent in every distinct self. Later, it suggests the possibility of altruism and patriotism: the self's commitments beyond itself. Moreover, through its play between Swift as writer and as subject, it suggests the emotional diversity within individuals. Referring to social and national as well as personal concerns and ricocheting among fragmentary multiple perspectives, it reminds its readers that the point of view of any single self is necessarily partial. This is poetry of emotion (though not only of emotion), yet it disclaims emotion as sufficient guide. It contrasts especially vividly with Egerton's defiant self-assertion, in which her sense of uniqueness, both painful and triumphant, provides a platform for utterance and a support in suffering.

*The Spleen* conveys a sense of self almost as complex as that of Swift's meditation on his own death. Here, too, the poet's double role as creator and at least intermittent subject enforces awareness of paradoxical possibilities. As creator, Finch has a position of authority. The self as social observer and commentator, as writer of the poem, however, often abandons critical distance in its hasty, uneven, rather disordered evocation of the psychological disorder that victimizes the self as subject. Imagining herself as victim of the spleen, Finch simultaneously asserts herself as commentator. Emotional energy suffuses her entwined suggestions of the self as at once fragile and powerful.

Pope, in his attacks on Timon and on Cutler, and Watts in his hymns convey the self not as subject but as voice. Both speak for and to their communities, but communities of different kinds, secular and religious. Watts conveys awe, trepidation, and hope, emotions appropriate to the believer. He subordinates any sense of personal self to his role: the self as representative of the community of faith. Pope assumes the voice of one possessed of, possessed *by*, intense clarity of moral vision. He declares the power of the inspired individual to function as seer, showing his fellows who they are and who they might be.

Inasmuch as they explore the powers and the weaknesses of the self, these early eighteenth-century poets call attention to an issue that will preoccupy many others as the century continues. They remind us that lyric, as conventionally construed, is not the only poetic form for self-exploration.

# 3

# The Power of Detail: Description in Verse

The particularities of early eighteenth-century verse locate objects in a universe of significance and enmesh readers in a web of meanings. Yet it proves difficult often even to notice the existence of particulars in poems that appear resolutely to concern themselves more with general perceptions than with sharply perceived specific scenes. Just as the emotion of the period's verse can elude the reader who brings to it expectations formed by poetry of a later era, so the detail of a nature poem that begins by invoking a mysterious and undescribed *"Silent Nymph"* can seem so vague and generalized that it virtually disappears.

The poem to which I allude is John Dyer's *Grongar Hill* (1726). Here are its opening lines:

> *Silent Nymph*, with curious Eye!
> Who, the purple Ev'ning, lye
> On the Mountain's lonely Van,
> Beyond the Noise of busy Man,
> Painting fair the form of Things,
> While the yellow Linnet sings . . .
> (1–6)

The Nymph, who soon gets invited to aid her sister Muse (10), is presumably the Muse of painting, invoked as a companion to that of poetry. Her curious eye underlines the implications of painting as a metaphorical allusion: this poem may be expected to dwell on the visual. *Grongar Hill* indeed provides many visual references. The first six lines suggest their nature. They depend, typically, on adjectives. In the quoted passage, *purple* and *yellow*, words of color, words that might come from a painter's consciousness, offer the closest approximation to vivid physical appearance. Yet "purple Ev'ning" evokes nothing very distinct, and the linnet's yellowness seems more classificatory than descriptive.

Other adjectives serve more ambiguous functions. "Busy," "curious," and "lonely" suggest psychological conditions as well as the physical manifestations that accompany them. "Busy Man," like "yellow Linnet," calls attention to a defining characteristic of the species adjectivally described, but the adjective also tells us that noise-making man is man in motion. We know the nature neither of the noise nor of the motion: only that both exist. "Busy Man" may belong to a painting, but the phrase hardly clarifies what the painting shows when it shows "Man." The curious eye and the lonely mountaintop, similarly, offer only hints about what the poem's reader should mentally "see."

The only other visual adjective, "fair," epitomizes vagueness. The scene is, the adjective tells us, pleasant, attractive. Exactly what makes it so remains unspecified. Perhaps the rest of the poem will tell us: "Draw the Landskip bright and strong," the poet commands the Muse (14). But although *Grongar Hill* extends for 158 lines, most of them nominally descriptive, the pictures it creates never conform for long to what post-modern readers might understand as "bright and strong." Clearly, the notion of description operating here requires special attention.

The poem itself offers clues about its procedures.

> Ever charming, ever new,
> When will the Landskip tire the View!
> The Fountain's Fall, the River's Flow,
> The woody Vallies, warm and low;
> The windy Summit, wild and high,
> Roughly rushing on the Sky!
> The pleasant Seat, the ruin'd Tow'r,
> The naked Rock, the shady Bow'r;
> The Town and Village, Dome and Farm,
> Each give each a double Charm,
> As Pearls upon an *Æthiop*'s Arm.
>
> (103–13)

According to this sequence, contrast provides the enlivening principle of the landscape – and, by extension, of the poem that evokes it. One need not focus on details of the fountain's appearance: what matters is that the fountain falls, whereas the river flows. The lowness and warmth of the valleys counterpoint the summit's wild height, as the rock's nakedness opposes the bower's fecundity. The onlooker cannot tire of the view when provided with so many diverse elements to look at. As pearls on a dark arm glow more intensely, but also call attention to the beauty of the darkness with which they contrast, so rock and bower, town and village set one another off.

Pattern exists both in individual oppositions, like that of "Dome" (in its Latinate sense, meaning private dwelling) and "Farm," and in the whole system of contrasts that the passage suggests. Every visual detail, therefore, demands to be seen – or imagined – in the context of other aspects of the scene that the poem conjures up. Although a detail may have value in itself, its participation in pattern intensifies that value.

The particular patterns Dyer imagines have special meaning because they show "the Face of Nature" (45), and show it, specifically, "In all the Hues of Heaven's Bow!" (46). The exclamation point, a form of punctuation on which the poet relies heavily, emphasizes the importance of this line about color and color's source. The various hues of nature belong also to heaven, since they derive, in Dyer's imagination, from the rainbow that constitutes God's promise to humanity. As a consequence, to dwell on the colors of a forest or farm approaches an act of worship, not because God inheres in nature, but because the natural world testifies to the operation of divine power.

So it is that when the poet contemplates a stand of trees, seeing them from his vantage point atop the hill, he sees mostly color:

> Below me Trees unnumber'd rise,
> Beautiful in various Dies:
> The gloomy Pine, the Poplar blue,
> The yellow Beech, the sable Yew,
> The slender Firr, that taper grows,
> The sturdy Oak with broad-spread Boughs.
> And beyond the purple Grove,
> Haunt of *Phillis*, Queen of Love!
> Gawdy as the op'ning Dawn,
> Lies a long and level Lawn,
> On which a dark Hill, steep and high,
> Holds and charms the wand'ring Eye!
> (56–67)

A visual symphony of color and form exerts direct power over the eye, which becomes enthralled by the scene's magic, a point emphasized by the final exclamation point. "Gawdy," in this period, means "brilliant" rather than "flamboyant"; and "purple" designates any form of rich color (by association with royalty, which wore purple). These generalized designations of the colorful reinforce the earlier stress on specific hues of the forest. The scene, however, offers no sound, no smell, no activity. Constructed like a painting, it exists only as a kind of vision, seen from a distance.

Charmed by color and by pattern, by hill in relation to lawn, lawn in relation to woods, the eye leads the mind not only to aesthetic pleasure but also to moral reflection. The picturesque ruined castle once housed the proud and mighty; its moldering remains remind the observer of the brevity of power. In the distance, the stream looks as though one could step over it; thinking about it, one knows better, and knows the possibility of self-delusion. As we see the mountain, beautiful from afar, and realize how rugged it would seem when approached, we realize how hope can disguise the dangers of the future.

> Thus is Nature's Vesture wrought,
> To instruct our wand'ring Thought;
> Thus she dresses green and gay,
> To disperse our Cares away.
>                        (99–102)

Like poetry, nature both instructs and pleases.

The poem's assorted morals do not exist as afterthoughts. Within the fiction of *Grongar Hill*, morals inhere in the landscape. The immediate observer, the verse asserts, not the poet reflecting from a distance, perceives the meaning of the mountain's contrasting aspects even as he perceives those aspects themselves. The scene forces its import upon him. Because, the poem implicitly argues, any observer may expect the same kind of experience – because, again, nature both instructs and pleases – Grongar Hill as a place becomes a type of nature as object of observation and as source of pleasure and wisdom, therefore recommended to every reader.

Dyer's heavy reliance on adjective–noun constructions to create aesthetic effects reappears in many poems of his period, as does his interest in and dependence on patterns created by concatenations of diversity. James Thomson composed *The Seasons* over twenty years, publishing individual parts of the long poem separately and revising them repeatedly. The sequential seasons provide him with a pattern of meaningful diversity, but his close examination of the natural and human scene supplies supporting data to illustrate the pervasiveness of such pattern throughout the created universe.

*Spring*, first published in 1730, exemplifies the poem's methods. The poet shows himself fully aware of description's difficulties:

> But who can paint
> Like Nature? Can Imagination boast,
> Amid its gay Creation, Hues like hers?
> . . . If Fancy then
> Unequal fails beneath the pleasing Task;
> Ah what shall Language do? Ah where find Words
> Ting'd with so many Colours?
>
> (468–70, 473–76)

Like Dyer, Thomson apparently considers color the crucial element in visual description. Of all the colors, green, "smiling Nature's universal Robe!" (83), is most important for spring, but the poem also abounds in color terms evoking the differentiated appearance of individual flowers and birds – to say nothing of the rainbow itself.

As the emphasis on color suggests, the eye once more assumes an important position. It is, variously, the "cherish'd Eye" (89) – cherished, presumably, for the abundance which it can absorb; the "raptur'd Eye" (111), the "hurried Eye" (519), the "roving Eye" (507). When a man achieves a height like that of Grongar Hill and contemplates the landscape beneath him, his eye is "snatch'd o'er Hill and Dale, and Wood and Lawn, / And verdant Field, and darkening Heath between" (951–52) – as well as quite a lot more. The emphatic verb, which makes the eye passive, possessed by rather than possessing the scene, calls attention to the poem's thematic stress on the natural world's power.

Over and over, the speaker commands the reader to "see." But not only to see: to smell, to hear, to feel, to imagine. The nature of the poetic enterprise makes imagining the most important of these capacities: only by virtue of imagination, after all, can the reader see, hear, or smell the luxuriance of spring as evoked by the poem. But the poet calls for more complicated forms of imagination than the kind involved in recapturing sense impressions. His demand for imaginative effort emerges often through particular forms of detail that may seem startling. Shortly after an evocative description of garden flowers, rich in precise visual detail, Thomson provides a short passage praising God as the source of all natural manifestations. Then comes this:

> By THEE the various vegetative Tribes,
> Wrapt in a filmy Net, and clad with Leaves,
> Draw the live Ether, and imbibe the Dew.
> By THEE dispos'd into congenial Soils,
> Stands each attractive Plant, and sucks, and swells
> The juicy Tide; a twining Mass of Tubes.
> At THY Command the vernal Sun awakes
> The torpid Sap, detruded to the Root
> By wintry Winds, that now in fluent Dance,
> And lively Fermentation, mounting, spreads
> All this innumerous-colour'd Scene of things.
>
> (561–71)

To think of plants as sucking and swelling, as consisting of a twining mass of tubes, requires an imaginative act quite different from that invited by a line like "The yellow Wall-Flower, stain'd with iron Brown" (532). If the mass of tubes creates a visual impression, that impression is vaguely unpleasant – far from aesthetically satisfying. But the line about the tubes actually makes it difficult to see anything at all, thus forcing the reader to ponder the *meaning* of conceiving a plant in such terms. That meaning depends upon the assumption that divine wisdom has created not only the garden's beauty but also its operating principles. The shock of such conjunctions of diction as "fluent Dance" and "lively Fermentation" – one phrase evoking appearance, the other, a chemical process – underlines the point. Both aspects of flowers, from the poet's point of view, possess equal importance. Both demand to be imagined. Each plant is "attractive" (565) in two senses: it attracts the viewer's eye, and it attracts the earth's moisture, converting it into sap. A word like *detruded*, quite alien to conventional poetic languages, calls attention to the scientific exactitude of Thomson's account, and to his insistence that science provides a form of vision vital to comprehending the visual spectacle of spring. Such a word acquires poetic power by virtue of its meaning rather than its sound. It inhabits a poem in which the visions of science have importance equal to that of what the eye alone sees.

Many of Thomson's details stress the intense activity that he perceives in the natural world. One final long quotation will suggest his inclusive view of nature's action.

> As the Sea,
> Far thro' his azure turbulent Domain,
> Your Empire owns, and from a thousand Shores
> Wafts all the Pomp of Life into your Ports;
> So with superior Boon may your rich Soil,
> Exuberant, Nature's better Blessings pour
> O'er every Land, the naked Nations cloath,
> And be th' exhaustless Granary of a World!
> Nor only thro' the lenient Air this Change,
> Delicious, breathes; the penetrative Sun,
> His Force deep-darting to the dark Retreat
> Of Vegetation, sets the steaming Power
> At large, to wander o'er the vernant Earth,
> In various Hues; but chiefly thee, gay *Green!*
> Thou smiling Nature's universal Robe!
> United Light and Shade! Where the Sight dwells
> With growing Strength, and ever-new Delight.
> From the moist Meadow to the wither'd Hill,
> Led by the Breeze, the vivid Verdure runs,
> And swells, and deepens, to the cherish'd Eye.
> (70–89)

The passage goes on to evoke trees in action – changing color, putting forth buds, "unfolding" – and the garden pursuing its own kind of activity.

The sources of energy in the quoted lines include ocean, soil, sun, sap ("the steaming Power"), human sight (which develops strength from its contemplation), breeze, and "Verdure." All contribute to natural harmony, not only as objects of contemplation but as agents of fruitful change. The color green itself composes a union, as though light and shade had actively merged to create it. Of the nouns I designated as "sources of energy," only ocean and breeze, and possibly sap, are ordinarily perceived as active. The green of spring leaves, like the solidity of soil, might for another poet contrast with the motion of wind and water. For Thomson, though, the soil is "Exuberant": luxuriantly fertile, overflowing with abundance, pouring out blessings, clothing the naked, supplying inexhaustible food. The verdure of spring runs and swells and deepens. Everything is in motion.

That motion, however, is partly invisible. One cannot see the soil pouring out blessings or clothing nations; the eye does not record the activity of the "penetrative Sun" or the wandering sap. Like the twining mass of tubes hidden in plants, much of spring's action is "seen" only by the eye of imagination. Thomson's imagination has its own exuberance: it overflows with its transmutations of scientific information and of remembered scenes, evoking a world of unbounded richness and promise.

The best-known sequence in *Spring*, the extended passage on the loves of the birds (as Thomson puts it, "*the Passion of the Groves*"; 580), which occupies more than 200 lines (581–789), varies the principle of realizing the invisible. Now the poet specifies in great detail exactly what the birds do – build their nests, guard their eggs and their young, encourage nestlings to fly – as their activity might be seen by a literal observer. Human beings become the material of analogies, as the birds take center stage: the birds resemble, for instance, a poverty-stricken couple who sacrifice their own food to the needs of their children. The exact nature of the resemblance depends on the poem's positing of feelings in the winged creatures it describes. Thomson attributes generosity, tenderness, and compassion, as well as love, to the birds who participate in the springtime ritual of mating. Such emotions are invisible; their attribution claims once more the imagination's power to see beneath surfaces, discovering connections and uncovering beauty.

In no simple sense, however, does "beauty" provide the goal for early eighteenth-century poets of detail. The aesthetic satisfaction of a line like "The torpid Sap, detruded to the Root" derives from a complicated process of abstraction and generalization – a process leading, like Dyer's generalized descriptions of farms and domes, hills and valleys, to perception of pattern. Thomson's patterns depend on the discovery of links between the human and animal world and between conventional manifestations of natural beauty and the unseen, divinely ordained processes that produce them.

Even for Thomson, as his successive enlargements of *The Seasons* demonstrate, and yet more emphatically for other poets of his time, man is the measure of all things. A few lines from Ambrose Philips's *A Winter-Piece* economically illustrate the point. Philips is describing the beauty revealed by the arrival of "The ruddy Morn" (30):

> ev'ry Shrub, and ev'ry Blade of Grass,
> And ev'ry pointed Thorn, seem'd wrought in Glass.
> In Pearls and Rubies rich the Hawthorns show,
> While through the Ice the Crimson Berries glow.
> The thick-sprung Reeds the watry Marshes yield,
> Seem polish'd Lances in a hostile Field.
>
> (33–38)

Responding to a natural scene, he evokes his reaction by comparing the natural to the artificial, as though the latter provided the standard of beauty – or, perhaps, of comprehensibility. The landscape he imagines indeed has a kind of spectral beauty, along with faintly sinister suggestiveness, but the language he chooses to convey his imaginings reveals that man's rather than God's creation provides his standard of judgment.

The clarity of Philips's aesthetic procedure calls attention also to a more hidden aspect of work by Dyer and Thomson. Both delineate nature as alike pleasing and instructive – classically ordained aspects not of nature, but of literature. Nature assumes these attributes, in the poems, because a poet has insisted that they exist and has pointed out the ways in which nature delights and educates. Without Dyer's instruction, we would not necessarily notice the pleasing contrast of rock and bower or understand how nature can discipline "our wand'ring Thought." Thomson teaches us that the sun wakens sap "detruded to the Root." Only as a result of this teaching can we take full pleasure in the multifarious patterns of activity in the natural world. Thus early eighteenth-century poets demonstrate their significance: the created universe provides beauty and instruction; the poets make these qualities available. Human control remains paramount.

Poets of nature are not alone in relying on meaningful detail. Pope's manipulation of minute particularities in *The Rape of the Lock* contributes powerfully to the poem's charm. It also exemplifies the deft balance of particular and general that characterizes much of the century's poetry.

In Canto 2, for instance, Pope describes the sylphs who act as guardian spirits for young women:

> The lucid squadrons round the sails repair:
> Soft o'er the shrouds aerial whispers breath,
> That seem'd but zephyrs to the train beneath.

Some to the sun their insect-wings unfold,
Waft on the breeze, or sink in clouds of gold.
Transparent forms, too fine for mortal sight,
Their fluid bodies half dissolv'd in light.
Loose to the wind their airy garments flew,
Thin glitt'ring textures of the filmy dew;
Dipt in the richest tincture of the skies,
Where light disports in ever-mingling dies,
While ev'ry beam new transient colours flings,
Colours that change whene'er they wave their wings.
(2: 57–68)

The sails around which the sylphs gather are those of the boat bearing Belinda, the poem's central figure, and her entourage down the Thames. The sylphs, in other words, inhabit an ordinary human setting, extraordinary though they are. "Too fine for mortal sight," of course never seen in actuality, these evanescent creatures achieve visual reality by virtue of a description that half-reveals, half-conceals. The "visual reality" attained in fact emphasizes the impossibility of precise definition. The description teems with color, yet no particular color is specified, except for the "clouds of gold" into which the sylphs sink – clouds presumably colored by the sun. As for the colors of the "lucid squadrons" themselves (*lucid* meaning bright or luminous, but also translucent or clear), the ambiguity of the introductory adjective persists throughout the passage. The sylphs glitter; they shed light about them in all the colors of the rainbow and of the heavens; yet like those of light itself, their colors cannot be captured by the eye. The poet through his details insists that he "sees" what no other mortal has seen. At the same time, he declares the impossibility of seeing what he describes.

Such a passage invites the reader into a rich imaginative world, but one defined by severe selectivity. Although the account of the sylphs creates an impression of ever-changing variety, all its details in fact concentrate on permutations of light and color. As "seen" by the poet, these beings consist entirely of patterns of light. They live in the mind's eye as fluctuations of color, yet the concentration on light creates a vivid sense of their natures.

The same principle of selectivity characteristically governs Pope's choice of detail. The famous dressing table scene in *The Rape of the Lock* provides another series of examples:

This casket *India*'s glowing gems unlocks,
And all *Arabia* breaths from yonder box.
The Tortoise here and Elephant unite,
Transform'd to Combs, the speckled, and the white . . .
                                                (1: 133–36)

The two couplets provide little visual data: the combs are either speckled or white; the gems "glow." The meaningful detail the lines offer concerns origins: gems from India, scents from Arabia, combs made of tortoise shell or ivory. The triviality of combs and scents contrasts vividly with the grandeur of elephants – or even tortoises; the exoticism and sheer distance of Arabia and India. The lines delineate Belinda as consumer of the world's goods – a suggestion that might raise either pride or concern in contemporary readers: pride over the international trade carried by British ships, which made Belinda's luxuries possible; concern over the possibility that increased opportunities for self-indulgence might weaken British moral fiber. The couplets also hint the magnitude of endeavor involved in producing and delivering the dressing table's ornaments – the magnitude of effort required to produce Belinda. Such a suggestion both mocks and glorifies the poem's central figure. On the one hand, Pope makes us feel the disproportion involved in Belinda's role as secular goddess: she is, after all, only a fashionable and vain young woman. On the other hand, we must take her beauty seriously. As William Butler Yeats would write, long after Pope: "One must labour to be beautiful"; and beauty (the beauty of a woman, of a constellation, of a poem) constitutes a genuine value.

In his poetry of detail, as in so many other respects, Pope towers above his fellows by virtue of his artistic control and his brilliant selectivity. But powerful detail marks much early eighteenth-century verse. *The Rape of the Lock* utilizes both psychological and physical detail; so did other works of the period. Poets who chose to write of the city rather than the natural world would almost inevitably concern themselves with human beings in action. Thus, in the eighteen lines of *A Description of a Morning*, Jonathan Swift suggests that various forms of corruption and laziness belong as inevitably as the rising sun to the urban scene, and he gives them concrete realization as part of that scene. The servant girl sleeps with her master; the apprentice is "Slipshod" (4); the youth who sweeps does so with the stump of a broom; unpaid tradesmen congregate at a lord's gate; prisoners return to jail from a night of stealing, undertaken to reward their guard; sheriff's officers lie in wait for evasive debtors. The poem's effect depends on the poet's and the reader's awareness of poetic tradition. Line two, which evokes "the Ruddy Morn's Approach," implicitly calls on readers to remember other poems that describe the advent of morning, perhaps using similar phrasing (as Philips does, in a line quoted earlier). Such verse typically dwells on erotic love (particularly in the aubade tradition, in which the coming of dawn concludes a night of passion) or, as in Thomson, on the beauties of nature. Swift's poem suggests erotic activity, but nothing approaching love; it insists on a cacophony of sound rather than rural harmony; it delineates domestic tasks, worn out gutters, and commonplace happening. It redefines the poetic.

Clarity provides the implicit ideal of such a work. The precision of detail that Swift brings to the task of describing the mundane would focus eighteenth-century readers' attention sharply on what they might see and largely ignore every day. For readers of a later period, the sharp focus clarifies exact and possibly unknown aspects of daily urban life in the past. Like a movie attentive to minutiae of an earlier time, the poem invites us to attend to just what things were like, without the sentimental haze that sometimes obscures bygone facts. The verses' poetic effect derives from their precision.

The same attention to things as they are marks *A Description of a City Shower*, another of Swift's urban poems. Drawing on Virgil (both the *Georgics* and the *Aeneid*) as specific model, the poet removes from his modern scene all classical dignity. The pain of corns, body aches, and hollow teeth foretells the shower; a character suggestively named Dulman "damns the Climate, and complains of Spleen" (12); instead of the queen who figures in the relevant passage of the *Aeneid*, Swift offers us a "careless Quean [hussy]" (19), who stains the clothes of passers-by (here figured as "you," a tactic for drawing the reader into the poem) with the drippings of a dirty mop. Rain and dust combine to contaminate the coat of the "needy Poet" (27), who makes one of a diverse cast of characters including servant girls, "daggled Females" (33), a law student, a seamstress, miscellaneous Whigs and Tories, and a frightened "Beau" (41). All suffer from the weather, which interrupts common pursuits and impels many to indulge in minor deception for the sake of finding shelter. The concluding triplet (three lines with a single rhyme) epitomizes the scene's sordidness:

> Sweepings from Butchers Stalls, Dung, Guts and Blood,
> Drown'd Puppies, stinking Sprats, all drench'd in Mud,
> Dead Cats and Turnep-Tops come tumbling down the Flood.
>
> (60–62)

Presumably in eighteenth-century London raindrops would glisten on the elegant façades of handsome buildings; a rainbow might arch over the streets; the rain could intensify the sweet odor of roses for sale in the market. Swift, however, ignores such possibilities. He selects his details to create specific effects, and the effects he seeks leave no room for rainbows. The poem's focus on the activities of people anticipating and then suffering the rain gives way in the final ten lines to a description of the progress of water through the streets, as it overflows the gutters, bringing with it from every part of London "Filth of all Hues and Odors" (53). That filth, most explicitly described in the three lines quoted above, comes to represent the city's corruption.

The stylistic references to Virgil throughout *A City Shower* remind the reader of an earlier world of heroic action and endeavor that appears to have no equivalent in the time of the poem's writing. The contrast between dignified style and sordid or trivial subject functions as social criticism, conveying a judgment of decline and decay. Other poets might use such contrast for comic purposes, but Swift communicates bitter distaste rather than comic acceptance. His tone darkens as the poem continues, beginning with debonair social observation but concluding with disgust. Once more, the exactitude of details – those "Turnep-Tops" – carries poetic meaning.

Disgust and outrage do not compose the only emotional responses to the city communicable by poetic selection of details. Swift's deliberate evocation of such feelings contributes to his program of reform: he sought to make the British see the actuality of their lives in order that they might be impelled to improve them. Others could express active pleasure in the multiplicity and stimulation of urban existence. John Gay wrote a three-book poem, *Trivia* (1716), with the revealing subtitle, "The Art of Walking the Streets of London". Like Swift, he uses Virgil as a point of reference, imitating the *Georgics*, which offered detailed advice to the farmer about crops and herds and such activities as tilling and beekeeping and predicting the weather. Like Swift's, his "imitation" of Virgil does not purport to duplicate the master's straightforward seriousness. Unlike Swift, however, Gay does not use his allusions to Virgil to criticize the decadence of modern times. To designate walking the streets an art sounds like, and partly is, a joke. Much of what the poet describes in London involves danger of one kind and another: from bad weather, from human carelessness, arrogance, and violence, from the sheer crowdedness of the streets. But despite the comic tone of the enterprise and the poem's full awareness of the city's negative aspects, Gay also conveys real delight in what London offers:

> Nor do less certain signs the town advise,
> Of milder weather, and serener skies.
> The ladies gayly dress'd, the Mall adorn
> With various dyes, and paint the sunny morn;
> The wanton fawns with frisking pleasure range,
> And chirping sparrows greet the welcome change:
> Not that their minds with greater skill are fraught,
> Endu'd by instinct, or by reason taught,
> The seasons operate on every breast;
> 'Tis hence that fawns are brisk, and ladies drest.
>
> (1: 143–52)

This passage demonstrates one of Gay's characteristic techniques. Delineating the "signs" of good weather, the poet adduces living beings as evidence: ladies, fawns, sparrows. He does not, however, offer details about each individual phenomenon, beyond a single characterizing adjective – wanton fawns, chirping sparrows, "ladies drest." To be sure, he adds an adverb for the ladies: they are "gayly" dressed. And the fawns range about with frisky pleasure, but this description only reiterates the adjective: wanton means frisky or frolicsome. We are meant to contemplate the scene as from a distance. Women with their various colors and sparrows with their chirps alike contribute to the overall harmony; they have no individual importance. One might complain, from a feminist point of view, about having women reduced to the level of fawns and sparrows, but the momentary aestheticizing of human beings and animals alike has its charm.

Throughout *Trivia*, Gay relies heavily on comprehensive rather than minute views of the city scene. He touches on an extraordinary number of urban manifestations – shoeshine boys, chandlers, cart drivers, beaus, coaches, wagons, carriages, prostitutes, soldiers, parks and palaces, river and riverside – providing an almost cinematic vision of early eighteenth-century London, teeming with life and with dark and bright possibility. "The busy city asks instructive song" (2: 220), he writes, and the instruction he offers enables the reader to imagine not only negotiating the streets but also appreciating the intricacies of a distant metropolis. The poet typically takes a long view: he sees everything but dwells on little.

On occasion, though, he pauses to focus on sensuous detail. Thus, his account of a street that his note identifies as Thames Street:

> Here steams ascend
> That, in mix'd fumes, the wrinkled nose offend.
> Where chandlers cauldrons boil; where fishy prey
> Hide the wet stall, long absent from the sea;
> And where the cleaver chops the heifer's spoil,
> And where huge hogsheads sweat with trainy [whale] oil,
> Thy breathing nostril hold; but how shall I
> Pass, where in piles *Cornavian* cheeses lye.
>
> (2: 247–54)

Another of Gay's notes tells us that *Cornavian* is an old name for Cheshire cheese. Unlike Thomson, the poet does not try to create an imaginative order here – the "order" he creates depends on an impression of disorder unified only by a series of bad smells. He is quite specific about those smells: the candle-maker's caldron of tallow, the old fish, the butcher's carcasses, the whale oil of lamps, the strong cheese. He offers no suggestion that anyone might enjoy the scene: the walker is advised to hold his nose. Yet in fact the exuberant detail creates its own enjoyment. The most powerful poetic effects in *Trivia* stem from the overwhelming sense of abundance it creates. Swift's verse, even the verse concerned with ugliness, insists on its own exactitude and gains moral force by its effort to describe things precisely as they are. Gay's, in *Trivia*, thrives on impressions rather than precision. It celebrates the experience of the city and implicitly declares the value of all experience.

Not that it deals always, or even typically, with the distasteful. Having evoked a fish stall with old fish, Gay shows himself also able to delight in a stall with more attractive wares:

> When fishy stalls with double store are laid;
> The golden-belly'd carp, the broad-finn'd maid [young skate],

Red-speckled trouts, the salmon's silver joul,
The jointed lobster, and unscaly soale,
And luscious 'scallops, to allure the tastes
Of rigid zealots to delicious fasts . . .

(2: 413–18)

Now he seems more closely akin to Thomson, or even Dyer, in his emphasis on color and pattern. The pleasure in abundance, however, remains the same as that manifested in Gay's account of smelly fish and hogsheads of oil.

As the poem's announced project of educating city walkers might suggest, Gay reveals more interest in human detail than Dyer, Thomson, or even Swift. We may glimpse that interest even in the last line of the passage quoted above: the allusion to strictly pious citizens who nonetheless allow themselves to be allured by delicious tastes even when allegedly fasting (i.e., eschewing meat). A final quotation will suggest how skillfully Gay weaves human vignettes into the texture of his treatise on city walking:

I've seen a beau, in some ill-fated hour,
When o'er the stones choak'd kennels [gutters] swell the show'r
In gilded chariot loll; he with disdain
Views spatter'd passengers all drench'd in rain;
With mud fill'd high, the rumbling cart draws near,
Now rule thy prancing steeds, lac'd charioteer!
The dust-man lashes on with spiteful rage,
His pond'rous spokes thy painted wheel engage,
Crush'd is thy pride, down falls the shrieking beau,
The slabby pavement crystal fragments strow,
Black floods of mire th'embroider'd coat disgrace,
And mud enwraps the honours [adornments] of his face.

(2: 523–34)

The speaker's involvement in the scene intensifies the episode's drama. The narrative begins in the present perfect tense: the speaker is about to tell us about something he has seen in the past. Immediately, though, it shifts to the present tense: the action seems to be occurring in the present. The arrogance of the rider, the resentment of the dust-man, both economically evoked, prepare us for the clash that will shortly ensue. The speaker himself is imaginatively drawn in, as he addresses the "lac'd [adorned with lace] charioteer," urging him to caution, only to see him fall, his vicarious pride crushed along with that of his frightened master. The poet's interest in the human situation does not outweigh his consciousness of physical appearances. He notes not only the black mud on the embroidered coat, but also the shards of glass on the "slabby pavement," inviting his readers to take pleasure in the visual contrasts even while responding to the social dynamics of the commonplace happening. The "scenes" *Trivia* offer usually have undifferentiated characters, but on occasion, as this example illustrates, Gay demonstrates his awareness of social psychology as well as of the city's proliferating appearances.

The range of examples offered here will suggest the variety and the purposefulness of detail as a component of early eighteenth-century verse. Readers and writers alike in this period assumed that literature should strive both to delight and to instruct. It could do both by enlarging the bounds of experience for its readers, providing imaginative experience to supplement and perhaps modify that of the literal world. Such poets as Dyer, Thomson, Gay, Swift, and Pope employed detail to define the nature of the experience they offered – experience, in every case, more than sensuous. How something looks or smells or sounds matters much less than the import conveyed by the appearance or smell or sound in question. From Pope's sylphs to Gay's coachman, from Dyer's hills and valleys to Thomson's courting birds, poets created effects to help their readers understand why they should take seriously the landscapes and cityscapes and social structures that poetry could evoke.

Descriptive poetry was by no means a dominant genre during the early years of the eighteenth century. Thomson and Dyer, although both popular, were unusual in their reliance on long descriptive sequences – and even they often subordinated description to moralizing or (in Thomson's case) to reflection on unseen particularities. Moreover, not even Thomson and Dyer often wrote description for its own sake. Descriptive passages serve purposes beyond that of creating immediate emotional response, often soliciting such response in the service of moral, social, or religious agendas.

Indeed, the poetry of detail often serves the purpose of generalization. Thus Thomson, despite his obvious excitement over the hidden workings of plants or the minutiae of birds' behavior, never loses his insistence on declaring that all individual natural manifestations demonstrate God's great plan. Swift, with less grandiose notions, uses sordid details of London scenes to support the tacit generalization that modern life is corrupt. Dyer maintains a vaguer generalization: everything in nature, rightly perceived, provides instruction. Gay and Pope, in contrast, delight in details more nearly for their own sake: the beauty of the sylphs and the excitement of London are self-justifying.

We don't find in early eighteenth-century poetry of detail any equivalent to the lush descriptions of the Romantics. This verse, however, often provides the satisfactions of precision as it builds connections between the particular and the general. Its creators choose their adjectives carefully, using them to locate objects in a comprehensive system. "Busy man," "fleecy race": such phrases evoke the functions served, within a cosmic plan, by different species. Readers are invited to think as well as to feel.

And to feel as well as to think. Despite the restraint characteristic of much of this verse, despite the fact that the adjective–noun combinations, the views from high places, the accounts of vegetable growth seem distinctly the product of reason rather than emotion, Gay and Swift and Pope and Thomson and Dyer invite their readers to learn through feeling as much as through thought. Their amassing of detail helps them teach new ways of understanding both the natural and the human world, and, as a result, to provide new objects for feeling.

# 4

# High Language and Low: The Diction of Poetry

Most people, most of the time, make unconscious choices about linguistic registers. Our vocabulary as we converse with our clergyman differs from that we use with an intimate friend. Single-sex groups tend to elicit different patterns of speech from those customary in mixed company. Talking to our young child, we don't sound the same as when we talk to our parents.

Eighteenth-century poets skillfully manipulated a wide range of linguistic possibilities. The classic epic – Homer's poetry, and Virgil's – that they considered the greatest of poetic achievements employed elevated diction and relied heavily on conventional formulations, but the classics also provided precedents for the use of more informal language, as in the satires of Horace and Juvenal. Imitation of the classics provided a significant part of the eighteenth-century poet's repertoire, but new possibilities were also emerging. Examining the linguistic range of the period's writers calls attention to both innovations and continuities.

Language functions always, among other things, to mark social class. The eighteenth-century poet could assume an audience, largely male, of cultivated readers conversant with poetry of the past. The period's poets themselves did not typically belong by origin to the upper classes. John Gay came to London as apprentice to a silk mercer; James Thomson, a Scot, served as a tutor. By virtue of their poetic accomplishment, though, they could speak directly to the educated gentry and aristocracy, often, indeed, becoming themselves accepted members of polite society. Literacy expanded during the eighteenth century (no consensus exists for exactly how much it increased); gradually, readers from lower social classes joined the audience for poetry. Still, most writers assumed the vocabulary of an elevated social class or adopted and adapted linguistic devices of their classical predecessors

– unless they chose to rely on more familiar diction to achieve special effects.

Pope provides a complicated example. At the age of twenty-one, in 1709, he published his *Pastorals*, claiming (perhaps accurately) that he had written them at sixteen. A group of four poems corresponding to the year's seasons, they follow Virgil in topic and language. Conspicuous artifice characterizes them. The shepherds who comprise the poem's characters employ a vocabulary no shepherd ever used and proclaim extravagant feelings in disciplined couplets. Thus Alexis, protagonist of *Summer*, appeals to his unnamed beloved, who fails to requite his love:

> Where-e'er you walk, cool gales shall fan the glade,
> Trees, where you sit, shall crowd into a shade,
> Where-e'er you tread, the blushing flow'rs shall rise,
> And all things flourish where you turn your eyes. . . .
> Your praise the birds shall chant in ev'ry grove,
> And winds shall waft it to the pow'rs above.
>
> (73–76, 79–80)

Although the lines rely heavily on one-syllable words, such terms as "gales," "chant," and "waft" belong to a poetic vocabulary. Moreover, the vision of the natural world glorifying the adored woman, with the gods themselves listening to her praise, constitutes an elaborate poetic conceit. The first two couplets in particular (memorably set to music by Handel) evoke a harmonious and essentially ornamental natural scene, its order originating in the power of a beautiful woman. Their elegant lines manifest great control: the open vowels of the initial "Where-e'er" slow the movement, which gradually speeds, until the end of the second line effectively imitates the movement of crowding. The delight of reading these poems stems largely from the poet's utter mastery as he elaborates fictions bearing only a tangential relation to actuality.

By inaugurating his career with verse of this kind, Pope announced his claim to belong to a high and ancient tradition and his capacity for elegant artifice. Several of his contemporaries attempted, usually much less successfully, to operate in the same mode. Counter-trends, however, were also at work. In 1714, Pope's friend, John Gay, offered his own version of pastoral, stimulated by a dispute that Pope had initiated in a contemporary periodical, the *Guardian*, over pastoral's proper nature. At once a joke and a serious commentary, *The Shepherd's Week* parodies more orthodox efforts in the pastoral genre. The structure of the week rather than the year organizes its six poems, but their subjects echo those that Pope and others had used. Here is Gay's unrequited lover, a woman rather than a man, complaining about her fate in *Tuesday; or, The Ditty*:

> Ah woful day! Ah woful noon and morn!
> When first by thee my younglings white were shorn,
> Then first, I ween, I cast a lover's eye,
> My sheep were silly, but more silly I.
> Beneath the shears they felt no lasting smart,
> They lost but fleeces while I lost a heart.
>
> (25–30)

And here is how the poem concludes:

> Thus Marian wail'd, her eyes with tears brimful,
> When Goody Dobbins brought her cow to bull.
> With apron blue to dry her tears she sought,
> Then saw the cow well serv'd, and took a groat.
>
> (103–06)

One could hardly imagine a more striking contrast with the tone and method of Pope's pastoral on a comparable subject. The reiteration of "woful" suggests Marian's linguistic impoverishment, as does the awkwardness of "I ween." The earthy idiom, "well serv'd," like the reference to a specific tiny coin, a groat, locates the situation firmly among people of small means and few pretensions. Pope's Alexis, considering a woman who does not respond to his overtures, finds graceful ways to glorify her, assigning her more than mortal power. Marian, speaking of Colin Clout, can only allude to his skill at shearing sheep and declare herself "silly" for losing her heart to him. Alexis acquires dignity through the eloquence of his praise; Marian's attempts at the dignity of romance do not get her far. Moreover, the concluding episode of the cow coming to be impregnated casts a harsh, if comic, light on the whole matter of romantic love. Marian's tears get dried with practical alacrity by recourse to her apron, and the paltry coin that pays her presumably comforts her as well.

Gay's poetry solicits no response comparable to that invited by Pope's – not because it lacks poetic skill, but because it does not deal in elegance or conspicuous artifice. Some of its couplets are neatly turned. We may note the comic effect of rhyming "brimful" with "bull" or the economy and point of the couplet about the sheep losing fleece while Marian lost a heart, but the verse does not call attention to itself as Pope's does. Nor does its language belong to a clearly "poetic" register. Although Marian's exclamations of woe and her archaic phrase, "I ween," derive plausibly from a farm girl's sense of what proclamations of love should sound like, they jar with the concreteness of "younglings," "shears," and "fleeces," to say nothing of aprons, groats, and bulls.

The mixed vocabulary and shifting tone, however, work effectively to sketch a character and a dramatic situation and to comment on the artificiality of pastorals like Pope's. Pope's shepherds face few obligations from their sheep. Such shepherds neither talk nor act like actual people. Marian, although as clearly fictional as Alexis, has work to do and does it, thinks in concrete terms, blames herself as well as the man who scorns her for her unrequited love, and in all these respects seems a more fully realized personage. By means of such genuinely imagined characters, Gay's pastorals achieve effects that merge comedy and pathos, asking readers at least briefly to think about country life and country people.

Inasmuch as they invite such response, the poems implicitly criticize more conventional forms of pastoral. Yet their criticism is not, and is not intended to be, devastating. Making gentle fun of poetic artifice, Gay's pastorals operate – as all poetry does – by means of their own forms of artifice and offer an alternative to, rather than a refutation of, the verse they parody. They call attention to the importance of linguistic level as a defining aspect of poetic impact.

Individual poets, of course, had diverse linguistic registers at their disposal. Pope himself can take advantage at will of far more informal diction than that of his pastorals. Within a single poem, he may move from dignified to colloquial idiom. *An Epistle to Bathurst* contains extended characterizations of two figures, the Man of Ross and the "citizen," Balaam. The account of the Man of Ross begins,

> Rise honest Muse! and sing the Man of Ross:
> Pleas'd Vaga ecchoes thro' her winding bounds,
> And rapid Severn hoarse applause resounds.

> Who hung with woods yon mountain's sultry brow?
> From the dry rock who bade the waters flow? . . .
>
> (250–54)

The invitation to the Muse, an echo of classical technique, establishes a formal tone reinforced by the personification of the river Wye as "Vaga," by the enlisting of inanimate nature as glorifying a human being, and by the attribution of supernatural power to the man being praised. The Biblical overtones of water flowing from dry rock lend heightened dignity to the rhetorical questions in the final couplet. The verse does not rely on a demanding vocabulary – once more, one-syllable words predominate – but its distancing from the commonplace locates it in a realm of high formality.

Here, in contrast, are some sequences from the account of Balaam:

> Sir Balaam now, he lives like other folks,
> He takes his chirping pint, he cracks his jokes:
> "Live like your self," was soon my Lady's word;
> And lo! two puddings smok'd upon the board. . . .
> Some Scruple rose, but thus he eas'd his thought,
> "I'll now give six-pence where I gave a groat,
> Where once I went to church, I'll now go twice,
> And am so clear too, of all other Vice."
>
> (357–60, 365–68)

The newly-knighted Balaam and his lady speak an impoverished language, more appropriate to their lowly origins than to their present elevated rank. The final line, with its awkward, choppy movement, suggests that the inadequacy of their moral reasoning corresponds to that of their speech. "Live like your self" conveys a similar effect in its banality. Moreover, the narrator too relies now on colloquial idiom, relatively devoid of genuine content ("he lives like other folks"), to characterize Balaam. The taking of a "chirping [merry] pint" and the cracking of jokes as human actions, in comparison to hanging a mountain with woods or bidding water flow from dry rock, call attention to the vast moral discrepancy between the Man of Ross and Balaam. The informality of the language conveys something close to contempt for a figure who invites no more elevated description.

In *The Rape of the Lock*, Pope's mastery of linguistic levels serves a special purpose. The poem begins in classical terms:

What dire Offence from am'rous causes springs,
What mighty contests rise from trivial things,
I sing – This verse to C –, Muse! is due.

(1: 1–3)

Moreover, it continues largely in Virgilian or Homeric mode, describing – as the opening suggests – trivial happenings in dignified language. Pope's notes remind the reader of specific parallels to the *Iliad* and the *Aeneid*. Belinda adorns herself at her dressing table; the poem describes her cosmetic rituals as acts of worship. She plays cards; the contest and its outcome become equivalent to epic battles. An aristocrat surreptitiously snips a lock of Belinda's hair; the act, a figurative rape, generates another epic struggle.

The technique of *The Rape of the Lock* is known as "mock heroic," a term designating the deliberate juxtaposition of epic rhetoric with mundane happening, usually for comic or satiric purpose. As Swift's Virgilian allusions in *A Description of a City Shower* point out how the behavior and assumptions of his present time have declined from those of the classic past, so Pope's insistent pattern of heroic language implicitly emphasizes the losses involved in a society that concerns itself with "trivial things" rather than great happenings. A woman who fusses about a stolen lock of hair makes herself ridiculous, from a classic perspective. The rites of self-adornment become only pettier when dignified by elevated language. Because, as we have already seen in contemplating the passage about the sylphs, Pope makes his imaginings beautiful; because, too, of the elegance of his verse; because he avoids the harshness of his account of Balaam – for such reasons as these, the narrative of Belinda does not register as fierce attack, only as gentle mockery ("like tickling," Pope himself wrote). The mockery inheres in the employment of grand language for small matters.

The effect of mock heroic, however, can be, and in *The Rape of the Lock* is, a good deal more complicated than mockery, as the poem's concluding passage suggests. The struggle over the lock is resolved when the hair disappears, rising to heaven as a new constellation. Finally, the poem's speaker offers advice to his subject:

Then cease, bright nymph! To mourn the ravish'd hair,
Which adds new glory to the shining sphere!
Not all the tresses that fair head can boast,

Shall draw such envy as the Lock you lost.
For, after all the murders of your eye,
When, after millions slain, your self shall die;
When those fair suns shall set, as set they must,
And all those tresses shall be laid in dust;
This Lock, the Muse shall consecrate to fame,
And 'midst the stars inscribe *Belinda*'s name!

(5: 141–50)

This reminder of human mortality continues to employ the high epic mode, addressing Belinda as "bright nymph," referring to her "ravish'd hair," giving that hair a claim to glory, and attributing to the young woman the metaphorical power to slay millions. It glorifies the Muse, though, more than it praises Belinda: by the transmutation of poetry, the lost lock has been preserved past the limits of mortality and elevated through the force of language to true importance. The triviality of the hair-snipping episode has less reality, these lines suggest, than the beauty of its linguistic embodiment possesses.

Beauty matters. At the beginning of Canto 2, Belinda appears, her cosmetic ritual complete, wearing on her breast a cross "Which Jews might kiss, and Infidels adore" (2: 8): her beauty transfigures a Christian symbol so that it holds power over members of every religious persuasion. "If to her share some female errors fall," the poet writes, "Look on her face, and you'll forget 'em all" (2: 17–18). The physical beauty that Belinda both embodies and symbolizes, the beauty that she consciously strives to heighten, contains power and value. Although *The Rape of the Lock* makes gentle fun of the importance assigned to the dressing table ritual, it does not mock the force of beauty itself. On the contrary: it finally assimilates the beauty created by poetry to that of the woman who exemplifies female charm. The beauty of a woman, the beauty of a poem: both possess a magic that Pope celebrates. The mock heroic technique thus simultaneously suggests the importance and the unimportance of daily ritual, small events, social exchange. It invites the reader to pay attention to the trivial – to laugh at it, but also to think about its meaning.

Mock heroic techniques can serve other purposes as well. In John Philips's 1705 exercise in Miltonic mock heroic, *The Splendid Shilling*, resounding language narrates the situation of an impoverished poet. The "splendid shilling," entirely hypothetical, inhabits the pocket of a more fortunate being, an imagined being, whom the possession of money enables to do all the things the poor poet cannot. Most of the poem dwells on that poet's fantasies of disaster, in the form mainly of arrest for debt; his imaginings of food and drink he cannot have; and the indignities he suffers of bad tobacco and worn out breeches. The comic juxtaposition of high language with a "low" subject constitutes the joke of the poem, a joke that apparently entertained many eighteenth-century readers. More cogently, the grandiose language functions to distance and displace the pathos of poverty. Treating poverty's misery as a joke enables Philips to write about real feelings without taking full responsibility for them. The mock heroic mode protects readers from the pain that underlies the joke. It makes the unacceptable – the suffering of the underprivileged – acceptable.

"Happy the Man," Philips's poem begins, in a conventional formulation ordinarily used to describe the situation of one separated from the corruption of court or city. The hypothetical happy man in this context, though, acquires his happiness in the first instance from what he does not feel: "He nor hears with Pain / New Oysters cry'd, nor sighs for cheerful Ale" (3–4). The lines set up a mild question in the reader's mind: why should anyone hear a cry of oysters with pain? Why sigh for ale; why not just drink it? Instead of answering such questions, the text goes on to describe the ordinary situation of one drinking with friends, smoking and laughing and joking, toasting his mistress as the glass goes round. Only then does the poem turn to the plight of its "I": "But I, whom griping Penury surrounds, / And Hunger, sure Attendant upon Want . . ." (11–12). And we begin to understand why a reminder of oysters might cause pain: to hear of what one desires and needs but cannot have generates suffering. The powerful adjective, "griping," which suggests both the stomach pains of hunger and the ferocious grip of poverty, generalizes misery that a cry of oysters only intensifies.

True to its Miltonic model, Philips's poem relies on blank verse rather than the couplets that have characterized every other poem discussed so far except for Thomson's *Spring* (also influenced by Milton). The couplet, the dominant form of the period, insists on its own discipline, supplying, in effect, automatic punctuation as its rhymes tend to enforce a pause after every pair of lines. Blank verse allows for more rambling, and Philips takes advantage of its possibilities, using an unobtrusive technique of free association. What makes the technique "unobtrusive" is the resounding language that both recalls Milton and suggests that the poem has grand concerns: one does not expect that its development will follow the movement of the poet's mind.

The poem's first series of reverberant names consists of Latinate terms for Welsh places, introduced by the speaker's reflections on the bad tobacco he smokes. This tobacco smells vile, and the pipe that holds it is short and black – like the pipe of a Welshman,

> when he
> O'er many a craggy Hill, and barren Cliff,
> Upon a Cargo of fam'd *Cestrian* Cheese,
> High over-shadowing rides, with a design
> To vend his Wares, or at th'*Arvonian* Mart,
> Or *Maridumum*, or the ancient Town
> Eclip'd *Brechinia*, or where *Vaga*'s Stream
> Encircles *Ariconium*, fruitful Soil,
> Whence flow Nectareous Wines, that well may vye
> With *Massic*, *Setin*, or renown'd *Falern*.
>
> (25–34)

The sonorous names will carry little clear meaning for most twenty-first-century readers, and even an audience of Philips's contemporaries would not necessarily have recognized their referents. Yet, as reading these lines aloud will readily demonstrate, the names generate poetic pleasure by sound alone. They appear to have entered the poem by virtue of the mind's random movements: thinking of himself smoking a pipe leads the speaker to think of Welshmen, those traditional pipe smokers; then to imagine the activity of the specific Welshman he summons up; then to trace his movements; finally, to imagine wines produced in Hereford ("*Ariconium*") and by extension to remember classical allusions to wine.

Philips's poetic capacities emerge most clearly when he follows Milton in the introduction of epic similes. His long meditation on the legal officers who lie in wait for debtors concludes with a pair of similes: a comparison of the bailiff with the cat lying in wait for mice and then, more elaborately, with the spider spreading her web for prey. The detail lavished on the spider and the flies recalls Thomson in its attentiveness:

> the Humming Prey,
> Regardless of their Fate, rush on the toils
> Inextricable, nor will aught avail
> Their Arts, nor Arms, nor Shapes of lovely Hue;

> The Wasp insidious, and the buzzing Drone,
> And Butterfly proud of expanded wings
> Distinct with Gold, entangled in her Snares,
> Useless Resistance make.
>
> (81–88)

The speaker's sympathy for the spider's victims presumably stems from identification: he sees himself, after all, as fly to the bailiff's spider. Yet his reflection on the insect's situation leads him to think about the beauty of the creatures in themselves, and one can feel and share his pleasure in the simile.

The linguistic pleasures that *The Splendid Shilling* provides counterpoint the wretchedness it describes. "Thus do I live from Pleasure quite debarr'd," the poet writes (115), and he vividly evokes how he

> Labour[s] with eternal Drought,
> And restless Wish, and Rave; my parched Throat
> Finds no Relief, nor heavy Eyes Repose.
>
> (106–08)

The detail of his misery is both persuasive and compelling. That misery consists of various forms of deprivation, but also of the operations of "Fancy," which remains awake even when its possessor sleeps. "Eager in a Dream" (111), it enables the poet to tipple "Imaginary Pots of Ale" (112). Awakening to his genuine thirst, he can only curse the "pleasant Phantom" (113) that has pretended to slake it.

As the poem carefully specifies, the suffering of poverty afflicts both body and mind. The epic simile that resolves the action suggests how each kind of affliction implies the other. Once more Philips demonstrates his skill at manipulating sonorous language, as he develops a comic comparison between the tearing of his breeches and the wreck of a ship. The disproportion of tenor and vehicle indeed generates a comic effect at the outset, but as the simile elaborates itself, it becomes ever more serious. Here are the last four lines, which begin by narrating the mariners' activities:

> They stare, they lave, they pump, they swear, they pray:
> (Vain Efforts!) still the battering Waves rush in
> Implacable, 'till delug'd by the Foam,
> The Ship sinks found'ring in the vast Abyss.
>
> (140–43)

The simile has developed its own actuality. By the final line, the reader can no longer feel even the shadow of a comic response. On the contrary, the shipwreck that engulfs the fancied ship seems all too plausible a metaphor for the disaster of poverty. Torn breeches can seem a matter for joking, because they are a relatively trivial sign of financial need. But the struggling seamen's lost lives carry meaning far beyond that of torn clothing. The simile enforces what the entire poem has suggested, beneath its mock heroic surface: poverty destroys lives.

As we shall see, later in the eighteenth century working class poets began to delineate the situation of those on their own social level. It would be difficult, though, to find many besides Philips in the first third of the century writing about the social inequities of their time and place. Sarah Fyge Egerton's railing about the situation of women provides the closest parallel. The devices of mock heroic allow Philips, however, unlike Egerton, to disguise his social criticism. They provide a protective screen for his serious purpose, soliciting comic responses even as the sonorities and similes of epic convention call attention as well to the genuine suffering, in mind and body, of the poor. Because the poet evidently writes – perhaps with exaggeration – about his own situation, he brings passion to his task, and the intensity of his feeling penetrates the mock heroic mask. Similarly, Pope's commitment to the aesthetic breaks through his screen of playfulness in *The Rape of the Lock*. He, too, offers social criticism: a light critique of the frivolity of the rich. And he too finds a kind of camouflage in the formalities of mock heroic.

The mock heroic mode provides an especially conspicuous example of early eighteenth-century awareness of linguistic register as poetic resource, but the shifting diction of individual poets also supplies evidence of such awareness. Anne Finch, Countess of Winchilsea, writes always in the cultivated language of her class, but she varies her vocabulary widely in relation to diverse poetic purposes, reminding us that more than social class is at issue in choices of diction. In Chapter 2, we considered her ambitious ode, *The Spleen*, with its elevated language and complicated metrical pattern. Such a poem by no means typifies Finch's accomplishment. Indeed, one could hardly declare any single poem "typical," so various are this poet's endeavors.

*The Appology* establishes a tone of bemused irritation as it pursues a project at once satiric and self-exculpatory:

'Tis true I write and tell me by what Rule
I am alone forbid to play the fool,
To follow through the Groves a wand'ring Muse
And fain'd Ideas for my pleasures chuse.
Why shou'd it in my Pen be held a fault
Whilst Mira paints her face, to paint a thought?
                                                    (1–6)

Beginning as though in the middle of a conversation, the lines employ direct, colloquial diction and straightforward syntax. The conceit of "a wand'ring Muse," to be followed through the groves, suggests light self-mockery, but this passage inaugurates a poem of self-defense, which proceeds by mentioning various conventional faults of women – Mira's make-up, Flavia's inappropriate self-flaunting – and suggesting that every woman has her weakness. The speaker's own failing, she reveals, "Is still to write tho' hoplesse to succeed" (16). Men don't find it easy to succeed as poets either, Finch points out.

Then the poem takes an unexpected turn:

(So weak are all since our first breach with Heav'n)
Ther's less to be Applauded then forgiven.
                                                    (19–20)

The sudden introduction of a theological context enforces a new perspective. The strong, harsh word, "breach," denoting violation of a legal or moral ban, forces a momentary pause in the fluent verse, demanding attention, and the turn to "all," in a poem of so much specific reference, emphasizes the change in substance and tone in these final lines. Eighteen of the twenty lines here have consisted in rather petulant self-defense or sniping at other, frivolous women, as well as at men of ambition comparable to the speaker's. Now the solemn "breach" signals sudden realization of how inappropriate such pettiness becomes in the light of the universal human situation. All need divine forgiveness; all should therefore forgive one another.

The shift, in a poem merely twenty lines long, from a rather off-hand social vocabulary to a language of religious allusion will not necessarily catch the attention of a casual reader. More striking is the deliberate shift of tone and diction in Finch's important poetic statement about her work, *The Introduction*. It begins in a resentful tone:

Did I, my lines intend for publick view,
How many censures, wou'd their faults persue,
Some wou'd, because such words they do affect,
Cry they're insipid, empty, uncorrect.
And many have attain'd, dull and untaught,
The name of witt, only by finding fault.
True judges, might condemn their want of witt;
And all might say, they're by a Woman writt.

(1–8)

Both in sentiment and in technique, this resembles *The Appology*. The notion that women inevitably attract reproach by presuming to write poetry; the implicit denigration of critics, who only "affect" a disparaging vocabulary; the idea of fault-finding for its own sake – all recall the other poem. The direct diction and straightforward utterance – a listing of one response after another – convey the speaker's desire to communicate. *The Introduction* contains its own disclaimer of female presumption. The first eight lines operate in a hypothetical mode, suggesting what "might" happen if the speaker were so foolish as to publish her work. Implicitly she claims, as she does in *The Appology*, to write only for her own pleasure.

As the poem continues, resentment becomes more palpable. Women who write, succeeding lines allege, are inevitably seen as intruders "on the rights of men" (10). No virtue can compensate for such a vice. The accomplishments to which women should aspire are "Good breeding, fassion, dancing, dressing, play" (14); intellectual activity "Wou'd cloud our beauty, and exaust our time, / And interrupt the Conquests of our prime" (17–18). A final indignity is that "some" believe "the dull manage, of a servile house" to be the utmost achievement of a female (19–20). The diction, in this part of the poem, remains unpretentious and precise, but a sense of indignation gradually builds.

In a surprising turn, the poem now changes direction and tone. Its subject becomes a series of Biblical stories: of the crowds of singers, including "holy Virgins" (30), that attend the return of the Ark to Jerusalem; of the "bright Chorus" (35) praising David's conquest, a chorus including "The fairest half, whose influence guides the rest" (43); and of Deborah, who "fights, she wins, she tryumphs with a song" (46). Each episode evokes a figure, or a group of figures, for the woman poet. Finch introduces the sequence by asserting that these Biblical stories cannot be merely "Fables" (21) – in other words, untrue. They demonstrate, she suggests, that God has assigned women in the past some share of wit and poetry. The language in which she recounts the Biblical stories echoes their source:

> Lo! the yong Poet, after Gods own heart,
> By Him inspired, and taught the Muses art,
> Return'd from Conquest, a bright Chorus meets,
> That sing his slayn ten thousand in the streets.
>
> (33–36)

The women's song, as reported in I Samuel, includes, "Saul hath slain his thousands, and David his ten thousands" (I Sam. 18: 7). Finch writes, "Saul upon the vast applause does frown, / And feels, itts mighty thunder shake the Crown" (39–40), adding that "Half of the kingdom is already gone" (42). The Bible says, "And Saul was very wroth, and the saying displeased him; . . . and what can he have more but the kingdom?" (I Sam. 18: 8). The poem's linguistic echoes evoke the authority of the Bible, the essence of Finch's argument.

In another startling shift, after completing the Biblical stories, the poem exclaims, "How are we fal'n!" (51). Given the religious context, the reader is likely to take this as an assertion about the human condition, fallen from grace by virtue of Original Sin. The rest of the line, however, immediately suggests other possibilities: we are "fal'n by mistaken rules." The "we" that have fallen, it turns out, are women; and their fall derives not from their own sin but from the fact that they are "Debarr'd from all improvements of the mind, / And to be dull, expected and dessigned" (53–54). So designed by God? No, the recapitulated Biblical stories have insisted that God has designed women with wit and the capacity to produce poetry. The designers now are men, who have controlled female education.

The tone of resentment, familiar from *The Appology*, that controlled the beginning of *The Introduction* has given way to something deeper and more serious, as Finch turns to more formal diction to address her Muse, recommending continued retirement, warning of the danger of being despised, advising "contracted wing" (60). The final couplet, nominally continuing the address to the Muse, clearly offers a message to the poet herself:

> For groves of Lawrell, thou wert never meant;
> Be dark enough thy shades, and be thou there content.
>
>                                          (63–64)

The final alexandrine (a line with six stressed syllables instead of the customary five) feels ponderous and gloomy. Counseling contentment, it suggests by its slow, somewhat awkward rhythm the effort required to achieve even the appearance of such a state, given the weight of expectation that burdens women, as the poem has revealed. In the Biblical past, perhaps women lived free lives of achievement. In the British present, achievement – even the "improvements of the mind" that might lead to it – is firmly "Debarred" for women. The endeavor to come to terms with that fact provides the explicit or implicit subject for several of Finch's poems.

She has, however, many other subjects as well and deploys appropriate diction for all of them. She writes moving religious poetry, as we have already seen. She produces love letters in verse and panegyrics to her husband. Finch's lyricism about nature, however, is the poetic mode that has generally appealed most to her recent readers. Several of her poems convey powerful feeling about the natural world. *A Nocturnal Reverie*, perhaps the best-known of the group, uses the period's conventional couplets to new ends, making of them a flexible form to communicate personal observations – from the sound of a horse chewing forage to the look of "freshen'd Grass" (10) in the cool of evening – about the experience of wandering on a summer night.

The vocabulary Finch uses here sounds familiar for two reasons. Part of it belongs to a well-worn poetic repertoire. We find many words and devices recognizable from other poems of the period: "gentle *Zephyr*," "lonely *Philomel*," "darken'd Groves," "falling Waters." Adjective–noun combinations make the poem's building blocks, as they do for a work like *The Choice*. Some of the adjectives, though, are surprising – often because they come from the other kind of familiar diction Finch employs here, that of everyday experience, belonging to no distinct social level. Thus we encounter "waving," "dusky," "sleepy," "temperate," "sunburnt," "swarthy": terms of specificity that derive not from poetry but from life. The conjunction of poetic decorum with what sounds like immediate personal experience creates the poem's special impact.

"In such a *Night*," Finch writes,

> when passing Clouds give place,
> Or thinly vail the Heav'n's mysterious Face;
> When in some River, overhung with Green,
> The waving Moon and trembling Leaves are seen;
> When freshen'd Grass now bears it self upright,
> And makes cool Banks to pleasing Rest invite . . .
>                                                           (7–12)

Cool banks invite one to pleasing rest in many a poem, but the idea of grass standing up by its own power in order to create the invitation – that is something new. Both the adjective and the verb in the line about grass call attention to themselves by their unexpectedness. The waving moon also offers a surprise, in its fresh evocation of the moon's look when reflected in moving water. "Heav'n's mysterious Face" suggests both the Christian mystery and the more immediate physical mystery of the meaning of celestial appearances. Every detail records the impact of direct experience, and the reminder of other verse in the idea of the banks' invitation only heightens the immediacy of the visual details.

More than vocabulary, syntax drives the poem, which consists of a single sentence, its meaning suspended for 48 lines. The repeated conjunction "when" links many of the sequences. The sentence's structure defines the night's happenings: "In such a *Night*" (1), "when" clouds give place, "when" the river reflects the moon, "when" glow-worms shed their lights, "when" sweet odors stray through the air, "when" darkened groves wear their shadows, and so on. None of these happenings is momentous in itself, yet the repetitive structure insists on the importance of the time period they define.

That period acquires its importance both from what it contains – the details of observation that generate much of the poem's interest – and from what it promises, by virtue of the long suspension of the sentence that describes it, a sentence that wanders like the poem's central figure. The promise is fulfilled by means of a shift from the physical to the spiritual, a shift that also hints a merging. A final "when" introduces the spirit: "When a sedate Content the Spirit feels" (37). The spirit's musings "urge the Mind to seek / Something, too high for Syllables to speak" (39–40). In this state of being, the soul, charmed to "compos'dness" (41), "Joys in th' inferior World, and thinks it like her Own" (44). The extra poetic foot of the alexandrine suggests the weight resting on this line: the earth, perceived in its beauty by the wanderer whose nighttime meanderings have enabled her to focus attention on it, comes to resemble, in the wanderer's perception, the heavenly kingdom.

The poem ends, though, with a return to mundane actuality: the actuality of the day rather than the night, the time when "All's confus'd again" (46). In the light of that posited confusion, the serenity and beauty of the nocturnal experience take on new meaning. Restorative in an obvious sense, as an alternative to the daytime routine of pursuing pleasures "seldom reach'd" (48), the wonder of nighttime perception also serves as a reminder of spiritual realities readily forgotten in the bustle of everyday life. Physical perception, in other words, can constitute a religious experience. *A Nocturnal Reverie* emphasizes this point partly by indirection: a vocabulary of dreary abstractions ("Our cares, our Toils, our Clamours . . ."; 47), in contrast both to the beautiful concreteness of nocturnal observations and the serene abstractions associated with the spiritual life, calls attention to the difference between ordinary daily experience and its spiritual alternatives.

Attention to the vocabulary and syntax of early eighteenth-century verse often enables us to locate a poem's intention and its preoccupations with special clarity. Such attention can help us understand the complicated workings of the period's poetry. To focus on diction, moreover, provides yet another way to register the variety of early eighteenth-century verse – variety that has emerged also through attention to the poetry's emotional aspects and to its descriptive detail. From Gay's blunt country diction to Pope's elegance and Finch's exaltations, poets showed themselves dexterous in manipulating linguistic modes. Communicating at various levels of diction, conversational to abstract, they implicitly claimed the capacity to reach diverse audiences, as the "public" function of poetry made imperative.

Well before Wordsworth articulated his view that poetry, as the activity of a man speaking to men, should employ the language of ordinary people, in other words, eighteenth-century poets on occasion do just that. To be sure, Gay, when he uses the diction of country folk, puts it in metaphorical quotation marks, inviting the reader to take it partly as a joke. Pope does the same thing when he surrounds Balaam with language from the working class: one can feel his distaste for the vocabulary as well as for those he has imagined using it. "Ordinary people" at a somewhat higher social level, however, supply natural sounding conversational diction for a poet like Anne Finch when she chooses to employ it. Egerton, too, proves adept at creating a poetic voice that sounds like an approximation of normal speech.

Such poets do not try to conceal their artifice. Preserving strict metrical forms, they thus preserve always also a sense of formality. Moreover, they may surprise us by, for instance, introducing a figure like the Muse of poetry into a context that has appeared realistic. Like poets of every period, they take advantage of whatever resources they find. In keeping with the cultural assumption of poetry's public function, they would hardly choose to deprive their work of dignity, except perhaps for such ironic commentary as Pope and Gay offer through their deployment of "vulgar" language. (And Pope and Gay, we must remember, display their poetic expertise, poise, and power in the accuracy of their ventriloquism and parody and the control with which they manage it.)

All the poets considered in this chapter take manifest pride in their ability to manipulate both traditional and new forms of poetic rhetoric. Their sense of poetry's social responsibility includes awareness that society operates partly by tradition. The language of poetry can remind its readers of tradition at the same time that it demonstrates fresh possibilities for using it. Expanding poetic language to accommodate more informal oral traditions allowed poets to enlarge the boundaries of decorum and to attract attention, on occasion, by startling their readers. The range of diction in early eighteenth-century verse calls attention to the growing flexibility of permitted forms.

# 5

# Alexander Pope and Lady Mary Wortley Montagu

In the summer of 1718, a lightning bolt killed a pair of rural lovers who had been working in the fields. Pope wrote three epitaphs for them. The first, only six lines long, compares the lovers' demise to that of Indians when a widow burns herself on the pyre that incinerates her husband's body. "Pitying heav'n" (*Epitaph on John Hewet and Sarah Drew* 3), seeing the mutual virtue of the lovers, killed both so that it might wound neither. "Hearts so sincere th' Almighty saw well pleas'd" (5); therefore, God sent his lightning.

As even the single quoted line will suggest, this does not sound much like any Pope we have encountered so far – not like the writer of the *Essay on Criticism*, or *The Rape of the Lock*, or *An Epistle to Bathurst*, or *Epistle to Burlington*, or the *Pastorals*. Already in his early poems, Pope assumes many different voices. Like the other Pope poems we have encountered, the epitaph relies on couplets marked by their compression and energy, but Pope does not often employ such an elaborate poetic conceit as this fantasy about a couple in effect rescued by being killed. Both the allusion to Indian custom and the construction of motivation for "th' Almighty" demonstrate his cleverness. The little poem glorifies the dead couple, to be sure, but it also displays the poet's gift of what he and his contemporaries called "wit": the capacity to bring together disparate ideas for the purpose of illumination.

In response to both this poem and Pope's second epitaph (equally sentimental and more insistently pious), which employed some phrases from the earlier piece and was actually inscribed on the lovers' tomb, Lady Mary Wortley Montagu offered her own reflections:

> Here lies John Hughes and Sarah Drew;
> Perhaps you'll say, what's that to you?

Believe me, friend, much may be said
On this poor couple that are dead.
On Sunday next they should have married;
But see how oddly things are carried!
On Thursday last it rain'd and lighten'd,
These tender lovers sadly frighten'd,
Shelter'd beneath the cocking hay
In hopes to pass the time away.
But the BOLD THUNDER found them out
(Commission'd for that end no doubt)
And seizing on their trembling breath,
Consign'd them to the shades of death.
Who knows if 'twas not kindly done?
For had they seen the next year's sun,
A beaten wife and cuckold swain
Had jointly curs'd the marriage chain;
Now they are happy in their doom,
FOR POPE HAS WROTE UPON THEIR TOMB.

(*Epitaph*, 1–20)

Pope had sent Lady Mary his two poems in a letter; she responded with this epitaph. Also couched in couplets, it relies on the four-stress lines that Swift used so deftly, instead of Pope's more dignified pentameters. Of course the poem makes no pretense at dignity. On the contrary, it adopts an off-hand tone intended to undermine Pope's moral and sentimental claims: that the thunder was "commissioned" by God, that erotic love constitutes or signals virtue; more fundamentally, that these lower-class lovers merit attention at all.

Neither poet sounds deeply moved by the unpredictable death. Pope's epitaph strikes a vaguely religious note, but the "Almighty" it evokes, although pleased by the spectacle of virtue, creates "Victims" at will and does not figure as an object of worship. Pope's little poem seems in love with its own cleverness. Clever indeed, it uses untimely death as a springboard for verbal acrobatics, contriving a poetically plausible explanation for an inexplicable event and conveying it with economy. Lady Mary speaks from a position of class superiority, signaled by her ostentatious use of idiomatic speech uncharacteristic of an aristocrat ("see how oddly things are carried") in a way that calls attention to the language's inadequacy to the event it purports to comment on. Her cynicism about marriage sounds class-based as well: she would hardly imagine a lord and lady as beaten wife and cuckold swain. Her refusal to sentimentalize the lovers' deaths, like her apparent doubt of God's participation in them, reiterates her superiority to common attitudes and comforting assumptions. Moreover, her version of events neatly undercuts Pope's verbal pyrotechnics – despite the compliment she pays him at the poem's end (a compliment that, in its context, sounds none too convincing).

Pope, we might conclude, has greater poetic gifts than Lady Mary, but his female contemporary is less self-preoccupied than he. Both deploy wit expertly in the service of their poetic ends. Lady Mary is cynical; Pope at least pays lip service to conventional attitudes. To be sure, he subsequently wrote yet another epitaph, this one consisting of a single couplet:

> Here lye two poor Lovers, who had the mishap
> Tho very chaste people, to die of a Clap.

("Clap" was a slang term for venereal disease.) Sentimental, bawdy, cynical: on the basis of these epitaphs one would not expect from either Pope or Lady Mary poetry of deep personal feeling.

Let us, however, consider two more examples of their work. Here are some lines from the concluding passage of Pope's *Windsor-Forest*, published in 1713:

> The Time shall come, when free as Seas or Wind
> Unbounded *Thames* shall flow for all Mankind,
> Whole Nations enter with each swelling Tyde,
> And Seas but join the Regions they divide;
> Earth's distant Ends our Glory shall behold,
> And the new World launch forth to seek the Old.
> Then Ships of uncouth Form shall stem the Tyde,
> And Feather'd People crowd my wealthy Side,
> And naked Youths and painted Chiefs admire [wonder at]
> Our Speech, our Colour, and our strange Attire!
> Oh stretch thy Reign, fair *Peace*! From Shore to Shore,
> Till Conquest cease, and Slav'ry be no more.
>
> (397–408)

The couplets move in more leisurely fashion than those of the epitaph. Although the verse is expert, it does not appear to function primarily for showing off the poet's gifts. The poem's speaker sounds possessed by a vision of possibility, imagining details of a future imperialist triumph that will also achieve vast unification, with seas becoming symbols of jointure rather than division. For a moment he even imagines, and accepts, that natives of other countries might perceive the English as grotesque. Inspired by the Peace of Utrecht, a treaty signed in 1713 that brought an end to the War of the Spanish Succession and helped to consolidate the strength of the British Empire, he evokes an ideal world, devoid of slavery and conquest, in which England's glory becomes an utterly benign force. And he sounds as though he means it: his imagination and his emotions are involved. This is not the dispassionate, self-displaying observer that the epitaph suggested. Desire to demonstrate his gifts perhaps always figures in a poet's undertakings, but Pope here sounds engaged by his subject as well as by his verse.

Lady Mary, too, can produce engaged poetry, but the reader may feel the poet's involvement at unexpected junctures. Although later in her life she wrote a few impassioned love poems, in the period that concerns us now her verse almost invariably exhibits a glossy surface, a façade of wit that might seem to exclude the possibility of directly expressing feeling. Yet the very expressions of wit on occasion suggest intense emotion. In *An Answer to a Love-Letter in Verse*, written during the 1720s, the speaker responds to an amorous epistle from a married man – who, as she points out in the poem, is possessed only by the desire for someone new. She definitively rejects his overtures, using them as pretext for a diatribe against "the Destroyer, Man" (14), who "In sport" "break[s] the Heart, and rend[s] the Fame [reputation]" (16). Even this outburst, though, is couched in witty couplets that compare the pet monkey who is punished for breaking a cup to the man who breaks hearts with impunity. She herself, the speaker continues, cannot be seduced: "Th' allready Plunder'd need no Robber fear" (18). Once she loved, but she has learned the art of self-protection. She breaks off her narrative of love betrayed with a moment of self-dramatizing self-pity: if she related all the wrongs of love "—this Tale would ever last; / Sleep, sleep my wrongs, and let me think 'em past" (27–28). Her final dismissal of the would-be lover suggests that he may find punishment for his counterfeit love by falling truly in love with someone who rebuffs him. Then the poem concludes with a simile:

So the Brisk Wits who stop the Evening Coach
Laugh at the Fear that follows their approach,
With Idle Mirth, and Haughty Scorn despise
The Passenger's pale Cheek, and staring Eyes;
But seiz'd by Justice, find a Fright no Jest
And all the Terror doubled in their Breast.

(35–40)

New intensity suffuses Lady Mary's verse at this point. Young men playing at being highwaymen suddenly face the possibility of "Justice" that may not distinguish between jest and earnest; that may, indeed, hang them for their joke. The passengers' terror is real, but less compelling than the fear that seizes their tormentors. The vignette provides material only for a simile, a piece of rhetorical decoration. This particular simile, however, serves a more crucial function than decoration: it urges the reader to take seriously a poem that has seemed in many of its devices mere *jeu d'esprit*. The "Destroyer, Man" threatens women's contentment; the counterfeit grief and ardency of a would-be lover has destructive power. The simile calls attention to the underlying urgency of this answer to a love letter.

Even these few examples may suffice to suggest how Pope and Lady Mary adopt different rhetorical modes for different purposes. To compare the two can at least hint the deftness of the period's poets in employing diverse techniques, exploring diverse subjects, and conveying diverse emotional tones. Pope and Lady Mary of course inhabited opposed social and literary situations. Pope, born to a Catholic family and deformed in infancy, probably by tuberculosis of the spine (his adult height was four feet, six inches and he had a hunched back), had friends among the noble and prominent but suffered social impediments. Because of England's laws governing religion, he could not attend a university or hold public office. He never married. Even by the early 1730s, though, he had achieved literary fame and was fully engaged on the literary scene. He thought of himself as a poet by profession: in 1717, at the age of 29, he had already published a sumptuous volume entitled *The Works of Mr. Alexander Pope*.

Lady Mary, in contrast, as the daughter of a duke could not with propriety publish her work, although some found its way to print – most often anonymously. She had social position but relatively little literary reputation. Poetry could be for her only an avocation; Pope's literary production, and its range, dwarfed hers. Unhappily married after a youthful elopement, she bore two children, then accompanied her husband to Constantinople, where he had an ambassadorial appointment. She and Pope for a time were friends – they corresponded during her stay in Turkey. Pope's letters at this time contained numerous erotic fantasies about her; it was later rumored that she had contemptuously rejected romantic overtures from him. For this or some other reason, the two became bitter enemies, and their poetry includes attacks on one another.

Conveniently for critical purposes, both poets wrote verse epistles to Lord Bathurst. Pope's *Epistle III. To Allen Lord Bathurst*, written between 1730 and 1732, contemplates, as its subtitle indicates, "the Use of Riches." More than 400 lines long, it focuses more intently on the *mis*use of riches. (The characterizations of the Man of Ross and of Balaam, considered briefly in Chapter 3, belong to this poem.) Beginning in a casual, conversational tone ("Who shall decide, when Doctors disagree, / And soundest Casuists doubt, like you and me?"), it establishes at the outset the fact that some men hoard, others squander, wealth and goes on to investigate examples of both human types, with elaborate footnotes that justify ferocious attacks on men assigned their actual names in the text. The poem includes quasi-philosophic reflection as well as personal attack:

> What Nature wants, commodious Gold bestows,
> 'Tis thus we eat the bread another sows:
> But how unequal it bestows, observe,
> 'Tis thus we riot, while who sow it, starve.
> What Nature wants (a phrase I much distrust)
> Extends to Luxury, extends to Lust . . .
>
> (21–26)

The lines exemplify important aspects of Pope's expertise in their rhythmic ease and their insistent wit. That wit manifests itself in dazzling shifts of perspective. The opening couplet sounds like a platitude. Read attentively, though, it may make us a bit uneasy. *Commodious* gold? The word means profitable, useful, convenient. Certainly such terms are applicable to gold, yet the idea of its usefulness and convenience takes on a certain edge when it turns out to mean that we eat what others sow. "Whatsoever a man soweth, that shall he also reap," Paul writes to the Galatians (Gal. 6: 7). Not in this world controlled by gold, though: we can simply buy what we want. The next couplet insists on good grounds for uneasiness: we riot while the sower starves. And note that it is *we* who riot: the poet rhetorically includes his readers as potential objects of attack. In the succeeding couplet, the poet turns on his own language, calling attention to the dual meaning of want as both need and desire. We are not on comfortable ground.

Indeed, Pope specializes in making his readers uncomfortable – but he does the job so deftly that we may not even notice. John Dryden, in *A Discourse concerning the Original and Progress of Satire* (1693), suggested that the satirist should resemble the executioner who cuts off a man's head so expertly that the victim remains unaware of the fact. Pope's verse moves gracefully; his movements of mind demand our answering agility and provide agility's pleasures; his linguistic exactness creates its own delight. The reader engrossed in the satisfactions of the verse may not feel like a target, yet the shock of recognition is likely to occur from time to time.

> Perhaps you think the Poor might have their part?
> Bond damns the Poor, and hates them from his heart:
> The grave Sir Gilbert holds it for a Rule,
> That every Man in want is Knave or Fool:
> "God cannot love (says Blunt, with lifted eyes)
> The Wretch he starves" – and piously denies.
>
> (101–06)

Even if we no longer recognize the proper names, we may find the sentiments familiar. Presumably, we will deplore them: the excuse that God disapproves of the poor, the equally meretricious willingness to leave their care to God, the assumption that poverty stems from wickedness or folly, Bond's irrational distaste for the poor. Just possibly, we may recognize in ourselves some tendency toward one or another of the attitudes of which we disapprove. If so, Pope will have made us uncomfortable again.

The verse, to be sure, suggests no clear intent to make us uncomfortable. On the contrary, its easy rhythms, its neat couplets, its brisk movement – all invite us to slide over the surface without lingering. It does not even announce itself as attacking the personages it so deftly characterizes. We must attend closely to the language in order to notice the attack. The moral dissonance of someone hating – instead of loving – "from his heart" may give us pause; Sir Gilbert's gravity may make us suspect that he lives his life by rules, and the moral inadequacy of the rule cited hints that such a way of proceeding has severe limitations. Blunt's "tearless" eyes betray the heartlessness that underlies his categorical dismissal of the poor. The Bishop's apparent meekness, only an "air," or pose, disguises the callousness that allows him to leave the poor to God, taking no responsibility himself. In every line, Pope thus inserts a hint of wrongness, of moral insufficiency in figures about whom he apparently offers only a factual sentence. As for us, his readers – well, we figure as "you," and we don't come off as altogether pure. Not that the poet accuses us of anything at all – but he hints at our faint-heartedness, in the "Perhaps" and the "might" of the first line quoted above. Conceivably, but not necessarily, we sympathize with the poor. We think they "might have their part"; we do not demand justice for them. If, unlike the named characters in the subsequent lines, we do not justify failure to help, neither do we insist that such failure will not do.

Pope appears not to insist either, but his implicit denunciation of the uncharitable rich grows increasingly intense. He summarizes:

> Yet, to be just to these poor Men of Pelf,
> Each does but hate his Neighbour as himself.
> (109–10)

Bond hates the poor from his heart; it turns out that he hates himself in the same perverse fashion. At every point, the men of riches denounced in Pope's poem reverse Biblical injunctions, in effect converting the sacred to the profane. *An Epistle to Bathurst* abounds in Biblical allusions that underline the seriousness of Pope's poetic project. The misuse of riches, as he figures it, constitutes not a social but a moral – indeed, a theological – sin.

The Man of Ross inhabits the poem as an ideal unattainable by ordinary mortals. More plausible is the standard embodied by Bathurst himself: a path midway between the extremes repeatedly denounced here.

> The Sense to value Riches, with the Art
> T'enjoy them, and the Virtue to impart,
> Not meanly, nor ambitiously pursu'd,

> Not sunk by sloth, nor rais'd by servitude;
> To balance Fortune by a just expence,
> Join with Oeconomy, Magnificence;
> With Splendour, Charity; with Plenty, Health;
> Oh teach us, BATHURST yet unspoil'd by wealth!
> That secret rare, between th' extremes to move
> Of mad Good nature, and of mean Self-love.
>
> (219–28)

Sense, Art, and Virtue recur in Pope's verse as terms of praise. Bathurst possesses all three and applies them to managing the wealth with which he is blessed. His middle course avoids the opposed traps of meanness and ambition, laziness and servility. He combines display with practicality, avoiding excessive self-concern and excessive, ill-considered generosity alike. Even he, though, is only conditionally successful: *yet* unspoiled, he may in the future succumb to wealth's seductions. The suggestion emphasizes how dangerous Pope considers the possession of riches – that possession for which most mortals yearn.

The intricate poem adduces many human examples, positive and negative, interspersing its characterizations and vignettes with verse paragraphs of reflection on the problem of money. Pope considers that problem both universal – gold has always existed underground, and men have always dug it up – and peculiarly modern, as his discursus on paper money indicates. His discussion of theological sin thus inhabits a specifically social setting. He implicitly justifies his attacks on named individuals by the scope and importance of the challenges he perceives in a society increasingly driven by money.

The figure Lady Mary sketches in her *Epistle to Lord Bathurst* bears little resemblance to the one who emerges in Pope's poem. This epistle too purports to offer criticism, social rather than moral in this case. For Lady Mary, however, Bathurst exemplifies rather than opposes the fault she wishes to delineate: misuse not of riches but of time. Bathurst, according to her indictment, shows himself consistently inconsistent. He may embark upon praiseworthy projects, but he will certainly not follow them through to the end.

The epistle begins in a tone suggesting praise:

> How happy you who varied joys pursue,
> And every hour presents you something new!
>
> (1–2)

As a happy man, Bathurst presumably has satisfied a human desire even more fundamental than that for wealth. What more can he possibly want?

It soon emerges that happiness does not last long. Bathurst's wealth gives him the power to turn architectural dreams into reality, but the work goes too slowly to suit him. "With dirt and mortar soon you grow displeased, / Planting succeeds, and avenues are raised" (13–14). Landscape gardening, however, proves no more satisfactory than architecture as an outlet for the nobleman's energies. The poem's tone grows increasingly dark as it considers Bathurst's excursion into public life:

> Ambition shows you power's brightest side,
> 'Tis meanly poor in solitude to hide:
> Though certain pain attends the cares of state,
> A good man owes his country to be great;
> Should act abroad the high distinguished part,
> Or show at least the purpose of his heart.
> With thoughts like these, the shining Court you seek,
> Full of new projects for – almost a week.
> You then despise the tinsel, glittering snare;
> Think vile mankind below a serious care;
> Life is too short for any distant aim,
> And cold the dull reward of future fame:
> Be happy then, while yet you have to live,
> And love is all the blessing Heaven can give.
>
> (27–40)

The subdued indignation marking these lines focuses on the misuse of moral language that Lady Mary ventriloquizes. Architecture and landscape gardening are all very well to occupy a rich man's time, but for him to claim a position of moral elevation ("A good man owes his country to be great"), only to treat public life as simply another way of passing his days – such behavior suggests something more serious than idiosyncrasy in the nobleman's inconsistencies. When Bathurst leaves statesmanship for love, in the poet's fantasy, he still uses a moral vocabulary to justify himself, deciding that "vile mankind" is unworthy of his care. The poem's subsequent account of his "loves" – he shifts from one woman to another with tempestuous speed, as a shape or a voice catches his fancy – underlines the man's ethical inadequacy. His inconsistency, which seemed at the outset a trivial, almost comic weakness, has come to function as something closer to a sin.

At eighty-four lines, Lady Mary's epistle has just over a fifth the bulk of Pope's. In the passages quoted thus far, it lacks the moral intensity as well as the wide range of *An Epistle to Bathurst*. Toward its end, though, it changes direction in unexpected fashion and acquires the intensity that seemed lacking earlier. The satiric account of Bathurst ends with a simile: Bathurst's mind resembles the sands of Africa's deserts; nothing leaves a mark on it, "So yielding the warm temper of your mind, / So touched by every eye, so tossed by every wind" (65–66). The extra metrical foot of the alexandrine line emphasizes its summary quality: this line generalizes the particularities that have been adduced about Bathurst. All the details add up to this.

This couplet, however, is not complete in itself. It turns out to be part of a triplet, three rhymed lines, and the third line provides a startling shift of focus: "O how unlike has Heaven my soul designed!" (67). This epistle addressed to Bathurst turns out finally to concern the poet herself. The concluding eight couplets provide a sketch of her personality and, implicitly, a view of her experience. In the first two couplets of the eight, the speaker claims to have no interest in the life that surrounds her. She does not wish praise, she does not feel love, she does not respond emotionally to any stimulus. The rest of the poem consists of an elaborated simile. If Bathurst's mind reminds her of shifting desert sand, her own is more like a rock. The passing flock leaves no footprint on it; the wind does not harm it; the waves beat on it in vain. The workman who tries to engrave it will face a difficult task. Finally she imagines a man carving his name "upon this marble breast." Ages pass; the name remains in the rock. Here is Lady Mary's final couplet:

> Tho' length of years with moss may shade the ground,
> Deep, tho' unseen, remains the secret wound.
>
> (80–81)

The poem's emotional force largely inheres in the single word, *wound*, which abruptly converts an engraved name into a concealed agony and demands reinterpretation of the preceding eighty lines. The ease and predictability of the couplets can lull the reader into seeing the poem as mere social performance, offering a conventional judgment through a structure of witty variation. Performance it may be – but it finally reveals its purpose as that of concealing pain, pain the more intense for being unarticulated.

Bathurst, as Lady Mary describes him, is hardly capable of being wounded. His feelings do not go deep. The poem does not emphasize this aspect of his volatility, but in retrospect it seems implicit in his facility for justifying every change as well as in his shallow commitment to each new activity. Lady Mary does not directly claim her own relative emotional depth. She does not dwell on her "wound," or explain it. She does not insist that steadfastness entails suffering as its inevitable penalty. All these implications remain for the reader to deduce from the understated simile with that powerful word at its conclusion.

The juxtaposition of manifest performance with poetically claimed suffering has a disorienting effect. The intensity of the final simile undercuts the decorum of the earlier satire, in effect discrediting the poem's conventional procedures as well as shedding a harsher light on Bathurst than the satiric couplets themselves have done. Moreover, the simile serves as something of a tease, suggesting a kind of subject matter Lady Mary might exploit and a kind of poetry she might write – but won't. If the satiric couplets on Bathurst constitute a poetic performance, so, in a different sense, do the concluding lines, disguising even as they reveal. And perhaps, after all, what they reveal is only another pose.

Poets always pose, to be sure. Here is Pope, at the end of *Eloisa to Abelard* (1717), a long poem written in the voice of its suffering female protagonist, confined to a convent after her angry relatives castrated her lover, who himself now inhabits a monastery.

> And sure if fate some future Bard shall join
> In sad similitude of griefs to mine,
> Condemn'd whole years in absence to deplore,
> And image charms he must behold no more,
> Such if there be, who loves so long, so well;
> Let him our sad, our tender story tell;
> The well-sung woes will sooth my pensive ghost;
> He best can paint 'em, who shall feel 'em most.
>
> (359–66)

Like Lady Mary, with slightly more indirection, since he adopts the voice of another to make his claims, Pope delineates himself as a sad, "Condemn'd" lover, consumed with the kind of grief he describes.

A familiar form of poetic pose is the persona, the personality, or mask, a poet adopts for the purposes of a specific poem. In *Eloisa to Abelard*, the poet assumes the name as well as the nature of another person. More usually, the adopted personality has no name or narrated history, but the voice of that personality informs and shapes a poem. Sometimes a poet assumes the same persona, or similar versions of the self, from one poem to another; sometimes a persona belongs only to a particular work.

The differences between the personas chosen by Pope and Lady Mary help to define the contrasts between their works. Pope characteristically assumes an authoritative voice. The exalted tone of the passage quoted earlier from *Windsor-Forest* suggests one form his authority might take: pronouncements from on high about national matters. *The Rape of the Lock* shows another. Toward the poem's end, Pope writes, of Belinda's shorn lock, "But trust the Muse – she saw it upward rise, / Tho' mark'd by none but quick Poetic Eyes" (5: 123–4). To all intents and purposes, Pope *is* the Muse: his eye of the imagination sees the lock rise to the heavens; his voice articulates its fate. Despite his verve and lightness of tone, as different as possible from the sonorities of *Windsor-Forest* toward the end, the poet speaks as one who *knows*:

> There Heroes' Wits are kept in pondrous Vases,
> And Beaus' in *Snuff-boxes* and *Tweezer-Cases*.
> There broken Vows, and Death-bed Alms are found,
> And Lovers' Hearts with Ends of Riband bound . . .
> (5: 115–18)

His debonair voice claims the reader's assent for even the most fantastic descriptions (like this one of the "Lunar Sphere"). Neither the certainty of his versification nor that of his assertion ever falters.

By the beginning of the 1730s, as he started writing his moral epistles, Pope had perfected a flexible persona that could sound at once authoritative and off-hand, confident and contemptuous. Although his tone may vary from line to line, his verbal control of the situations he narrates and assesses never wavers. The opening of *Epistle to Burlington* provides a case in point:

> 'Tis strange, the Miser should his Cares employ,
> To gain those Riches he can ne'er enjoy:

Is it less strange, the Prodigal should wast
His wealth, to purchase what he ne'er can taste?
Not for himself he sees, or hears, or eats;
Artists must chuse his Pictures, Music, Meats: . . .
Think we all these are for himself? No more
Than his fine Wife, alas! or finer Whore.

(1–6, 11–12)

The speaker's rhetorical questions and his direct assertions ring with equal certainty. Beginning with a generally accepted view of misers – they heap up money but can't enjoy its spending, because they wish only to keep it – he uses it as a starting point for arguing the case that spendthrifts endure lives of comparable restriction, since they lack the taste either to select or to enjoy the goods they purchase. The triple-barreled sexual insult at the end (the spendthrift's wife is unfaithful; he too is unfaithful; his whore is unfaithful) consolidates the series of contemptuous judgments that have preceded it. Pope here sets his sights on a human category rather than a named individual, but his stipulations about prodigal behavior make that category immediate: not abstract, but imagined in human terms. The prodigal's lack of taste, which receives only casual mention, will turn out to matter: throughout the poem, absence of taste accompanies moral insufficiency. Only the sexual allusions at the end of this first vignette hint that moral accompanies aesthetic weakness in this prodigal; later sketches will insist more strongly on the connection. Later sketches will also underline the point implicit in this characterization: that a person's inadequacies create their own punishment. The prodigal's inability to choose subjects him to the will of others; he lives in confinement of his own making.

Like the other moral epistles, *To Burlington* intersperses moral pronouncements ("Something there is more needful than Expence, / And something previous ev'n to Taste – 'tis Sense"; 41–42) with vivid exempla in order to construct a complicated argument. An intricate gloss on the meanings of "Sense," it explores more subtle misuses of riches than those that *An Epistle to Bathurst* addresses. The failure to employ wealth for active good constitutes a sin in this poem. Correspondingly, a vision of riches as the basis of civic betterment elicits Pope's most exalted tone. Throughout the epistle, his capacity to deploy a voice of authority and conviction proves an essential resource.

Lady Mary's personae, more varied than Pope's, serve different purposes from his. Two poems in which the speaker is assigned a name as well as a nature will suggest the difference. *Saturday. The Small-Pox*, written probably in late 1715, was published as the last of Lady Mary's *Six Town Eclogues*, in which she employs pastoral conventions for accounts of court activity. Her granddaughter testified to the auto-biographical bearing of *Saturday*, composed after Lady Mary herself had suffered small pox. She does not, however, speak openly about herself. Instead, she adopts the voice of someone named Flavia to articulate the despair of a young woman who considers her beauty her only resource.

Flavia has understood her beauty as a promise of happiness. "Where's my Complexion?" she inquires rhetorically: "where my radiant Bloom, / That promis'd happiness for Years to come?" (7–8). Contemplating her ravaged face, she describes herself as "A frightful spectre, to myself unknown!" (6). The rest of the poem confirms the implication, at once poignant and horrifying, that she has known herself only through her beauty.

The complex balancing of tones in this ninety-six-line poem demands from the reader constantly shifting emotional responses. In several respects, at several junctures, Flavia represents herself as a superficial and frivolous creature. She glories in the gifts of opera tickets and cherries she has received; she boasts of the contempt she has displayed for the raffle prize offered to her; she insists that other beauties can reign now only because of her absence: "'Tis to my ruin all your charms ye owe" (58). If she showed up in her former beauty, no one would pay the slightest attention to them. She remembers with pleasure the hours she has spent at her toilette and recalls how she gloried in the sight of herself in the mirror. The emphasis on her vanity and frivolity suggests that even this first-person account has a satiric thrust: from the extremity of Flavia's self-adoration (adoration, that is, of her past self) we may learn how meretricious is devotion to mere appearance.

Yet that is not quite what we learn. For one thing, the narrative of lost beauty suggests the almost magic power of female charms. In a central stanza, Flavia reports her effects on past lovers. Soldiers wrote soft verses; beaus tried to turn into wits; wits spoke nonsense. In some instances, the beauty's power effects reform. Gamesters stop demanding their money; the bold and haughty tremble; the bashful squire "Has dar'd to speak with spirit not his own" (87). Beauty embodied in a woman has largely controlled the social scene. One can hardly blame its former possessor for mourning its loss.

Moreover, Flavia has moments of penetrating self-awareness:

> But oh! How vain, how wretched is the boast
> Of beauty faded, and of empire lost!
> What now is left but weeping, to deplore
> My beauty fled, and empire now no more!
>                           (60–63)

Reading the first of these couplets, one may think that Flavia is making an analogy between her beauty and the empire of great men. The second couplet, however, makes it clear that she speaks literally of her own empire, perhaps analogous to that of princes and conquerors, but an empire obtained entirely by the power of beauty. She recognizes the vanity – both the futility and the narcissism – of remembering her happy past life; she acknowledges that the time has come for deploring rather than boasting. By the poem's end, she has declared her intention of retiring to the country, with a realistic sense of the likelihood that in the city, false friends will "mourn my ruin with a joyful heart" (92). The concluding couplet articulates her rueful farewell to all she has known: "Ye, operas, circles, I no more must view! / My toilette, patches, all the world adieu!" (95–96). Concern with toilette and patches still seems frivolous, but "all the world" sums up Flavia's situation: the world she has inhabited is no longer available to her. When she speaks of her "lost inglorious face" (94), she speaks literally: her face has been the source of her glory; that glory exists no longer. One can hardly fail to sympathize.

The poem, then, uses its persona to evoke both something like amused contempt, for the woman who thinks the labors of her dressing table enormously important, and sympathy, for the woman who has lost everything she had. If her empire was trivial in comparison to that of male conquerors, it was yet all that she, as a woman, had available to her. Her competitiveness operates in a limited sphere, but, like her ambition, it links her with those who can strive and achieve in less confined circumstances.

Had Lady Mary written about her smallpox in a voice avowedly her own, she would have run the risk of appearing self-pitying, if not maudlin. With the voice of Flavia she can protect herself – even, perhaps, mock herself a little. (Smallpox did not, in fact, desperately damage the poet's appearance, although she feared its ravages.) She gains distance from personal subject matter. Her voice, unlike that of Pope's typical persona, does not at all assert its own authority. On the contrary, it both declares and exposes weakness; yet this poetic manipulation of asserted weakness serves as a guard.

A more surprising choice of persona is that of Arthur Gray, a footman convicted of trying to rape his employer and condemned to death for the crime, although not in fact executed. In *Epistle from Arthur Gray the Footman, after his Condemnation for attempting a Rape*, Lady Mary imagines herself into the situation of a working-class man seized with passion for an upper-class woman. The epistle addresses this woman. The first three couplets clearly establish its emotional circumstances:

> Read, lovely nymph, and tremble not to read,
> I have no more to wish, nor you to dread:
> I ask not life, for life to me were vain,
> And death a refuge from severer pain.
> My only hope in these last lines I try;
> I wou'd be pitied, and I then wou'd die.
>
> (1–6)

The verses narrating his hopeless, desperate love indeed rouse pity, but their poetic effectiveness derives more fundamentally from the satiric implications of Gray's story. As he tells it, his torment arises not only from his hopeless love but from seeing his beloved wooed by "those triflers who make Love a trade" (44). He loves truly and deeply; they "sigh not from the heart, but from the brain; / Vapours of vanity, and strong champagne" (49–50). Their notions of wit and of pleasure are alike meretricious; he, as the "Vapours of vanity" line suggests, can exercise wit and can dream of real pleasure. He decides on suicide, but the sight of the woman he loves in morning disarray when he brings up her breakfast overwhelms him. He grows "giddy" and makes his attempt.

To use a servant's voice to convey social criticism is a daring move. Equally daring is Lady Mary's assigning of strong feelings and powerful language to a footman. This imagined Arthur writes energetically, economically, often wittily.

> Th'extremest proof of my desire I give,
> And since you will not love, I will not live. . . .
> But when you see me waver in the wind,
> My guilty flame extinct, my soul resign'd,
> Sure you may pity what you can't approve,
> The cruel consequence of furious Love.
>                                          (87–88, 91–94)

Such verse demands emotional response – and the demand itself would seem remarkable to a contemporary audience. Pity and sympathize with a footman who tries to rape a lady? What an extraordinary idea!

The boldness of Lady Mary's enterprise depends on her choice of persona. Writing from the point of view of a social outcast, she can imply questions about the established order, suggesting ideas that she could hardly articulate in her own voice. Once more, she gives power to a voice that does not embody obvious authority.

Pope chooses larger subjects than Lady Mary does: the use of riches rather than the insufficiencies of a single man. Lady Mary, however, at her best employs relatively limited subjects to large purpose. The varied repertoires of both poets exemplify the wide poetic possibilities explored in this period. Both the contrasts between them and the similarities they reveal underline aspects of their time.

Pope has made an appearance in every chapter so far: appropriately, given his status as a literary giant of the early eighteenth century. The closer focus on him in the context of a single other poet continues to reveal his participation in his period's important trends. "How to live" preoccupies him especially in *An Epistle to Bathurst*, which follows the pattern of Pope's other moral epistles in adducing positive as well as negative examples of individual living and in offering general as well as specific commentary. The poet's sense of the individual's position in society – that issue generally considered the special concern of the novel – shapes his satire. He considers "society" to mean the structured organization of the broad community he inhabits, including financial and political arrangements. Thus his observations about the use and misuse of wealth bear indirectly on the nation as well as the individual.

For Lady Mary, "society" means mainly the small group of privileged persons like herself. Her investigations of "how to live" focus on the situation of aristocrats like Flavia and Lord Bathurst, who inhabit a realm of luxury. Moral choices make their demands even in such a realm.

Flavia, after her illness, appears to make better choices than Bathurst does, but, in contrast to the nobleman's, her conceivable choices are limited. Directly or indirectly, Lady Mary often suggests her awareness of restrictions on women. Even her own hinted role as victim of male heartlessness, like her account of Lord Bathurst as flitting from one female to another, conveys a sense of women as inevitably subjected to male whim.

As male and female, as penalized Catholic and secure aristocrat, as famous professional poet and ambitious amateur, Pope and Lady Mary contrast with one another. Yet both deploy a skillful rhetoric of feeling, half-concealed; both deftly manipulate heroic couplets to varied purposes; both directly and indirectly advocate, in disciplined verse, a disciplined moral life. In these ways they epitomize trends of their period, in which poets tried both to articulate and to preserve values of the classic past – moderation, control, responsibility – and to hint, on occasion, some longing for lives of ease and personal expressiveness.

Their differences matter too, not just as reflections of their different social positions but also as indications of the range of acceptability in eighteenth-century poetic practice. The voice of high moral authority that Pope developed, the voice always implicitly or explicitly articulating "The strong Antipathy of Good to Bad" (*Epilogue to the Satires* 2: 198), exerted such power that later critics often termed it the voice of the era. It indeed represents the strong satiric impulse widespread in the early eighteenth century. To define it as the voice of the era, however, hardly does justice to the range of poetic impulses expressed during those years. Lady Mary's multiple voices, while sometimes used for satiric purposes, also call attention to the potential poetic force of positions of ostensible weakness rather than strength. The condemned prisoner, the victim of smallpox, the woman scorned: all speak for those who seldom speak for themselves. Although Lady Mary, like Pope, deployed wit and concision as poetic tools, she used them, often, for new purposes.

No two figures could in their verse sum up the divergent impulses and practices of a period, but the writers considered in this chapter call attention, through their convergences and their contrasts, to how far from univocal their period's poets were.

# 6

# How to Live: The Place of Work

*The Choice*, at the beginning of the eighteenth century, articulates an ideal of ease, retirement, and harmony and suggests that everyone might wish to live as peacefully, as effortlessly, as possible. By mid-century, however, poets expressed serious doubts about Pomfret's vision. Ease, retirement, and harmony, once the dream of a war-torn society, could also be seen as forms of shirking responsibility. At the center of human existence, arguably, was work. Prescriptions for the good life might focus on admonitions about work – yet accounts of work as actual experience, while recognizing it as an economic necessity, suggested that such occupation could prove deadening rather than enlivening.

The tension between these two positions depended partly, though only partly, on social class. Those who wrote as participants about the experience of work often belonged to the laboring class, whereas spectators and theoreticians commented from the perspective of more elevated social reaches. At least one important poem from the second third of the century, however, incorporates the tension itself as at least a covert concern. Work as moral imperative provides the ostensible subject of *The Castle of Indolence*, a long narrative poem in Spenserian stanzas and pseudo-Spenserian language published by James Thomson a few months before his death in 1748. The poem tells how the wizard Indolence lures men to his estate with the promise of ease; then it reports their subsequent lives of lassitude, explains how they are thrown into a dungeon when they grow "displeasing," and finally narrates their rescue by the Knight of Arts and Industry. The poem's first stanza articulates the work's explicit moral:

> O Mortal man, who livest here by toil,
> Do not complain of this thy hard estate;

That like an emmet [ant] thou must ever moil,
Is a sad sentence of an ancient date;
And, certes, there is for it reason great;
For, though sometimes it makes thee weep and wail,
And curse thy star, and early drudge and late,
Withouten that would come an heavier bale [evil],
Loose life, unruly passions, and diseases pale.

                                        (1.1. 1–9)

The Biblical account of the Fall of Man made labor part of man's
punishment for sin – that's the "sad sentence of an ancient date." In
Thomson's interpretation, the punishment becomes blessing. A worse
fate would overtake us if we lacked work as a resource.

Yet the ambivalence of *The Castle of Indolence*, despite its project's
clarity, betrays the fact that high valuation of work as a way of life
does not come cost free. The first canto of the two-canto poem dwells
on details of life at the castle – details that in many respects echo those
of Pomfret's idyllic vision. Here "the calm pleasures always hover'd
nigh" (1.6. 7): pleasures of landscape, of varied scenery, of singing birds,
of freedom from passion, ambition, and avarice. The poet imagines himself as a one-time inhabitant of the castle and berates himself for his
self-indulgence. Still, he describes the seductive pleasures of indolence
in luscious detail:

Was nought around but images of rest:
Sleep-soothing groves, and quiet lawns between;
And flowery beds that slumbrous influence kest,
From poppies breath'd; and beds of pleasant green . . .

                                        (1.3. 1–4)

The Castle of Indolence holds more obvious emotional appeal than does
the strenuous knight who rescues its inhabitants for courts, military
camps, senates, the pursuit of the Muses, "the thriving mart," or "the
rural reign" (2.60. 6, 7). The second canto, devoted to the rescue, contains verse that often sounds more dutiful than inspired. It ends with
a lurid account of two allegorical figures, Beggary and Scorn, who plague
castle inmates unwilling to accept the gospel of work. In other words,
economic failure and social contempt, two powerful sanctions, threaten
the laggard. The reader may feel that the poet is whipping himself into
compliance with his own doctrine.

The alternatives of delightful ease and arduous toil reflect the collective consciousness of a period of mercantile expansion. Great Britain's ships sailed the known world, trading with many nations, bringing back many goods, fostering a growing taste for new commodities. Merchants were making money – enough money to threaten traditional class distinctions, as impoverished aristocrats saw the advantages of marrying their daughters to the sons of rich commercial men. Industry, both as individual and as collective activity, provided a plausible and profitable way of life. Thomson shows himself aware of that truth, even as he also betrays his nostalgia for less demanding standards.

Most of the period's poems dealing with work as a recommended pattern for existence do not, like Thomson, discuss alternatives to it. If they feel ambivalent about their recommendations, they avoid betraying such feeling. John Dyer, earlier the poet of *Grongar Hill*, in the last year of his life published *The Fleece*, a poem fully modeled on the Georgic tradition to which poets like Swift and Gay had earlier alluded. It both celebrates work (of many kinds) and elucidates the system of values that honors it. "Whate'er is excellent in art proceeds / From labor and endurance," Dyer writes (3. 349–50). As an immediate example, he cites the oak, which must sink its roots in stubborn earth if it hopes for its branches to ascend. The oak provides an analogy to human achievement, not a model for men: Dyer repeatedly suggests that human beings alone can set a meaningful standard. Thus, in the process of weaving wool, "hammers, rising and descending, learn / To imitate the industry of man" (3. 166–67). A few lines later, the woven cloth, spread out to dry,

> Expands;
> Still bright'ning in each rigid discipline,
> And gath'ring worth; as human life, in pains,
> Conflicts and troubles.
>
> (3. 172–75)

Inanimate objects, like the manifestations of nature, imitate human beings and thus in turn provide moral models or reminders.

*The Fleece* seems a strange poem now, reminding us of the cultural and social chasm created by the passage of almost three centuries. Dyer's evident assumptions about human life and about the nature of poetry emanate from a society that took literature seriously as a record of and a guide to experience. British manufacture, like British trade, was flourishing. Although aristocrats of landed heritage might condescend to the prosperous merchants who exercised increasing political power, the wealth that attended the manufacture and circulation of British products exhilarated many. Dyer writes not as a wealthy man himself, but as one excited by the energies that generated wealth. Perceiving the human force at work in national productivity, reflecting about the meaning of such vitality, he promulgated a vision of the universe as likewise dependent on the proper deployment of energy.

> Ev'n nature lives by toil:
> Beast, bird, air, fire, the heav'ns, and rolling worlds,
> All live by action: nothing lies at rest,
> But death and ruin: man is born to care;
> Fashion'd, improv'd, by labor.
>
> (3. 20–25)

In setting forth this doctrine, Dyer assumed the role of poet as sage, instructing his countrymen and women in the ways of industry and in its importance. The ambition of *The Fleece* is staggering. The poet sets out not only to record every stage in the production of wool and its manufacture into cloth, but also to delineate the place of this production and manufacture in national life, to examine the role of Great Britain in the community of nations, to investigate various British institutions, to suggest the significance of commerce, and, above all, to glorify the productive use of human energies. Such an enterprise might seem more suitable to a prose treatise, but Dyer draws on epic models (notably Milton, his precursor in the use of blank verse for high purpose) as well as on Virgilian georgic. He makes both poetic and intellectual claims on his audience. He even calls on that audience for emotional response – often in surprising contexts.

A particularly egregious case in point, for current sensibilities, is the poet's praise of the workhouse, an eighteenth-century institution intended to employ the poor in useful activity while also providing them with room and board. To a modern consciousness, the workhouse appears a tyrannical and exploitative establishment, based on injurious assumptions about the causes of poverty. Dyer sees it otherwise. "Ye children of affliction," he writes, addressing the poor, "be compell'd / To happiness" (3. 247–48). Before the reader can fully grasp the notion of "compelled" happiness, the poem moves on to describe the spontaneous happiness of onlookers, among whom the speaker counts himself:

> By gentle steps
> Uprais'd, from room to room we slowly walk,
> And view with wonder, and with silent joy,
> The sprightly scene; where many a busy hand,
> Where spoles, cards, wheels, and looms, with motion quick,
> And ever-murm'ring sound, th'unwonted sense
> Wrap in surprise. To see them all employ'd,
> All blithe, it gives the spreading heart delight,
> As neither meats, nor drinks, nor aught of joy
> Corporeal, can bestow.
>
> (3. 263–72)

If the reader too possesses the capacity for a "spreading heart" – a heart that expands with benevolent feeling – that reader presumably will share the emotion attributed to those who literally visit the workhouse. Yet because Dyer relies heavily on assertion rather than demonstration, it is difficult to imagine that anyone who has not already been uplifted by the spectacle of enforced labor would participate in the feeling ascribed to the onlookers.

The conclusion of Book 3 demonstrates more persuasive exaltation:

> See the silver maze
> Of stately Thamis, ever chequer'd o'er
> With deeply-laden barges, gliding smooth
> And constant as his stream: in growing pomp,
> By Neptune still attended, slow he rolls
> To great Augusta's mart, where lofty trade,
> Amid a thousand golden spires enthron'd,
> Gives audience to the world: the strand around
> Close swarms with busy crouds of many a realm.
> What bales, what wealth, what industry, what fleets!
> Lo, from the simple fleece how much proceeds.
>
> (3. 622–32)

The final exclamation sounds heartfelt. Not everyone would be exhilarated by the thought of bales and fleets, but Dyer's tone makes his own exhilaration convincing. Like Pope at the end of *Windsor-Forest*, on whose rhetoric he appears to model his own, he finds the spectacle of trade in action thrilling. Although the presence of Neptune comes as something of a surprise, the pervasive sense of crowded activity emerges vividly, and activity, after all, provides the primary subject of *The Fleece*. Process interests Dyer far more than product – what proceeds from "the simple fleece" rather than the fleece itself.

His effort to find language for describing process, however, often blocks his poetic energy. A final example will suggest the problem:

> That stain alone is good, which bears unchang'd
> Dissolving water's, and calcining sun's,
> And thieving air's attacks. How great the need,
> With utmost caution to prepare the woof,
> To seek the best-adapted dyes, and salts,
> And purest gums! since your whole skill consists
> In op'ning well the fibres of the woof,
> For the reception of the beauteous dye,
> And wedging ev'ry grain in ev'ry pore,
> Firm as a diamond in gold enchas'd.
>
> (3. 203–12)

The pronoun "your" in the sixth line comes as a shock, and nothing in the larger text explains it. It suggests that Dyer, having done his homework, knowing exactly what the process of dyeing entails, now imagines an actual person performing that process, a person whom he addresses. From the reader's point of view, however, no one is there. The process remains theoretical. Words like "beauteous" and similes like that of the diamond set in gold insist on the aesthetic interest of dyeing as an activity and of its poetic embodiment, but that interest hardly makes itself felt.

Dyer writes, and writes at great length, like a man possessed by his project, that of demonstrating the high value of action in every realm. His distance from most of the activity he describes, however, makes it difficult to grasp the subject's emotional resonance, despite the fact that the poem's language often seeks emotional response. It remained for other writers – writers closer to the experience of physical work – to make the subject more immediate, although not, like Dyer, to glorify it. Those who know first-hand what labor entails do not advocate it. They consider it a necessity, the center of their own experience, but not a matter for aestheticizing. The kind of work they have done gives them grounds for recommending how *not* to live – if, that is, one is fortunate enough to have any choice in the matter.

I am thinking in particular of two working-class poets, Stephen Duck and Mary Collier. Duck, known as "the thresher poet," established his fame with a poem called *The Thresher's Labour*; Collier, angered by that work's treatment of women, responded with *The Woman's Labour*. Collier attracted little attention and remained a laborer. Duck, in contrast, won royal patronage and eventually became a clergyman. His life, however, ended in suicide.

*The Thresher's Labour* delineates in detail the daily experience of the farm laborer. James Thomson, in the 1730 version of *Spring*, wrote, "Ye generous BRITONS, venerate the Plow!" (67), but the plow exists for him only as a means to the end of producing crops that will make Britain "th' exhaustless Granary of a World!" (77). For Duck, flails and scythes and wagons have immediate physical reality and immediate purpose, purpose fulfilled at the end of the day, when crops are reaped or hay is made, rather than the end of the year, when a vague though prolific harvest emerges in Thomson's rendition. Instruments of work rather than objects of veneration, they excite no specific feeling, serving simply as functional tools.

The speaker, a farm laborer, emphasizes the hardships of his lot:

> Each Morn we early rise, go late to Bed,
> And lab'ring hard, a painful Life we lead:
> For Toils, scarce ever ceasing, press us now,
> Rest never does, but on the Sabbath show,
> And barely that, our Master will allow.
> (245–49)

The poem is full of sweat, a rare manifestation in eighteenth-century poetry. Stripped for action, the threshers find their sweat falling "In briny Streams" (44), trickling down their faces, dropping from their hair. Mowing hay, their "Streams of Sweat run trickling down a-pace" (123). The speaker compares himself to a fast horse, triumphantly galloping over hills and flat land, until, at noon, "piercing Beams hath bath'd his Sides in Sweat" (132) and his pace slackens. The physicality of such allusions lends immediacy to an account that sticks close to actualities of the day's work. The speaker makes no attempt, like Dyer, to explain processes involved in cutting hay or threshing grain or peas. Instead, he tries to convey how each activity feels to those who perform it. Sweat is essential.

As a close observer of his own life, the laborer specifies the emotional responses of the workers – looking and feeling like guilty schoolboys when rebuked by the master, eager to begin work in the long days of summer, at first joyful in the open air, then weary and discouraged after a morning's scything, and so on. Such specificity has an important function in the dual project of *The Thresher's Labour*: first, to convey as vividly as possible the exact nature of the labor; second, to declare the humanity of the working class, a group often ignored by those higher in the social scale. The ever-shifting emotions of the workers demonstrate the responsiveness and sensitivity often denied to them by cavalier assumptions of their social superiors.

Another aspect of the same demonstration focuses on responsiveness to nature. Early in the poem, the speaker comments on the absence of natural beauty around the workers. He inquires, rhetorically, whether threshers, like shepherds, can tell stories to one another, but notes that the noise of the flail would drown speech. Perhaps they can think instead? Obstacles present themselves even to such a choice. They do not, however, include or suggest mental incapacity in the laborers.

> – Alas! what pleasing thing
> Here to the Mind can the dull Fancy bring?
> The Eye beholds no pleasant Object here:
> No cheerful Sound diverts the list'ning Ear.
> The Shepherd well may tune his Voice to sing,
> Inspir'd by all the Beauties of the Spring:
> No Fountains murmur here, no Lambkins play,
> No linnets warble, and no Fields look gay;
> 'Tis all a dull and melancholy Scene,
> Fit only to provoke the Muses spleen.
>
> (54–63)

The implicit question of the passage concerns how to make poetry of rural experience that bears little similarity to that of the conventional pastoral. In the opening address to his patron, Duck had claimed that even the endless toils of the worker's year can be rehearsed in poetry "When you, and Gratitude, command the Verse" (12). When he thinks specifically of what is missing from the scene of country work, he begins to doubt the possibility. Yet attention to that scene reminds him of what natural pleasures remain to him and his fellow laborers. "The Birds salute us as to Work we go," he writes (105), and as he prepares for reaping, he appreciates the "different Beauties" (224) of the unmown field. Then he contemplates, "with a more tender Eye" (225), the fact that it will soon lie in ruins:

> For once set in, where-e'er our Blows we deal,
> There's no resisting of the well-whet Steel:
> But here or there, where-e'er our Course we bend,
> Sure Desolation does our Steps attend.
> Thus when *Arabia*'s Sons, in hopes of Prey,
> To some more fertile Country take their way;
> How beauteous all things in the Morn appear,
> There Villages, and pleasing Cots are here;
> So many pleasing Objects meet the Sight,
> The ravish'd Eye could willing gaze 'till Night:
> But long e'er then, where-e'er their Troops have past,
> Those pleasant Prospects lie a gloomy Waste.
>
> (227–38)

The simile conveys a complicated emotional response. As one who appreciates the natural scene, the speaker regrets the desolation he inflicts. Comparing the reapers to Asian invaders who lay waste to beautiful country, he defines them as destroyers of beauty and emphasizes the presence of beauty to be destroyed. Unlike pastoral poets, he does not need to conjure up scenes of lambkins and fountains. He appreciates the beauty that lies about him, and his capacity for such appreciation makes an implicit claim on his audience to recognize, even to share, his awareness and sensitivity.

This speaker, however, appreciates more than beauty: he values also the power and energy that farm workers bring to their destructive activity – which is, of course, also productive. The "well-whet Steel" of their scythes is resistless; their force cannot be opposed. An aesthetic response to the lovely spectacle of wheat waving in the fields, although appropriate, is insufficient. It remains important to acknowledge as well the worth of those who, in the service of their master, but also, as Thomson pointed out, of their country, mow it down.

The simile serves yet another important function. Duck wishes not only to declare his "common humanity" with his readers; he wants also to claim uncommon attributes. Like other self-educated poets of the period, he imports classical allusions and methods in order to suggest that he shares with his audience not only emotional capacity and sensitivity to nature, but also a body of knowledge that traditionally belongs only to upper-class males. His poem's several extended similes recall those of classical epic. His references to Hercules, Cyclops, Vulcan, Thetis, and, most importantly, Sisyphus also allude to the classic past. If *The Thresher's Labour* positions its writer firmly among his fellow laborers, it also insists on his specialness. He demands to be taken seriously both as a worker in the fields (look how hard I work, look at the endlessness of my toil, look at the exhaustion I feel . . .) and as an embodiment of the Muse who can transmute labor into art.

Although the speaker does not traffic extensively in self-pity, he clearly wishes to elicit the reader's pity. Through most of the poem, pride in accomplishment wars with claims of exhaustion and discouragement. The thresher sounds resentful about the fact that he cannot escape even in sleep – he dreams about the day's toils – but also pleased with his endurance and strength. Only at the very end does one suspect the encroachment of despair. The verse reports the harvest feast, with the master urging his workers to consume abundant beer. The next morning however, "soon reveals the Cheat, / When the same Toils we must again repeat" (273–74). The realization of that recurrence leads to a comparison with Sisyphus and to the desolate concluding couplet:

> Now growing Labours still succeed the past,
> And growing always new, must always last.
>                           (281–82)

The poem makes no overt claim for sympathy at this point, yet the culminating realization, simply and directly stated, sets the conversion of labor into poetry in a new light. The Muse's enterprise, according to the poem's logic, can provide at best only a temporary respite. The laborer's life contains no escape clause.

Even for a twenty-first-century audience, *The Thresher's Labour* retains poetic vitality by virtue of its evocative physical specificity and its emotional detail. One sequence of manifest feeling demands special attention: Duck's treatment of women, which would provoke Mary Collier. First, wives figure as vague presences providing dumplings and bacon. Then, at length (almost forty lines), Duck narrates the arrival and activity of "a Throng / Of prattling Females" (163–64), the hay-makers. The unmistakable force of his distaste animates the account. Mostly, according to this narrative, the women talk instead of work. They sit on the grass in order to eat; after they've eaten they remain sitting and keep talking. Only rain can dispel "The tattling Croud" (187). Their dispersion by a shower provokes in the poet an extended belittling comparison to a flock of sparrows.

The entire passage speaks of strong emotion: resentful contempt of these females who chatter while men work. The feeling inspires some of the poem's best verse: economical, pointed, forceful:

> All talk at once; but seeming all to fear,
> That all they speak so well, the rest won't hear;
> By quick degrees so high their Notes they strain,
> That Standers-by can naught distinguish plain:
> So loud their Speech, and so confus'd their Noise,
> Scarce puzzled Echo can return a Voice;
> Yet spite of this, they bravely all go on,
> Each scorns to be, or seem to be, outdone.
>
> (177–84)

By the time Duck refers to them as "The tattling Croud," the phrase has the force of definition, like Thomson's references to birds as "the plumy People" or to sheep as "the woolly kind." The poet has cat-egorized women so forcefully that he can dismiss them. Men exist as workers; women, only as talkers.

Mary Collier's angry reaction, on behalf of herself as a hard-working woman and of her sex, seems both predictable and justifiable. Unlike Duck, she has few classical allusions available to her, and her verse does not achieve his level of ease. She too, however, can draw on a wealth of specific detail, and powerful feeling infuses her lines. Resentment of Duck provides a starting point: resentment of the social and financial advancement he has achieved, as well as of his attitudes. Collier soon moves beyond this emotion, though, to more intense anger about prevailing attitudes toward women and about the condi-tions of female labor. The energy of that anger gives her poem power, despite its sometimes crude versification.

The poem's speaker describes herself as a slave, continuing,

> No Learning ever was bestow'd on me;
> My Life was always spent in Drudgery:
> And not alone; alas! with Grief I find,
> It is the Portion of poor Woman-kind.
>
> (7–10)

She looks back to an imagined Golden Age in which men respected and adored women. Now, she says, men scorn the other sex. Duck adds insult to injury when he does not simply ignore women, but speaks "As if our Sex but little Work could do" (44). Most of the rest of the 246-line poem details the nature of the work women actually do. They too "freely toil and sweat" (57), sharing the labor of haying and reaping, but also bearing the entire responsibility of life indoors. Only after a hard day's work in the fields do they produce the bacon and dumpling that a man expects on his return home. Unlike the men Duck describes, they cannot rest at every stile on the way home: "We must make haste, for when we Home are come. / Alas! we find our Work but just begun" (105–06). Women take care of their children as well as work for family income. Men can rest at night; women lose sleep because their "froward [naughty] Children cry and rave" (114). All in all, women have a harder time. They must take their children to the fields with them, either carrying them or compelling them too to participate in the gleaning or haying. Not only can they not rest at the stiles: they can never rest.

The most persuasive and most passionate portion of the poem concerns work in domestic service, which Collier portrays as more demanding and exhausting than its equivalent in the fields. Doing the washing, scrubbing the pots, brewing the beer, women work morning and night, sometimes beginning one morning and working until the next night. The mistress comes to check on their work, warning them not only to work hard but also to save on soap and fire:

> Now we drive on, resolv'd our Strength to try,
> And what we can, we do most willingly;
> Until with Heat and Work, 'tis often known,
> Not only Sweat, but Blood runs trickling down
> Our Wrists and Fingers; still our Work demands
> The constant Action of our lab'ring Hands.
>
> (182–87)

The horrifying detail of blood as well as sweat dripping down receives no special emphasis. The important fact is that "constant Action," the action demanded by and defining women's work.

Three times in the poem the speaker refers to herself as a slave, or to the condition of women as slavery. By the time she has supplied the detail of her labor, the metaphor seems hardly metaphorical. She has dramatized the condition of her sex as one of unremitting hardship. Her poem's resolution sounds as despairing as that of *The Thresher's Labour*. First Collier declares the futility of her poetic enterprise: "But to rehearse all Labour is in vain, / Of which we very justly might complain" (235–36). Then she supplies one of the poem's two classical allusions: if the male thresher can see himself as Sisyphus, women workers can as plausibly describe themselves as Danaids, doomed forever to fill leaking jars with water. Their situation emblemizes futility and frustration. The poem does not end here, though. It goes on to another simile, which seems positive at the outset and turns sharply negative:

> So the industrious Bees do hourly strive
> To bring their Loads of Honey to the Hive;
> Their sordid Owners always reap the Gains,
> And poorly recompense their Toil and Pains.
> (243–46)

The productiveness of bringing back honey seems at odds with the futility of women forever pouring water into leaking jars, but the final couplet suggests the connection between the two comparisons. Productivity has no meaning for the workers themselves. Because their masters and mistresses reap the benefits, those whose industry produces those benefits find their work as meaningless as that of the Danaids.

This bitter conclusion to Collier's poem may retrospectively call attention to the absence of bitterness in Duck's. Although the threshers' master urges them on to ever more work, the worker hardly complains of this. He appears to accept it as given that some men work for others and that those others have the right to dominate. Collier's final couplet, in contrast, has the force of sudden realization. After her dreary recital of miserable labor, she abruptly grasps the meaning of it all: her work benefits "sordid Owners," not herself. She tells us not "how to live" but "how *I* live," how she labors and suffers by necessity – thus revealing a potential difficulty in the widespread assumption that work inevitably possesses moral value. The existence of a contemporary audience for such poems as Collier's, an audience including members of the gentry as well as possibly the aristocracy, testifies to the possibility of widespread uneasiness about the subject of work.

Another kind of ambiguity emerges in allusions to her own work by Mary Jones, a woman of a higher social class than Collier's, sister to a clergyman and friend to several aristocrats. Jones's work is poetry, but she claims it only with diffidence: the notion of a woman's nondomestic work raises real social questions. *An Epistle to Lady Bowyer*, in which the poet discusses her vocation most fully, imitates Pope's *Epistle to Arbuthnot* and uses allusions to Jones's male precursor as a means of self-denigration. *Lady Bowyer* opens in exclamatory fashion:

> How much of paper's spoil'd! what floods of ink!
> And yet how few, how very few can think!
> The knack of writing is an easy trade;
> But to think well requires – at least a Head.
>
> (1–4)

She does not claim to possess "a Head" herself; instead she announces that only one "Genius" arises in an age, and that Pope holds the position for her time.

> Whilst lofty *Pope* erects his laurell'd head,
> No lays, like mine, can live beneath his shade.
> Nothing but weeds, and moss, and shrubs are found
> Cut, cut them down, why cumber they the ground?
>
> (9–12)

Having relegated herself and her poetry to the status of weeds and ordered her own excision, she goes on to review the various reasons her friends offer her for writing, and to refute each in turn. She doesn't wish fame; she lacks a friend at court who might help her; she does not wish to flatter the great. She exhibits a fastidious distaste for the very possibility of moral contamination by becoming a "slave" (98) – a term she uses in quite a different sense from Collier's – to some unworthy great man. She outlines the nature of the lord for whom she would be willing to write and to whom she would be willing to dedicate: one of "great unspotted soul" (84), who is nonetheless "too honest to be great" (95), a paragon of virtue and of moral isolation.

The poem concludes with an account of her worthy parents and of her own peaceful, solitary life. If the addressee of the epistle approves of her verse, she will be content:

> Enough for me. I cannot put my trust
> In lords; smile lies, eat toads, or lick the dust.
> Fortune her favours much too dear may hold:
> An honest heart is worth its weight in *gold*.
> (123–26)

This position of moral superiority contrasts oddly with the self-abasement of the opening. The speaker has no hesitation about making moral claims, but she demonstrates her unwillingness to claim importance for her poetry.

Yet she writes it. She introduces the final sequence by declaring her desire for only a few friends, who love her well: "What more remains, these artless lines shall tell" (105). By writing – or claiming to write – *artless* lines, she distinguishes herself from Pope, who is nothing if not artful. At the beginning of her poem, she has announced her unworthiness in comparison to him. Perhaps she imitates *Arbuthnot* – its rhythms, much of its sentence structure, and several of its topics – in order to emphasize her inferiority? The differences between *Arbuthnot* and *Lady Bowyer* suggest another, more surprising purpose: to emphasize, rather, the contrast between Pope's purposes and her own. *An Epistle to Arbuthnot* is centrally a poem about poetry. Its speaker proclaims his inability *not* to write. Like the speaker in Jones's poem, he also proclaims his virtue – but that virtue intimately connects itself with the writing of poetry. He writes to attack the evil and to please the good. If his virtuous parents and his love of them suggest attractive human qualities, his vocation as poet only supports those qualities.

Jones, in contrast, creates an opposition between poetry and virtue. To write poetry for a wider audience than her friends, according to the epistle's logic, necessarily involves flattery and corruption. The choice of a simple life supports her preservation of the honest heart on which she prides herself. Her poems will exist to please only those she personally wishes to please. If she feels some desire to reach a wider audience – and her exploration in verse of the possibilities suggests that – her fear of corruption and her desire for virtue will protect her against implementing it.

As *An Epistle to Arbuthnot* progresses, every successive line makes increasingly clear the poet's vocation that provides the poem's subject. The movement of *To Lady Bowyer*, in contrast, raises increasingly compelling questions about whether the speaker can properly assert poetry as vocation. Perhaps, rather, her work is goodness: trying to achieve and maintain the ethical stability and certainty that she proclaims at the poem's ending. Other Jones's poems suggest the same possibility. *Soliloquy on an Empty Purse*, for instance, starts by labeling the speaker a poet, possessor of "A Poet's fortune! – not immense" (7). At the poem's end, she declares once more that hers is "a Poet's purse" (50). Much has changed, however, between the first and the second assertion. The poem's two central stanzas (20–45) insist on virtues associated with lack of wealth. Such qualities as temperance and fortitude attend the woman who lacks disposable income. Poverty creates serenity: the speaker feels no interest in trinkets or pastry or clothes she cannot afford. Her poetry, as a consequence, redefines itself:

> softly sweet, in garret high
> Will I thy virtues magnify;
> Outsoaring flatt'rers' stinking breath,
> And gently rhyming rats to death.
> (50–53)

The poem has described no alternative function for poetry, but the allusion to flattery reminds us that the poet might possess a fuller purse, were she willing to flatter the great. Her choice to use her verse to glorify the virtues forced on her by her refusal to pander for patronage reflects the same progression as that in *To Lady Bowyer*, from a generalized longing for the distinction of being known as a poet to a determination to concentrate, rather, on virtues she can attain, employing her capacity for verse only in privacy.

In *Of Desire. An Epistle to the Hon. Miss Lovelace*, Jones sets out most explicitly the kind of ethical dilemma that concerns her. Like others in her period, she sees desire as the source of human difficulty. "Whence these impetuous movements of the breast?" her poem begins. "Why beat our hearts, unknowing where to rest?" (1–2). A few lines later, she characterizes desire as "This unremitting sickness of the soul" (6), identical, it seems, with the dangerous "lawless Passion" (7) that wars with reason. She imagines the existence of some who "think, and wish, just only what they ought" (10). For such people, true greatness, wisdom, and virtue must be inevitable. For others, the majority, such attainments come only at the cost of struggle.

After a series of exempla illustrating the miseries of undisciplined desire, the poem concludes that only hope provides that "anchor of the mind" (136) that allows lasting serenity. Jones concludes by wishing for herself a life "full of thee" (156), a life, consequently, peaceful and devoid of false joys – "No ties forgot, no duties left unpaid, / No lays unfinish'd, and no aching head" (165–66). Poetry provides a reference point, but the speaker hopes for completion rather than for creativity. Moreover, she embeds this hope among references to moral responsibilities, ties and duties, and the state of her health. Her concluding wish echoes those expressed in other poems:

> This wish howe'er be mine: to live unknown,
> In some serene retreat, my time my own,
> To all obliging, yet a slave to none.
> Content, my riches; silence be my fame;
> My pleasures, ease; my honours, *your* esteem.
> (171–75)

The life of modest seclusion answers her modest desires. Yet the reference to riches, fame, and honor reveal her full awareness of other alternatives for a poet. The vocation of goodness as a private endeavor demands of her a struggle against commitment to that other vocation of poetry as public performance.

One can readily surmise that the conflicted position articulated in Jones's poems speaks of the female situation in eighteenth-century England. The vocation of goodness would undeniably seem more acceptable for women than that of poetry. In fact, though, the conflicting impulses toward public life and virtuous seclusion expressed themselves in men as well. Pomfret's vision did not in fact die. *The Castle of Indolence,* with its idyllic portrayals of the life of leisure, treats public life as duty and retreat as pleasure. The harsh details of Duck's poetry and Collier's suggest how onerous work could become, despite the moralistic praise that such as Dyer lavished on it. Activity was manifestly making the nation powerful; still, the vocation of goodness might seem a luxurious alternative.

That choice, however, often implies a life of relative reclusiveness, perhaps including benevolent action, but not facing the pressing demands of existence more fully involved in the tumult of the marketplace –

or, for that matter, the hayfield. The imperative to work entailed an obligation to function fully in the community. It thus carried political overtones as well as personal obligation. The Castle of Indolence tempted people toward ease and pleasure; the Knight of Arts and Industry urged them toward the world – a world in which national power was increasingly equated with industrial and commercial achievement. If living properly implied working productively, it implied also consciousness of social obligation as more than realization of the moral ties between individuals.

Perhaps the period's most eloquent statement of work as itself a form of virtue is a short poem by Samuel Johnson, *On the Death of Dr Robert Levet*. Levet, one of a number of needy individuals who inhabited Johnson's household, achieved no conspicuous public accomplishment. He practiced as a physician in London slums, a fact of great importance to his patients but of little obvious significance otherwise. When he died at the age of 76, however, Johnson declared his significance in verse that makes no obvious emotional announcement, yet conveys both grief and admiration for an obscure man.

The admiration focuses on the work that Levet did and the way he did it. Johnson's first stanza establishes a large context for his elegy:

> Condemn'd to hope's delusive mine,
>     As on we toil from day to day,
> By sudden blasts, or slow decline,
>     Our social comforts drop away.
>
>                                   (1–4)

Beginning not with Levet, but with "we," the poet invites us to contemplate the situation shared by all humanity. In his view, all labor in the same mine. We hope, but hope often in vain; we work ("toil"), but toil simply to get from one day to another; we suffer, one way or another, the loss of friends whose presence has helped to alleviate the daily toil. Although Johnson never directly says so, he conveys the sense that Levet has been conspicuous among his "social comforts." He articulates his loss by praising the unsung accomplishment of a lifetime.

Levet has been, the poet says, "Well tried" (5) through his life. He has manifested many virtues; he "fills affection's eye" with tears (9), although men of "letter'd arrogance" (10) might consider him unworthy of attention because of his lack of refinement. The poem acknowledges both his obscurity and his coarseness, but demonstrates the irrelevance of such qualities in comparison with the importance of Levet's constant effort to alleviate misery and want and to answer all calls for help, accepting meager financial recompense for unremitting and arduous work. The word *toil* reappears, as the poem tells us how the doctor supplied his own modest wants with "The toil of ev'ry day" (24). Johnson sums up his friend's achievement by reference to Christian standards:

> His virtues walk'd their narrow round,
>     Nor made a pause, nor left a void;
> And sure th' Eternal Master found
>     The single talent well employ'd.
>                                   (25–28)

Levet's virtues accompany him in his confined circuit of the poor. Like their possessor, they never stop. Johnson refers to the Biblical parable of the talents, in which two men are each given a single coin, a talent. One man buries it in the ground for safekeeping. The other uses it as a starting point for gaining further wealth. At the end of a year, the men's employer declares the one who has used his talent superior to the one who has buried it. The modern pun on the word, enabled by the fact that *talent* now (as in the eighteenth century) designates an innate human quality rather than a coin, allows Johnson to speak of Levet's "single talent" – his possibly modest gift for medicine – as well used, worthy of both divine and human praise.

The poem concludes by narrating Levet's peaceful death, an appropriate ending for his virtuous life. It says no more, even indirectly, about Johnson's grief. Yet the poem's eloquent celebration of an obscure career has demonstrated the speaker's deep appreciation of the dead man and has expanded the sense of loss: a loss experienced by humankind, the loss of a good person who models the power of virtue, not only deprivation felt by a single mourner. Levet, as rendered by Johnson, shows us, simply and eloquently, "how to live."

# 7

# Matters of Feeling: Forms of the Personal

By the century's middle years, personal feeling had come to seem more acceptable than it had seemed earlier as a subject for verse. Such reticence as that of *On the Death of Dr Robert Levet* did not always attend the poetic making of emotional claims. The lyric assumed an increasingly prominent place in the poetic repertoire, and many poets ventured both to discuss and to express emotion more openly and more frequently than most of their predecessors had done. Nonetheless, the question of how emotion could best be represented remained perplexing. Indeed, one of the period's most poignant lyrics, Thomas Gray's *Sonnet on the Death of Richard West*, makes this problem a central concern. The speaker, who has suffered an intense personal loss, muses about what resources remain for him. Around him, the sun rises, birds sing, the fields look beautifully and cheerfully green – and none of these appearances conveys meaning to him. He writes of his pain, and of the impossibility of communicating it.

Wordsworth chose Gray's sonnet as an instance of bad – dead – poetic diction, failing to see how systematically the poet deploys such phrases as "smileing Mornings" (1), "cheerful Fields" (4), and "the busy Race" (9) (referring to humankind). All allude to a body of poetry, nominally concerned with nature, that has, like the natural world itself, no power to speak to the human sufferer. When he speaks directly of his own feelings, the mourner uses straightforward, unornamented diction:

> A different Object do these Eyes require.
> My lonely Anguish melts no Heart, but mine; . . .
> I fruitless mourn to him, that cannot hear,
> And weep the more, because I weep in vain.
>
> (6–7, 13–14)

The two adjectives in these lines, "different" and "lonely," specify rather than elaborate. They do not reflect the kind of artifice that substitutes aesthetic effect for acknowledgment of pain. The sufferer's misery stems from his realism: his awareness that no one shares his anguish, that the dead man cannot hear him, and that his weeping serves no restorative purpose. The same realism makes him register the irrelevance of natural beauty and of poetic artifice to his immediate suffering. Only a poetry of direct statement, the sonnet implies, can relate the truth of experience. Such statement provides no consolation beyond the cold comfort of acknowledging actuality, but it may seem less bitter than the device of representing mornings as smiling in order to cheer men, or the rising sun as a Greek god.

The loneliness that intensifies grief's anguish in this poem does not for Gray attend only mourning: this poet typically represents himself in his verse as solitary and melancholy. The authority of his emotion empowers his moral statement. In the early *Ode on the Spring*, a poem which, like the sonnet on West, manipulates poetic artifice with apparent skepticism (this time to faintly comic effect), Gray turns an ironic eye on this aspect of his writing. He fancies himself in an elaborate and highly stylized rural scene, complete with "rosy-bosom'd Hours" (1), "Cool Zephyrs" (10), and an agreeable Muse (17). With the Muse, and with apparent satisfaction, he contemplates the vanity of worldly ambition and achievement and the universal inevitability of death – only to hear the insects around him ("The sportive kind"; 42) reply,

> Poor moralist! And what art thou?
> A solitary fly! . . .
> On hasty wings thy youth is flown;
> Thy sun is set, thy spring is gone—
> We frolick, while 'tis May.
> (43–44, 48–50)

A solitary fly provides as accurate a figure as any for the way the poet represents himself: alone, insignificant, unloved and unloving. In the *Hymn to Adversity*, which extols the value of suffering as an impetus to moral improvement, the speaker employs first-person pronouns throughout the final stanza, appealing to the goddess Adversity

> To soften, not to wound my heart,
> The gen'rous spark extinct revive,

> Teach me to love and to forgive,
> Exact my own defects to scan,
> What others are, to feel, and know myself a Man.
>
> (41–45)

The idea of himself as devoid of generosity and uneducated in love and forgiveness, needing help in order to feel the reality of others – this melancholy idea assumes various permutations, but it reappears frequently.

Perhaps the most compelling deployment of the emotionally charged figure of himself that Gray frequently evokes occurs in works where it may initially appear to have no importance. Two of Gray's best-known and most affecting compositions, *Ode on a Distant Prospect of Eton College* and *Elegy Written in a Country Church Yard*, exemplify the point. In the Eton ode, the speaker looks from a near-by height down on the grounds of the school he attended as a careless child, "A stranger yet to pain!" (14). The breezes that blow on him now "seem to sooth" his "weary soul" (17): once more he evokes himself as a melancholy figure. After this introduction, however, the rest of the poem concerns the activities of the schoolboys, the meaning of those activities, and the prospects the boys face in the future. The first-person presence who inaugurates the poem does not appear again, yet his sense of himself as weary, pained, and troubled informs every observation and judgment.

At first, watching the play of children who, as he fancies, bear no psychic burdens, the speaker enters sympathetically into the possibility of carefree recreation. By line 52, however, he perceives the players as "little victims," ignorant of the horrors they face.

> Yet see how all around 'em wait
> The Ministers of human fate,
> And black Misfortune's baleful train!
> Ah, shew them where in ambush stand
> To seize their prey the murth'rous band!
> Ah, tell them, they are men!
>
> (55–60)

The only specific personage who has been addressed previously is "Father Thames" (21) – who, as Dr. Johnson pointed out, is ill-equipped to answer the questions presented to him. Such a being seems even more unlikely as object of the imperatives in the last three lines above, but the poem has identified no other interlocutor. The speaker's command sounds more like a desperate plea, addressed to anyone at all who might be able to illuminate the state of ignorance in which the young inevitably exist. The poem itself tries to provide illumination: increasingly specific and horrifying evocations of the miseries that face all humankind. To tell the boys that they are men, the command of line 60, is to tell them of inevitable suffering: "To each his suff'rings: all are men, / Condemn'd alike to groan" (91–92). The poem concludes with the famous observation, "where ignorance is bliss, / 'Tis folly to be wise" (99–100).

Ignorance, in the logic of the poem, belongs to the students on their playing fields; wisdom, to the atrabilious speaker. The ode has strongly suggested that the wisdom in which the speaker takes mournful pride derives only from age – from experience that necessarily includes suffering. That experience gives him authority, as the experience of feeling cut off from others lends authority to his plea in *To Adversity*. The joyous boys at Eton may take pleasure in their ignorant bliss, as the observer takes pleasure in watching it: soon enough, they will, like the doleful speaker himself, lose it. Alternatively, the boys may in fact be neither ignorant nor blissful: the speaker posits both states, himself ignorant of the actual thoughts and feelings possessed by the young people he watches. His fantasies about the feelings of youth serve him as literary conveniences; the real nature of those feelings remains irrelevant. Finally, the poem reads as a delineation of the speaker's sense of self: cut off from others, struggling to communicate his useless "wisdom."

The presence presiding over *Elegy Written in a Country Church Yard* initially receives no definition in the poem: he exists only as an observer in a rural landscape tinged with melancholy by his observation of it. Thus he understands the curfew bell as tolling a knell for dying day; he emphasizes the plowman's weariness; he fancies the owl complaining. Most of the elegy concerns his imagining of the dead villagers in the churchyard around him. His voice tells us of the evils they avoided, of the community they shared, and of the mourning for them expressed in the inscriptions on their graves. Then this "voice" enters a new and confusing situation. The elegy began in the first person, with the speaker describing his position in the solitary churchyard. It continues as the reflections, presumably, of the same speaker. At line 93, a "thee" enters the poem – sounding perplexingly like the "I" at the beginning.

> For thee, who mindful of th'unhonour'd Dead
> Dost in these lines their artless tale relate . . .
>
> (93–94)

Surely the relater of the artless tale is the churchyard observer. The text goes on to imagine a "kindred Spirit" who inquires "thy" fate (96). A local swain describes a young man who, after displaying a range of intense emotions, disappears. The swain invites the kindred spirit to note the epitaph inscribed on the youth's gravestone. The first stanza of the three-stanza inscription reads:

> Here rests his head upon the lap of Earth
> A Youth to Fortune and to Fame unknown,
> Fair Science [knowledge] frown'd not on his humble birth,
> And Melancholy mark'd him for her own.
>
> (117–20)

The account bears enough affinities to Gray's own situation in his early thirties to intensify the suspicion that this epitaph records his imagining of his own death. Although it is possible to devise other assignments of identity for the personages who suddenly appear toward the end of the elegy, the poem most plausibly seems to play with evanescent notions of self, the shifting pronouns corresponding to the play of identities that the poem explores.

The "Melancholy" assigned to the youth who relates tales of the dead corroborates the tone of those tales. Indeed, the churchyard elegy explores the possibility of melancholy as revelation. Willingness to brood over graves and their fancied inhabitants is the prerequisite for the poem's reflections on the contrasting situations of the "great" and the obscure and on the universal human need for sympathy and remembrance. Only by allowing his melancholy full dominance can the observer discover what the churchyard has to offer him – as well as his reading audience.

Melancholy is by no means the only emotion expressed and explored by mid-eighteenth-century poets. William Collins, often coupled with Gray in literary history, in fact takes a sharply different approach. In many of his odes, he makes emotion his explicit subject; in others, an implicit one. Odes addressed directly to pity and to fear appeal to these powers to inspire him. He writes *The Passions. An Ode for Music* (a poem that was actually performed to musical accompaniment), and ends it with an appeal to music to "Arise as in that elder Time, / Warm, Energic, Chaste, Sublime!" (105–06). The adjectives, like the ode's subject, indicate the poet's concern with emotion as an empowering human capacity. "Chaste" signifies that music, ideally, will not arouse erotic feelings – Collins doesn't want it to be *too* "Energic" (vigorous) – but it will have the "warmth" to energize other emotions, including those that elevate consciousness to the pitch of sublimity, that sense of exaltation that can make human beings feel close to, or awed by, the divine. Only with help, many of Collins's poems suggest, can people develop the capacity for emotion.

More particularly, he concerns himself with the poet's capacity (his own capacity) for feeling, frequently hinting or asserting the diminished emotional power of poetry at his historical moment. *Ode to Pity* cites Euripides and Otway as predecessors who incorporated pity's resources in their dramatic poetry. The speaker begs pity to come to him, "by Fancy's Aid" (25) – not so that he can feel pity as a response to others he encounters, but in order to enable him to imagine those others and his reaction to them. He conjures up a temple to Pity that will "raise a wild Enthusiast Heat" in all who view it (29). There he wishes to spend his days, melting away "In Dreams of Passion" (38)

> Till, Virgin, Thou again delight
> To hear a *British* Shell!
> (41–42)

British poetry, figured by the "Shell" (the lyre, thought to have been originally made of a stringed tortoise shell), has lost the power to utilize pity as a resource. Some day, it may regain that power – perhaps by means of the speaker.

The gap between dreaming of passion and actually feeling it seems to escape Collins's notice. Characteristically, he imagines imagining emotion. *Ode to Fear* both emphasizes and tries to demonstrate the imaginative power that fear releases. Fear is invoked as an emotion enabling vision of "th'unreal Scene" – but only when "Fancy lifts the Veil between" the real and unreal world (3–4). More fully than in the companion *Ode to Pity*, Collins envisions his subject as an allegorical personage, a personification. He evokes not the appearance (except for "thy haggard Eye"; 7) but, vaguely, the actions and, more specifically, the companions of this being. The attendants of Fear include the "hideous Form" (12) of Danger; Vengeance, of unspecified appearance; a thousand phantoms who prompt the mind to evil deeds, an unspecified number of fiends who preside over disruptions of nature, and "that rav'ning Brood of Fate, / Who lap the Blood of Sorrow" (22–23), identified by Collins's footnote as the Greek Furies. The Greek tragedians, according to the ode's epode, best exemplified the literary power of fear, to which Collins's speaker responds:

> O *Fear*, I know Thee by my throbbing Heart,
>    Thy with'ring Pow'r inspir'd each mournful Line,
> Tho' gentle *Pity* claim her mingled Part,
>    Yet all the Thunders of the Scene are thine!
>
> (42–45)

In the poem's concluding section, the speaker imagines a setting for Fear, makes a clear distinction between fear as a source of literary achievement and as an experienced emotion (he rejects the latter for himself), and appeals to fear, as the emotion that inspired Shakespeare, to "Teach me but once like Him to feel" (69).

The choice of emotion as subject has relatively little importance in itself: after all, good poems can be written on virtually any subject. For Collins, though, this choice provides a means for stimulating feeling both in himself and in his readers. The sequence of personifications – Fear, Danger, and Vengeance, attended by fiends and furies – in *To Fear* provides an example. The poet first imagines fear as a means of perceiving "the World unknown" (1). Then he demonstrates how the idea of fear enables him to create just such a world. Pondering the nature of fear and its causes, he imagines Fear as embodying rather than causing fear: this haggard being has a hurried step; he starts; he flees in disordered fashion. The monsters around him evoke causes of fear in the animate and inanimate world. Vengeance remains undescribed, except for a single action: she "lifts her red Arm, expos'd and bare" (21). Is the arm flayed, skinless, and therefore red? Is it covered with blood because of the unspeakable acts in which Vengeance engages? We receive no clues, only a vague sense of horror. What matters is the effect of imagining – for the writer and for the reader:

> Who, *Fear*, this ghastly Train can see,
> And look not madly wild, like Thee?
>
> (24–25)

To "see" this group of beings through the eyes of fancy – the only way they can be seen – is to achieve a kind of identification with the power of fear itself, that power Collins has already connected with vision. Both writer and reader presumably know that such creatures do not exist in the actual world, but both must respond to the suggestive details that demand emotional reaction.

When the speaker at the end of the poem begs to be taught to feel like Shakespeare, he concludes that, given such emotional capacity, he would willingly "dwell with" Fear (71). Like many of Collins's poems, *To Fear* conveys dissatisfaction with life as actually experienced, a longing to inhabit an imaginative world that would offer more emotional richness, and passionate excitement at the possibility of such an outcome. Populating his poetry with large casts of imaginary beings, Collins invites his readers to share his excitement, by participating imaginatively in, for example, an elaborately described scene of an Eden atop a cliff, inhabited by the figure of Milton, listening to music from heaven (*Ode on the Poetical Character*). The scene's point is that such poetic inspiration is no longer available. Its effect, however, is immediate exhilaration. By imagining in detail the setting and the action and imagining himself "viewing" it (63), Collins finds material for emotional poetry – poetry that constantly asserts the impossibility of its own existence.

The mode of Collins's verse is not always so flamboyant as in the examples I have cited. With calmer personifications and fuller awareness of external reality, the poet writes, for instance, *Ode to Evening*, an innovative lyric in unrhymed verse. Evening, like the four seasons and such entities as fancy, friendship, science, and peace, is personified, but the personification consists of no more than the occasional epithet (e.g., "pensive"; 2) and the use of such nouns as "Nymph" and "Maid" to designate evening. The scenes composed by the poem do not concentrate on the actions of personifications but on the atmosphere of evening:

> Now Air is hush'd, save where the weak-ey'd Bat,
> With short shrill Shriek flits by on leathern Wing,
> > Or where the Beetle winds
> > His small but sullen Horn
> As oft he rises 'midst the twilight Path,
> Against the Pilgrim born in heedless Hum.
>
> (9–14)

Invited imaginatively both to see and to hear, the reader is urged also to participate in the writer's loving responsiveness to detail. He appeals to Evening to teach him "To breathe some soften'd Strain" (16), and the poem that contains that line exemplifies the softening of his music.

Similarly effective, in the space of only twelve lines, is *Ode, Written in the beginning of the Year 1746*, which both mourns and celebrates the death of soldiers in battle. The poem begins with an exclamation:

> How sleep the Brave, who sink to Rest,
> By all their Country's Wishes blest!
> (1–2)

Its subsequent tone, however, is far from exclamatory. The assertive physicality of the verb "sink" prepares for the emphasis of the entire first stanza, on the "Mold" (4) (meaning the earth of the burial ground, but also suggesting the earlier meaning of the "earth" that is the substance of the human body) and "Sod" (5) of the graves. Few elegies or odes dwell with such determination on the literal fact of burial. The reality of the grave anchors the stanza, which insists finally that this sod is "sweeter" "Than *Fancy*'s Feet have ever trod" (5–6). One may feel some surprise at such an assertion coming from Collins, that great relier on and celebrator of fancy, but at least for the moment he unambiguously contends that one must face the reality of death as well as that of military courage.

The second stanza, however, turns in a different direction. Now we find "Fairy Hands" ringing the soldiers' knell (7), "Forms unseen" singing their dirge (8), Honour arriving as a pilgrim "To bless the Turf that wraps their Clay" (10), and Freedom coming for "a-while" (11) in the form of a weeping hermit. The line about the turf wrapping the clay returns rather disturbingly, given the new context, to the preceding stanza's physicality, but emphasis falls on multiple examples of "*Fancy*'s Feet": the metrical feet of the poem itself, and the imagined feet of the graves' visitors.

The poem's emotional effect depends on the impossibility of reconciling its contradictory ideas. We must remember that these soldiers are dead and buried – no glimmer of an after-life. They can be glorified through acts of the imagination, but such acts do not modify the reality of their death. Nonetheless, the imagining that gives them a melancholy other-worldly entourage provides precarious comfort. The poet does what he can to exalt the dead, by associating them with honor and freedom and by supplying them with imaginary mourners. He also demands that the living come to terms with the fact of loss. The imaginary and the factual coexist, with neither canceling, but each challenging, the other.

The questions about the sources of poetic energy raised by *To Pity* and *To Fear* (and also by other odes including *To Simplicity*, *The Passions*, and *Ode on the Poetical Character*) persist in new terms in *To Evening* and the *1746* ode, where Collins explores the possibility that attention to the actual can, in conjunction with the repertoire of fancy, provide poetry with substance that also generates feeling. Whether or not he dwells on emotion as subject, Collins consistently writes verse that solicits emotional response.

So do many of his contemporaries whose means, at this distance in time, seem less original than his, but who were received when they wrote as offering something new and exciting. Especially popular – wildly popular – was *The Complaint: or Night-Thoughts on Life, Death, and Immortality*, by Edward Young, first published in 1743. Because it purported to be a record of personal grief and reconciliation, it had something of the appeal of memoir, but its original title indicates how centrally it concerns itself with individual emotion – indeed, with emotional self-indulgence. (The poem has more recently become known as *Night-Thoughts*.) Young had endured the deaths, in close succession, of his wife, his wife's daughter, and the daughter's husband. The poem narrates his losses, but it also tells the story of the fictional Lorenzo, an "infidel" who is converted by the speaker's disquisitions on mortality and religion. It thus provided the satisfactions of didacticism along with those of vicarious emotional indulgence.

An early passage will suggest the tone of Young's "complaint":

> I wake, emerging from a sea of Dreams
> Tumultuous; where my wreck'd, desponding Thought
> From wave to wave of *fancy'd* Misery,
> At random drove, her helm of Reason lost;
> Tho' now restor'd, 'tis only Change of pain,
> A bitter change; severer for severe:
> The *Day* too short for my Distress! and *Night*
> Even in the *Zenith* of her dark Domain,
> Is Sun-shine, to the colour of my Fate.
>
> (1: 9–17)

Young does not, like Collins, invent elaborate figures to convey his state. His emotional extravagance consists, rather, in finding repeated ways to assert that no one ever suffered as he has suffered: night is sunshine compared to the darkness of his fate. Although the speaker believes in a glorious after-life for the virtuous, he uses even this faith as a means for self-pity:

> Let heav'nly pity fall,
> On me, more justly number'd with the Dead:
> *This* is the Desert, *this* the Solitude; . . .
> All, all on earth is *Shadow*.
>
> (1: 112–14, 119)

Both the speaker's lugubriousness and his faith, however, serve to direct Lorenzo away from his commitment to the things of this earth and toward preparation for death, which, the poem assures him, can never come too soon. In later books, charnel house imagery – attention to graves much more insistent than that Collins offers – reinforces the horrors of a merely earthly perspective.

The middle years of the century saw something of a vogue for what was called "graveyard poetry," its most conspicuous representative Robert Blair, whose *The Grave* appeared in 1743, dedicated to painting "the gloomy Horrors of the *Tomb*" (5). Meditation on death was a conventional religious exercise, but poetry of this sort clearly satisfied more than religious needs. It provided a legitimate venue for emotional indulgence, permissible because of the religious atmosphere that enveloped it. Poets who explored the possibilities of graveyards could appropriately express a range of emotions: not only melancholy, but horror, fear, anxiety, as well as faith and hope.

Melancholy remained a popular subject. Milton's *Il Penseroso* had long provided a model for poems on this topic, but mid-century poets branched out from the conventional discussion of moody, solitary wandering. Thus Thomas Warton's *The Pleasures of Melancholy* (1745) starts with its protagonist yearning to sit amid the moss-grown ruins of an abbey but soon turns to self-congratulation about the fine feelings being revealed.

> Few know that elegance of soul refin'd,
> Whose soft sensation feels a quicker joy

> From Melancholy's scenes, than the dull pride
> Of tasteless splendor and magnificence
> Can e'er afford.
>
> (92–96)

To equate melancholy (specifically, pleasure in melancholy) with elegance of soul marks an important cultural development. For the rest of the century, many writers and non-writers alike would cultivate what they called "sensibility," a ready responsiveness to emotional stimuli that declared the responder's subtle and "elegant" capacity for feeling. Novelistic heroines fainted and wept; even men proclaimed their sensitivities; and poets provided material to which their readers might sensitively respond. Warton lists among the pleasures of melancholy that of unrequited love:

> Is there a pleasure like the pensive mood,
> Whose magic wont to sooth your soften'd souls?
> O tell how rapturous the joy, to melt
> To Melody's assuasive voice; to bend
> Th'uncertain step along the midnight mead,
> And pour your sorrows to the pitying moon . . .
>
> (168–73)

Such a poem as his produces some of the satisfactions of narrative: the sketch of the melancholy lover adumbrates a story that the reader can fill in and respond to. Moreover, the array of "pleasures" outlined here presumably allows many readers to identify with the emotions evoked, retrospectively or prospectively delighting in their own experiences of sadness – at the least, as evidence of their fineness of soul.

Responsiveness to nature also began to be seen as demonstrating the elevated soul. *The Pleasures of Melancholy* includes several accounts of satisfying experience in the natural world. *The Enthusiast: Or the Lover of Nature* (1744), by Thomas Warton's brother Joseph, makes not nature but human sensitivity to nature its primary subject. The claim of moral superiority suggested in *The Pleasures of Melancholy* (the person who takes pleasure in melancholy towers over the one who enjoys tasteless magnificence) becomes more emphatic here. From the very beginning, we learn of "art's vain pomps" (4), as compared with nature's beauties. Versailles tortures its waters in fountains; the "foamy stream" from "some pine-top'd precipice" (30, 29) provides superior satisfactions.

To contemplate such contrasts leads the speaker to an ecstasy of responsiveness.

> O taste corrupt! that luxury and pomp
> In specious names of polish'd manners veil'd,
> Should proudly banish nature's simple charms!
> All-beauteous nature! by thy boundless charms
> Oppress'd, O where shall I begin thy praise,
> Where turn th'ecstatick eye, how ease my breast
> That pants with wild astonishment and love!
>
> (142–48)

To convey the sense of astonishment – *wild* astonishment – and love becomes the poem's endeavor. The observer of nature does not respond merely with aesthetic appreciation, as John Dyer, early in the century, had done in remarking the patterns to be perceived from a height. The response of the later observer declares his emotional capacity, now almost equivalent to moral virtue.

The poems we have considered thus far in this chapter make their concern with emotion apparent. The speakers in them explicitly or implicitly declare their own highly wrought emotional reactions, and they characteristically use exclamatory rhetoric to generate comparable response in their readers. If the emotion invoked is rarely romantic love, that staple of both earlier and later poetry, it remains nonetheless intense and exalted. Even in this period, though, when heightened value attached to the expression of emotion, some poems of great emotional intensity make few, if any, obvious claims to the feeling they convey.

It is no accident that one of the most remarkable such poems, Samuel Johnson's *The Vanity of Human Wishes* (1749), is written in heroic couplets. Earlier in the century, as we have seen, most poets relied heavily on such couplets. The poems considered in this chapter, in contrast, often employ blank verse or other unrhymed forms – forms that lend themselves more readily to following movements of consciousness. Returning to the highly disciplined mode of the earlier period, Johnson announced even in his poetic structure his allegiance to restraint. Moreover, his poem "imitates" a satire by the first-century Roman poet, Juvenal. The imitation was an established eighteenth-century form: not a translation, but a loose adaptation of a (usually) classic model to contemporaneous purposes. Johnson, in the course of demonstrating, as Juvenal had done, that all desire leads to destruction, can comment on the corruptions of his own time as well as on human weaknesses that he believed universal.

As the poem goes on, it develops increasing intensity in its portrayals of individuals and types.

> Enlarge my Life with Multitude of Days,
> In Health, in Sickness, thus the Suppliant prays;
> Hides from himself his State, and shuns to know,
> That Life protracted is protracted Woe.
> Time hovers o'er, impatient to destroy,
> And shuts up all the Passages of Joy:
> In vain their Gifts the bounteous Seasons pour,
> The Fruit Autumnal, and the Vernal Flow'r,
> With listless Eyes the Dotard views the Store,
> He views, and wonders that they please no more.
>                                         (255–64)

"All the Passages of Joy." The phrase refers to the five senses, imagined in their emotional rather than their physical functions. To concentrate on these few words suggests the poet's vigorous conception of his enterprise: not only to reveal the self-destructiveness of human desire, but to indicate how richly the "Gifts" provided to human beings might satisfy them – if properly understood and appreciated. The gifts of fruit and flowers belong to the external world but can supply pleasure if valued aright; the gifts of smelling and tasting and feeling and seeing and hearing provide inlets of delight typically unappreciated until they disappear.

Johnson's portrayal of the dying man reverberates with unstated feeling. His general (and characteristic) observation that "Life protracted is protracted Woe" enlarges the scope of the evoked suffering to all who fail to endure the earlier suffering of untimely death. The "Dotard" is not said to suffer. His "listless" eyes and confused wondering, however, like his refusal to know his state, indicate his desperate pushing away of what he cannot bear to face directly. The reader, forced to know what the dying man repudiates, is forced also toward experiencing what Johnson understood as the universal pain of the human condition. That pain entails not only the deprivation that results from age but the even more widespread sense of deprivation derived from ungratified wishes – wishes that, if fulfilled, would, like the prayer for length of days, bring only disappointment.

For such a view of the human situation, the only likely compensation is religious faith. After many intricate turns, *The Vanity of Human Wishes* concludes not in a profession of faith but in an ardent wish for faith, love, and patience. Only such yearning avoids the disappointments of misguided desire; only such a wish has a chance for real gratification. The poem formulates the wish as instruction: this is what you, reader, *should* wish for. After specifying the petition's value, the poem concludes,

> With these celestial Wisdom calms the Mind,
> And makes the Happiness she does not find.
>
> (369–70)

The yearning for a calmed mind accrues poignancy from the lines that precede this final formulation. Throughout the poem, the speaker, despite his rigorous poetic discipline, betrays a mind in turmoil, pained and agitated by the futility he sees everywhere in the human situation – a situation, of course, of which he too partakes. Passionate, and conceiving of passion ("Yet with the Sense of sacred Presence prest, / When strong Devotion fills thy glowing Breast, / Pour forth thy Fervours"; 359–61) as part of the search for peace, he ultimately imagines a happiness he cannot specify. The poem's force derives in large part from the emotional energy it controls and directs. Fully acknowledging the destructive power of emotion, it yet channels its own emotion into the desire for transcendence.

We must return also in this context to Pope, who died in 1744 and wrote his most passionate and powerful poetry in the late 1730s and early 1740s. The passion assumed several forms: political, literary, personal. Its intensity ignites the verse.

As we might expect from our glimpse of Pope's more youthful productions, the poet frequently expressed his passion in satiric form. In 1743 he published the final version of his longest and most ambitious work, *The Dunciad*, an anti-epic for his age. Poets and literary critics continued to assume that epic constituted the greatest literary form: *The Iliad* and *The Aeneid* held the position of uncontested masterpieces. By writing a long poem, complete with supernatural forces, a parodic visit to the underworld, and quasi-epic contests of skill and valor, Pope made a claim for literary supremacy. His epic, however, has a ludicrous anti-hero at its center, and the Goddess of Dullness serves as its presiding deity. Marked by brilliant versification, full of imaginative energy, propelled by its own inexorable logic, *The Dunciad* cannot be readily dismissed. Its very existence constitutes a devastating criticism of the society that generated it.

Pope had anonymously published an earlier version of the poem, in three books, with the minor poet Lewis Theobald as its central figure, in 1728. In the final revision, Theobald's place is assumed by Colley Cibber, a vain (by his own admission) playwright and weak poet who had become poet laureate. Such a position made him a symbolic representative of the monarchy and of the society at large, and Pope attacks both. He evokes a decadent, self-destroying populace, stubbornly dedicated to corrupt values. The evocation, conveyed with immense vitality and variety, ultimately becomes metaphysical: the poem ends with a vision of the entire world destroyed by the power of dullness.

The last three couplets of *The Dunciad*, even deprived of the context that supports and enriches them, will suggest the fervor Pope brings to the task of denouncing corruption and upholding the good. These lines provide the culminating details of the portrayal of chaos triumphant.

> Nor *public* Flame, nor *private*, dares to shine;
> Nor *human* Spark is left, nor Glimpse *divine*!
> Lo! thy dread Empire, CHAOS! is restor'd;
> Light dies before thy uncreating word;
> Thy hand, great Anarch! lets the curtain fall;
> And Universal Darkness buries All.
>
> (4: 651–56)

At first thought, dullness sounds like a rather trivial sin. It makes its possessors seem boring to others; perhaps it causes someone to miss the point of a joke or to muddle an equation. How could it have the power to destroy the social and the cosmic order? How might it restore the empire of Chaos?

Pope exhaustively and imaginatively explains Dullness's power. In the first book of *The Dunciad*, he describes the goddess as "Daughter of Chaos and eternal Night" (1: 12), those powers that Milton locates at the gates of hell. The adjectives applied to her suggest how she operates: "Laborious, heavy, busy, bold, and blind, / She rul'd, in native Anarchy, the mind" (1: 15–16). Dullness is a force of energy, busy and bold, moving forward by sheer weight. Busy and bold – but also blind, so that her energy applies itself in random fashion. Her activity lacks coherence. She therefore preserves, rather than controls, the mind's native anarchy. The mind needs discipline, Pope assumes, to function usefully. Lack of discipline, however, provides the path of least resistance. The whole long poem demonstrates its consequences. Its ultimate result is ultimate chaos.

Perhaps the most charged line in the heavily charged sequence quoted above is "Light dies before thy uncreating word." The Word of God has creative power, as the New Testament tells us; the word of Dullness possesses the terrifying power of unmaking. The death of light – all illumination by intelligence, wit, imagination – marks the death of civilization. Like the death of the sun, literal source of life, which would bring an end to the animal and vegetable world, the death of this metaphorical light constitutes an end to all things. The public and the private, the human and the divine: all categories and all meaning disappear. The relentless force of dullness, obviating distinctions, makes understanding impossible.

Dullness is a choice: Pope makes the point over and over. He does not wish to attack native stupidity; he says that directly. His target, rather, is *willed* stupidity, product of laziness, vanity, worldly ambition, or simple inertia. As the poem takes aim at those in different walks of life – cooks, clergymen, teachers, lawyers, noblemen, writers, and many more – it focuses also on the different forms dullness can take, and on the ways it remains the same through all its manifestations. The emotion of the poem as a whole, as of those last six lines, is complicated. It includes a sense of pathos that finally becomes despair, as the writer contemplates misuses of words and of things, and, most importantly, of human capacity. Inviting his world to contemplate what it has made of itself, he invites his readers also to realize the immense rejection – the rejection of divine creativity – implicit in easy, corrupt choices. Other parts of *The Dunciad* sound angry. The conclusion sounds desperately sad. Its vision of cosmic destruction, more than rhetorical, derives from following out the logical consequences of dullness's increasing power. To see those consequences as Pope does registers despair, the powerful emotion of the poem's conclusion.

*The Dunciad* has political, educational, psychological, emotional, and moral implications. It proceeds sometimes by scurrilous attack on individuals, sometimes by elevated generalization, but with a consistent vision imbued with feeling. It constitutes Pope's most complex achievement in the satiric mode. The satiric mode, however, is by no means his only register. A final instance of the moving verse of his later years comes from one of his imitations of Horace, *Epistle II, ii,* published in 1737. He wrote several such imitations, of Horatian epistles and satires, finding in the form opportunity for both public and personal commentary. The passage below clearly speaks of the personal:

> Years foll'wing Years, steal something ev'ry day,
> At last they steal us from our selves away;
> In one our Frolicks, one Amusements end,
> In one a Mistress drops, in one a Friend:
> This subtle Thief of Life, this paltry Time,
> What will it leave me, if it snatch my Rhime?
> If ev'ry Wheel of that unweary'd Mill
> That turn'd ten thousand Verses, now stands still.
>
> (72–79)

In literal translation, the lines Pope imitates read as follows: "The years, as they go, steal from us things one after another; they have robbed me of my jokes, my loves, my feasts, my games; they are now striving to wrest from me my poetry." The tone is rather off-hand, the possible deprivation of poetry receiving no special emphasis. Nothing in Horace's lines corresponds to Pope's terrifying suggestion that we finally are stolen from our selves. Pope conveys – with great dignity – the anguish of loss, not his alone, but his in particular, as he moves from plural to singular first-person pronouns. Everyone of a certain age will recognize the climate of loss the poem evokes, and even the young know loss's inevitability. The speaker eschews personal reference, subsuming his own losses in those of all humanity, until the final couplet, which raises the dreadful possibility of lost vocation. Borrowing from Milton, for whom time was the subtle thief of youth rather than of life itself, the verse explodes in the adjective *paltry*, one of only two adjectives in the six lines, meaning "Rubbishy, trashy, worthless; petty; despicable." Time, that subtle thief, takes everything, including our selves, yet it remains valueless. Its value inheres in what it contains – what, at last, it steals, possessing vast power though no inherent worth. The poetry it takes, too, has a double valence. The speaker realizes that, from one point of view, he might be said just to turn out verse with mechanical precision, like a grinding mill. From his own perspective, though, poetry is essential to life: without it, nothing would remain.

The high discipline and rhetorical restraint of these lines communicate deep feeling, one of Pope's many poetic resources. This feeling does not strike the same note as Gray's plangencies or Collins's magnificent performances or even Johnson's conflicted vision of the human condition. In conjunction with the work of these others, however, Pope's lines can remind us how steadily and insistently eighteenth-century verse continued to rely on and to convey emotional intensity.

They may remind us also of the range of emotions articulated in verse. Anger, fear, religious exaltation as well as melancholy, mourning, love of nature, self-pity, despair, confusion: the list could go on. The feelings evoked arise sometimes from an immediate personal situation – someone mourning the loss of a friend or expressing ecstasy over the beauties of nature – but sometimes from reflection on the human condition (e.g., Young's meditations on death, Gray's on the ignorance of the young) or a perceived national predicament (Johnson, Pope). Like earlier works, these poems thus may imagine the individual human being as embedded in social or theological contexts – but their speakers may also question the value of the social matrix, as Gray does through his persistently communicated sense of isolation and Pope through his ferocious attack on existing institutions. Emotion, now more often conspicuous in verse, has become a public means of confronting problems and of communicating meaning.

For the most part, neither the stated causes for emotion nor the kinds of emotion evoked in the poetry this chapter has surveyed resemble their counterparts in the verse probably most familiar to a twenty-first-century reader. Collins's odes sound neither like Shakespeare's sonnets nor like John Ashbery's lyrics. Despite the fact that in the second third of the century emotion has become a respectable poetic subject, much of its expression seems oddly mediated. We read less of a speaker's pity or fear than of his yearning to experience such feelings, less of the suffering of melancholy than of the melancholic's self-congratulation. Gray's meditations on the probable fates of schoolboys turn into covert reflections on himself. Even *Night-Thoughts*, a prolonged reflection on death, becomes an uplifting conversion story. Emotion may be the stuff of poetry, but only, it seems, in rather elaborately constructed contexts.

That is to say, established principles of decorum continue to govern the writing of poems. The sense of a poem as a *made* thing, a piece of work intended to communicate with an audience, and still to instruct as well as to please: such ideas caused poets to try to use the expression of emotion as a way not only to speak of the personal, but also to promulgate large truths. Indeed, some of the poems touched on here (*The Vanity of Human Wishes*, *The Dunciad*) represent large truths as the proximate cause of emotion. Johnson's feelings about the human condition presumably gain intensity inasmuch as they are also feelings about his own situation in the universe. Pope, imagining the self-destruction of the culture he knows, bitterly feels the prospect of a chaos he has tried, but necessarily failed, to stem throughout his poetic career. Even poets more directly focused on themselves, like Collins and Gray, embed their personal revelations in reflections about larger matters.

In short, the announced causes for emotion multiply and the nature of poetically rendered emotion diversifies as the century continues. The conspicuous expression of poetic discipline, conveying the control of reason, remains constant.

# 8

# Structures of Energy, Structures of Leisure: Ode and Blank Verse

Partly as a result of the increasing stress on poetry as a means of communicating emotion, innovative poetic forms flourished during the middle years of the century. The ode, an important medium for Collins, Gray, and the Warton brothers, among others, was by no means a new genre; those using it typically claimed to model their work on the classics. Nor was blank verse new. As we have seen, Thomson employed it in the 1730s, and so did many others, particularly those who wished to ally themselves with Miltonic tradition. In the 1740s, however, blank verse began to be imagined in fresh ways and used for fresh purposes, and the ode came to be seen as a mode of expansive possibilities.

To label a poem an ode tells us little about its shape: odes assume many poetic contours. "Ode" designates an attitude more than a form. Collins and Gray and the rest associated it particularly with "enthusiasm," the exaltation that they considered characteristic of the inspired poet. Although their odes' content might suggest the poet's anxiety about equaling the inspiration of his great predecessors, the mode they chose signals their effort to unite themselves with a grand tradition.

Collins entitled his 1746 collection *Odes on Several Descriptive and Allegorical Subjects*, a designation that suggests his technique. Emphasis on personification, which provides these odes with their allegorical features, and on visual effects pervades all the poems. Almost equally characteristic are a tone of excitement and an elaborate rhyme scheme, although *Ode to Evening* uses no rhymes at all, and many of the odes contain sections composed of couplets. Such aspects separate Collins's poems from much that had preceded them in the eighteenth century, and the separation was presumably deliberate. The atmosphere of excitement permeating Collins's odes stems partly from consciousness of doing something new.

The adjectives "Descriptive" and "Allegorical" might suggest a static kind of poetry. In fact, conspicuous energy marks the odes of 1746 – energy sometimes apparently in excess of the poet's power to contain it. *Ode on the Poetical Character*, for instance, begins with a story from Spenser's *Faerie Queene*; continues by imagining Fancy's participating in a version of that poem's Florimel plot, her magic girdle given to "gird [the] blest prophetic Loins" of the gifted (21); and in the epode goes on to a bizarre creation myth, in which God appears to copulate with Fancy, who subsequently gives birth to Apollo. The allusion to Apollo generates a multitude of personifications and vague *"Pow'rs"* (49) to accompany him, as well as an adumbration of some ("dang'rous Passions"; 41) that remain outside the scene. The personifications include Truth and Wonder, as well as "shad'wy Tribes of *Mind*" (47). Contemplating them leads to the apparent non sequitur that concludes the epode:

> Where is the Bard, whose Soul can now
> Its high presuming Hopes avow?
> Where He who thinks, with Rapture blind,
> This hallow'd Work for Him design'd?
> (51–54)

Only superficially do these questions constitute a non sequitur. They bear no clear connection to the assemblage of Apollo and his allegorical crew, born from the conjunction of God and Fancy; yet in a deeper sense, the questions contain the essence of the poem. Everything before them leads to them; everything after elaborates them. My efforts to summarize the first two sections of the ode produced confusing multiplicity; the ode itself confusingly keeps moving in new directions. Yet it has a clear and well-defined subject, the poet's calling. The movement of ideas (which finds further new directions in the antistrophe) signifies the poem's energy, expressed in a bewildering series of imaginative leaps, all intended to delineate a single problem: what possibilities remain for a poet in the middle of the eighteenth century? Collins simultaneously demonstrates his poetic power – his imaginative energy, his capacity for varied versification, his awareness of literary tradition – and expresses his doubts about it. For such a self-contradictory endeavor, the ode's freedom provides an appropriate theater.

Indeed, Collins employs the ode – as did Gray – as a kind of the-
atrical venue, assigning his personifications stagy actions calculated
to display their natures, and piling up visual details to heighten dramatic effect. Even an *Ode to Mercy*, which one might expect, given its
subject, to be a quieter kind of performance, begins calmly enough
with Mercy sitting as a bride with Valour, but by the second stanza
has Mercy, with bare bosom, pleading for the life of a fallen soldier
and witnessing the "Country's Genius" (12), heavily wounded, decking
her altar. The antistrophe represents the *"Fiend of Nature"* (15) rushing
in wrath "to make our Isle his Prey" (16), only to have Mercy overtake him and stop his wheels. In the final stanza, "his sable Steeds"
(20) recoil at the sight of Mercy. Finally, Britain emerges as a place
"Where *Justice* bars her Iron Tow'r" (24), but where "we" build "a roseate
Bow'r" (25) in which Mercy shall rule, "and share our Monarch's
Throne!" (26). A lot of action for a twenty-six-line poem: action tumul-
tuous, various, appropriate but unpredictable. It relies for effect on
such visual details as the black horses recoiling. Like the odes to fear,
pity, simplicity, and other abstractions, the poem uses its action and
its sense of imaginative profusion to lend emotional specificity to a
generalized quality.

Rhyme scheme and content interact in Collins's odes. To return to
*Ode on the Poetical Character*: the poem begins the strophe, its first section, decorously with four short couplets (four stresses a line, instead
of the five stresses characteristic of the so-called heroic couplet, which
Pope and many others employed) . The eight lines move rapidly to narrate a situation: once "I," the speaker, read Spenser and learned about
Florimel, the only woman entitled to wear the magic girdle of chastity.
(Collins has in fact misread Spenser: the girdle could be worn by any
chaste wife.) The second stanza, also eight lines long, consists of two
quatrains in which the first and fourth lines rhyme, framing an internal couplet. Now the lines are longer, with five stresses each, and their
rhythms more various. The poem's movement has accordingly become
more leisurely, as the speaker contemplates and moralizes about the
situation he has imagined, in which one "Nymph" (9) after another tries
the girdle, only to have it leave "unblest her loath'd dishonour'd Side"
(13). The third stanza again varies the form, six lines long instead of eight.
Two short couplets are framed by two rhymed lines, the first line containing five stresses, the last line with six. The long final line brings to
an emphatic stop the strophe's reflective movement, after the poem has

established the analogy between Spenser's girdle of chastity and the new magic girdle of poetic inspiration.

Each stanza explores a different aspect of the strophe's topic, the magic girdle, with the language becoming steadily more exalted as the focus moves to the divine gift of poetic power. Metrical and stanzaic variations call attention to the movement and to the poetic energy that shapes the ode.

Considerably longer than the strophe (32 lines), the epode nonetheless moves rapidly, with its four-stress couplets. Until the crucial final questions, already quoted, it consists of rather economical narrative about Apollo's conception, his companions, and their activity. The concluding questions slow the rapid flow by beginning with a strongly stressed syllable, "Where." Despite their emphatic positioning, the questions receive no direct answer. Indirectly, the "I" of the concluding antistrophe suggests that it is he himself "who thinks, with Rapture blind, / This hallow'd Work for him design'd."

The antistrophe formally responds to the strophe. Its identical stanzaic pattern again follows an eight-line group of couplets with a more elaborately rhymed eight-line stanza and a concluding six-line stanza with an extended final line. The movement of ideas, however, pursues an unpredictable course. The first stanza moves briskly to sketch the new Eden that flourishes on top of a cliff, suggesting the mystery that envelops it: "Strange Shades o'erbrow the Valleys deep, / And holy *Genii* guard the Rock" (58–59). The second stanza, however, without transition introduces the "I" who contemplates the scene. Contorted syntax marks this figure's advent:

> I view that Oak, the fancied Glades among,
>   By which as *Milton* lay, his Ev'ning Ear,
> From many a Cloud that drop'd Ethereal Dew,
>   Nigh spher'd in Heav'n his native strains could hear.
>
>                                             (63–66)

Even when one untangles the syntax, the sense remains obscure: what is the relation between the cloud dropping dew and the hearing of native strains? The difficulties signal the transition to the experienced plight of the ode-writer himself. The stanza ends in mid-sentence and further obscurity. Someone is greeting Milton's glory, retreating "From *Waller's* Myrtle Shades" (69), and offering "many a Vow from Hope's aspiring Tongue" (70). Someone – but who?

The final stanza answers the question, with its reference to "My trembling Feet" (71). The poem's "I" does the greeting, retreating, and offering, but all in vain:

> Such Bliss to One alone,
> Of all the Sons of Soul was known,
> And Heav'n, and *Fancy*, kindred Pow'rs,
> Have now o'erturn'd th' inspiring Bow'rs,
> Or curtain'd close such Scene from ev'ry future View.
>
> (72–76)

Thus the poem ends, with the finality of the six-stress line and the more troubling finality of the inspirational vision closed off or overturned.

The intricacies of the ode as Collins conceives it allow him freedom to explore his subject and formal equivalents for his sense of paradoxical possibilities. His contemporary, Thomas Gray, used the ode for different purposes, often conceiving it as an opportunity to employ high rhetoric and to articulate a public stance. His two most ambitious odes, Pindaric in form, both deal with the problem of poetry's situation. Pindar, the most famous of Greek poets, wrote in the sixth century B.C. Many of his odes are still extant, elaborate lyric structures often composed to celebrate victories at war or in public games. Abraham Cowley, in the seventeenth century, composed odes in English that he called "Pindaric," and others imitated him – not necessarily on the basis of solid know-ledge of Pindar. Gray, in contrast, learned in Greek, devised intricate forms that provided English equivalents for Pindar's elaborate struc-tures. Like Pindar, he employed elevated rhetoric. He also relied heavily on sometimes obscure literary allusions. As a result, his original audi-ence found the odes impenetrable. In 1768, nine years after the poems' first publication, Gray appended explanatory notes, along with an "Advertisement" explaining that he had originally "had too much respect for the understanding of his Readers" to take the liberty of providing explanations, and with an epigraph from Pindar, in Greek, which trans-lates, "Vocal to the intelligent – for the rest they need interpreters."

Twenty-first-century readers, too, are likely to need interpreters. The fact, however, has less to do with intelligence than with historical and literary knowledge. What Gray assumed as a common fund of knowledge had long been the property of a minority. As the audience for poetry enlarged, ever fewer of its members had thorough classical educations. Immensely learned himself, Gray made his learning implicitly part of the argument in *The Progress of Poesy*, the first of the two odes published together. Like Pindar's compositions, Gray's ode organizes itself around a narrative: a story of the decline of poetry. After introductory sections about poetry's psychological and moral value, Gray reviews the accomplishments of the classic past, then of Shakespeare, Milton, and Dryden. He concludes, however, that the "Thoughts, that breath, and words, that burn" (110) formerly scattered from Fancy's urn are now heard no more. His note, a long one, speaks of the lack in English of "odes of the sublime kind." Apparently, the sublime ode – the kind of ode he himself writes – defines for him poetic accomplishment. The poem that deplores the lack also attempts to remedy it, demonstrating in the process that learning makes part of the equipment of the poet who would aspire to the composition of odes. Presumably the decline in learning that has accompanied the decline in poetry helps to account for it.

Given the ode's associations with sublimity, with learning, and with a great age of poetic accomplishment, Gray's choice of the mode becomes easy to understand. His working out of *The Progress of Poesy* also makes it apparent that he, like Collins, found poetic freedom and energy in devising odes. In the epode of the first section, the third stanza, for instance, he describes, as his note explains, the "Power of harmony to produce all the graces of motion in the body." This large subject allows the poet to describe Venus, surrounded by the Graces and by such personifications as "antic Sports, and blue-eyed Pleasures" (30), dancing on the green.

> With arms sublime, that float upon the air,
> In gliding state she wins her easy way:
> O'er her warm cheek, and rising bosom, move
> The bloom of young Desire, and purple light of Love.
>
> (38–41)

Gray's note to the final line directs the reader to a Greek source: the allusion to sexuality does not, he thus explains, derive from his own imagination. But his evocation of female arms at once sublime (powerful, majestic) and floating, his imagining of ease, beauty, and warmth as the concomitants of Venus – such aspects of the verse both suggest the poet's pleasure in his imagery and engage the reader's.

Despite the emphatically public aspect of a Pindaric ode, Gray manages to use *The Progress of Poesy* finally for personal statement. Commenting on the situation of the eighteenth-century poet, he implicitly alludes to himself, as he did at the end of the churchyard elegy. The ode concludes with these lines:

> Yet oft before his infant eyes would run
> Such forms, as glitter in the Muse's ray
> With orient hues, unborrow'd of the Sun:
> Yet shall he mount, and keep his distant way
> Beyond the limits of a vulgar fate,
> Beneath the Good how far – but far above the Great.
>
> (118–23)

This insistence on the poet's visionary capacity, although qualified by the suggestion that it implies no moral virtue, immediately follows lines that, like Collins's at the end of *Ode on the Poetical Character*, assert the loss of inspiration in modern times and the eighteenth-century poet's necessary incapacity in comparison with Pindar. Yet Gray claims more than Collins does. His gift for creating images of beauty allows him to inhabit a position "far above the Great": above aristocrats and public men. If he acknowledges the moral insufficiency of image-generating as life occupation, his proud assertion of social superiority appears to compensate for this recognition.

That assertion has, of course, more than personal significance. It bears on the question of public authority that the Pindaric ode, with its high rhetoric and commanding tone, generically implies. In his victory odes, Pindar spoke for his country, articulating national pride and supporting the value system that honored competitive triumph. Gray, in a later time, knows that he will not be considered a national spokesman. He believes, however, that the poet should enjoy just such status. His demonstration of his capacity to write a Pindaric ode, making a public statement about the importance and the arduousness of poetry, maintains his right – not personally, but in his role as poet – to the authority of one who speaks important truths.

The other Pindaric ode originally published with *The Progress of Poesy*, *The Bard*, makes the same claim, through its narrative of a thirteenth-century Welsh bard, an oral poet, who prophesies the future of the line of British kings and leaps to his death with an assertion of triumph.

His peroration reiterates the power of poetry through a series of personifications and an anachronistic allusion to Milton. To the king who has ordered the execution of all bards, as the voices of a conquered country, he defiantly prophesies: "Be thine Despair, and scep'tred Care, / To triumph, and to die, are mine" (141–42). The triumph, product of the poet's inspired vision, effectively nullifies the power of death: the bard's words remain; his prophecy is true; his force survives through the ages.

Unlike *The Progress of Poesy*, *The Bard* suggests specifically political power for the poet. Commentator on the royal succession, so dangerous that he must die, the bard as figure of the poet foretells the future and declares his triumph in his knowledge. The king will survive in despair; he himself will die victorious. The poem, in its virtuosity, its impetus, and its direct assertion demonstrates the continuing authority of the poet's voice.

Others also explored the ode's possibilities. Joseph Warton, in the "Advertisement" to his 1746 collection of odes, makes explicit the programmatic intent of his experimentation with the ode. "The Public," he writes,

> has been so much accustom'd of late to didactic Poetry alone, and Essays on moral Subjects, that any work where the imagination is much indulged, will perhaps not be relished or regarded. . . . But as [the author] is convinced that the fashion of moralizing in verse has been carried too far, and as he looks upon Invention and Imagination to be the chief faculties of a Poet, so he will be happy if the following Odes may be look'd upon as an attempt to bring back Poetry into its right channel.

Like many of the period's other poets, Warton chose to write mainly in Horatian rather than Pindaric terms. The Roman Horace wrote many short odes, typically in two- or four-line stanzas, intimate and reflective in tone, about such matters as friendship, love, and the writing of poetry. He provided a less challenging model than Pindar's. Although Joseph Warton praised Pindar, he produced many odes on the Horatian model, typically addressed to abstractions: Fancy, Health, Liberty, Superstition. Like Collins, he relied heavily on elaborate pictorial personifications, often lavishly multiplied in a single poem. His diction often recalls the earlier part of the century. Thus *Ode on the Spring. To a Lady* contains this stanza:

> All nature feels her vital heat around,
> The pregnant glebe now bursts with foodful grain,
> With kindly warmth she opes the frozen ground,
> And with new life informs the teeming plain.
>
> (5–8)

Despite its Thomsonesque language, however, the ode concludes with an appeal to a beloved woman: Spring brings "soft desire" (17) to all, yet "Amoret " remains a foe to the season's influence. The emotional atmosphere of mid-century odes differentiates them from most of the verse that had preceded them.

The Horatian ode, with its classical precedents, seemed to sanction the new stress on emotion. Horace himself was typically restrained in articulating feelings, but feelings often provided his subject. Mid-eighteenth-century experimenters with the ode often restrained themselves as well: countless odes, for instance, express similar feelings of serenity about the advent of evening. Yet the Horatian model also liberated some writers to express intense feeling within a structure of restraint. Thomas Warton, Joseph's brother, provides a good example in *Retirement: An Ode*, which concludes with a curious mixture of invocation and satire:

> O Virtue's Nurse! Retired Queen,
> By Saints alone and Hermits seen,
> Beyond vain Mortals' Wishes wise,
> Teach me *St. James*'s to despise;
> For what are crowded Courts, but Schools
> For Fops, or Hospitals for Fools?
> Where Slaves and Madmen, Young and Old,
> Meet to adore some Calf of Gold.
>
> (33–40)

The conventional invocation of Retirement as "Virtue's Nurse" leads to the specificities of the energetic attack on the court, which combines Biblical allusion (the "Calf of Gold") with the fresh imagining of courts as schools for fops or hospitals for fools. One suddenly feels the force of conviction within a poem that has earlier only trodden familiar ground.

Another of Thomas Warton's odes, *Ode written at Vale-Royal Abbey in Cheshire*, employs the stanzaic form of Gray's churchyard elegy and alludes to that earlier poem frequently, by diction and reference. Warton, too, begins his poem with the slow arrival of evening. Here, as in Gray, we find "forgotten graves and scatter'd tombs" (24), a clock, a spire, and a plowman. Yet this composition calls itself ode rather than elegy. The fact may both call attention to the lack of formal requirements for the ode as understood in the mid-eighteenth century and alert us to seek what elements caused Warton to think of this as an ode.

The first nine stanzas pursue a line of thought much like Gray's, evocation of the scene and reflection (brief) on the dead who lie beneath. At line 37, though, a new element enters. Between this point and the poem's ending, at line 92, we encounter Charity, Pity, Candour, Superstition, Sloth, Oblivion, Hospitality, Glory, Ambition, Religion, and four or five other personifications. Only Hospitality merits extended description. Sitting "Forlorn . . . upon the brambled floor" (52), surrounded by broken emblems of her former power, she embodies the loss of community entailed by the abbey's decay. For the other personified figures, Warton typically offers only a single characterizing element, sometimes one adjective – "unsocial Sloth" (45) and "cold Oblivion" (46), for instance.

Such adjectives, like the slightly longer characterizations of Ambition as "a pilgrim sage" (58) or "Wan Indolence" rocking a "drowsy cradle" (48), partake of convention but also emerge from reflection about the meanings of abstractions and about how those meanings change with situation. Warton's poem works out largely through meditation on abstractions the problem of how one should feel about the loss of such institutions as the abbey. Sloth and Oblivion and Ambition do not belong, in his telling, to the abbey's decay, but to its flourishing years. Sloth's unsociability is a cause, not an effect, of community's decline. Oblivion and Indolence inhabit the cloister, commenting on the monks' removal from the ordinary life of society. Ambition's role as pilgrim, in contrast, notes the abbey's function as place of refuge: one worn out in the search for glory can repose in the shelter of religion.

Through the personifications, the poem establishes an alternating emotional sequence, noting both positive and negative aspects of the functioning medieval abbey. Finally it turns to the Muse, observing that she surveys the ruined building

> With fond regret . . .
> And with fair images of antient things
> The captive bard's obsequious mind beguiles.
> (78–80)

We forgive the Muse, though, the ode continues, because she is dominated by Fancy.

Here are Warton's last ten lines:

> Severer Reason forms far other views,
> And scans the scene with philosophic ken.
>
> From these deserted domes, new glories rise;
> More useful institutes, adorning man,
> Manners enlarg'd, and new civilities,
> On fresh foundations build the social plan.
>
> Science, on ampler plume, a bolder flight
> Essays, escap'd from Superstition's shrine:
> While freed Religion, like primeval light
> Bursting from chaos, spreads her warmth divine.
>                                                    (83–92)

In short, everything's better now; we need not regret the loss of past institutions. Such is the message of Reason, as opposed to Fancy.

The contrast between the conclusions of Gray's elegy and of Warton's ode could hardly be more striking. Gray, having used his tight quatrains to pursue an orderly sequence of meditations, now apparently overtaken by the melancholy he evokes, suddenly changes direction to muse on his own death: how he could be memorialized. Warton employs the neat stanzas to different purpose, using them to express a pattern of emotional vacillation. Then he pulls himself out of it. After all, we must listen to the voice of reason, which tells us of progress, not loss. The "social plan" of the present presumably does not entail sloth, oblivion, and indolence. The religion "freed" by the establishment of the Church of England and the destruction of the monasteries does not involve the dangers of superstition. All the bad abstractions have vanished; only good ones remain. The poem justifies itself as an ode by its final celebration of things as they are, its achievement of public purpose. The earlier vacillations are private and fanciful. The concluding certainties speak in authoritative tones of the national situation.

To write odes, Horatian or Pindaric, was not the only poetic strategy available to those wishing to achieve a greater sense of freedom than the couplet provided for poets less accomplished than Pope. Blank verse increased in popularity and was turned to new purposes. Milton offered the most distinguished and most obvious model for those employing blank verse, and poets maintained *Paradise Lost* as a point of reference. James Thomson, revising and enlarging *The Seasons* into the 1740s, continued to employ the lofty vocabulary and extended similes associated with Milton, as did Mark Akenside, who published *The Pleasures of the Imagination*, a long poem in Miltonic blank verse, in 1744. Unlike Thomson, whose evocations of the natural world mixed with accounts of scientific or geographical truths, Akenside focused mainly on abstractions. His opening lines suggest the nature of his subject matter and the ponderousness of his verse:

> With what attractive charms this goodly frame
> Of nature touches the consenting hearts
> Of mortal men; and what the pleasing stores
> Which beauteous imitation thence derives
> To deck the poet's, or the painter's toil;
> My verse unfolds.
>
> (1–6)

Others, however, found a somewhat less formal mode of using unrhymed iambic pentameter. The Warton brothers, for instance, both wrote reflective blank verse poems that pay homage to Milton. Joseph Warton's *The Enthusiast: Or the Lover of Nature* (1744) occasionally echoes *Paradise Lost*, but also draws on *Comus* and *L'Allegro*; Thomas Warton's *The Pleasures of Melancholy* (1745) is strongly influenced by *Il Penseroso*. The Wartons' admiration for Milton, however, does not draw them into extended passages of epic diction. Instead, blank verse becomes for them a form inspiring leisurely associative development.

Here is Joseph Warton, implicitly criticizing Pope, who had praised the beauties of Lord Cobham's estate at Stowe:

> Can Stow
> With all her Attick fanes, such raptures raise,
> As the thrush-haunted copse, where lightly leaps
> The fearful fawn the rustling leaves along,
> And the brisk squirrel sports from bough to bough,
> While from an hollow oak, whose naked roots
> O'erhang a pensive rill, the busy bees
> Hum drowsy lullabies?
>
> (8–15)

He makes his case against Pope on the basis of poetic subject matter and the sensibility it betrays, displaying his own sensibility in his evocation of nature unshaped by human interference. Although, like Thomson, he flirts with humanizing the wild (those busy bees and their lullabies . . . ), he also appreciates the fawn and the squirrel and the thrush in themselves – for the sake of the "raptures" they raise.

To contrast this sequence from Warton with a passage from *Grongar Hill*, published less than twenty years earlier, not only illuminates the shift in sensibility that had occurred in the interim; it also suggests the special effect of blank verse. Here is Dyer, toward the end of his poem:

> Now, ev'n now, my Joy runs high,
> As on the Mountain-turf I lie;
> While the wanton *Zephir* sings,
> And in the Vale perfumes his Wings;
> While the Waters murmur deep;
> While the Shepherd charms his Sheep;
> While the Birds unbounded fly,
> And with Musick fill the Sky,
> Now, ev'n now, my Joy runs high.
>                                    (137–45)

Dyer's four-stress couplets create a brisk pace. Each couplet contemplates and completes contemplation of a different subject (indeed, lines 141 and 142 each disposes of its subject in a single line). The doubled assertion of joy that frames the passage gains emphasis by the reiteration, and the evocative details – wanton zephyr with perfumed wings, deep-murmuring water, charming shepherd, musical birds – justify the joy and invite the reader to share it. This joy involves no apparent reflection: only immediate sensuous response.

In contrast, Warton's blank verse allows him leisurely contemplation of a scene calculated to raise "raptures." Those raptures derive from interpretation: the haunting of the copse, the pensiveness of the rill, the bees' lullabies. Like the passage from Dyer, that from *The Pleasures of Melancholy* consists of a single sentence. Its more intricate structure, however, creates a sense of a mind moving over its subject, rather than a sensibility receiving it. The question here asked is rhetorical – its answer assumed – but the interrogation, in contrast with the assertively framed description of Dyer's verse, intensifies the atmosphere of brooding consciousness. Parts of the scene are not separated: the fawn inhabits the thrush-haunted copse, as does the squirrel; the bees, the oak, and the rill belong to the same site. Dyer employs simultaneity as a unifying device; Warton insists on place.

Although the rhetorical question lends a certain formality to the Warton passage, the unhurried movement of the blank verse and the emotional language urge the reader toward an experience of contemplation comparable to that conveyed by the poem's speaker. The expansiveness of blank verse made it appealing to many writers interested in considering movements of consciousness, particularly as consciousness engaged nature. Joseph Warton's *The Enthusiast: Or the Lover of Nature* (1744) provides an excellent case in point. Much of the 251-line poem consists of didactic passages about the superiority of nature to art, but Warton also offers long sequences of natural description:

> All-beauteous nature! by thy boundless charms
> Oppress'd, O where shall I begin thy praise,
> Where turn th'ecstatick eye, how ease my breast
> That pants with wild astonishment and love!
> Dark forests, and the opening lawn, refresh'd
> With ever-gushing brooks, hill, meadow, dale,
> The balmy bean-field, the gay-clover'd close,
> So sweetly interchang'd, the lowing ox,
> The playful lamb, the distant water-fall
> Now faintly heard, now swelling with the breeze . . .
> (144–54)

Such listing might continue endlessly; it actually goes on for six more lines. Like many earlier poets, Warton relies heavily on adjective–noun pairings to evoke nature's delights. One may feel some disproportion between the claim to feel ecstasy, wild astonishment, and love and the relatively bare description that follows. The forests have no distinct color; the brooks gush (as a brook might be expected to do); only its openness distinguishes the lawn. Yet the rather commonplace imagery has its effect because of the very disproportion between the claim of intense feeling and the lack of fresh specificity in the description. Part of the poem's point is that the most ordinary aspects of the natural world have the power to elicit strong emotion in the observer properly sensitive to nature.

Blank verse imposes little obvious discipline on its user. Both Wartons clearly take pleasure in the freedom to move from one subject to another, lingering as long as they choose on a given topic. Miltonic precedent, even when poets did not adopt Miltonic diction or subject matter, justified elevation of tone. For Joseph Warton, nature itself provides the fundamental cause for elevation. The subject, however, leads him to rhetorical devices that seem far removed from nature. Toward the end of his poem, a group of personifications appear, to dispense wisdom. To compare the way these personifications work with the function of personifications toward the end of Pope's early *Windsor-Forest* may illuminate further the effects of blank verse in mid-century poetry.

Here is Warton, interrupting his own musings on nature:

> As thus
> I wander musing, lo, what awful forms
> Yonder appear! Sharp-ey'd Philosophy
> Clad in dun robes, an eagle on his wrist,
> First meets my eye; next, virgin Solitude
> Serene, who blushes at each gazer's sight;
> Then Wisdom's hoary head, with crutch in hand,
> Trembling, and bent with age; last Virtue's self
> Smiling, in white array'd, who with her leads
> Sweet Innocence, that prattles by her side,
> A naked boy! – Harrass'd with fear I stop,
> I gaze, when Virtue thus –
>
> (213–24)

The "awful forms" – awful in the eighteenth-century sense meaning "awe-inspiring" – make up a parade that the poet has visualized in some detail, giving each character a group of visible attributes. The expansive visual development that has marked the treatment of nature in earlier sequences of the poem continues to characterize Warton's method. He dwells on what he sees, carefully alternating male and female, ending with a child. The pageant hardly seems fearful: it comes as a surprise when the speaker describes himself as "Harrass'd with fear." His fear presumably derives from his recognition that these are super-natural beings – or perhaps from a premonition of Virtue's subsequent announcement that she and her company are leaving England.

The passage's unhurried movement depends partly on the openness of blank verse. For Warton, as for many of his contemporaries, blank verse becomes the medium of something close to what we call free association. Fancying himself musing through the nighttime woods leads him to fantasize embodiments of abstractions, no more (and no less) unlikely than the "little Fayes" that dance through the dales a few lines earlier (211). The imagining of Virtue as a lovely woman leads him to a moment of erotic fantasy, as he contemplates "her round and rosy neck," "long ambrosial hair," and rich perfumes (230–32). Fantasies of America as a place of escape follow. The entire poem is organized in similar fashion.

Glancing at Pope's personifications, we may feel struck at once by their purposefulness. His evocation differs sharply from Warton's in tone, since he imagines hateful rather than attractive beings:

> Exil'd by Thee [Peace] from Earth to deepest Hell,
> In Brazen Bonds shall barb'rous *Discord* dwell:
> Gigantick *Pride,* pale *Terror,* gloomy *Care,*
> And mad *Ambition,* shall attend her there. . . .
> There hateful *Envy* her own Snakes shall feel,
> And *Persecution* mourn her broken Wheel:
> There *Faction* roars, *Rebellion* bites her Chain,
> And gasping Furies thirst for blood in vain.
> (*Windsor-Forest,* 411–14, 417–20)

Scrupulous adjectives, chosen to define economically the quality of the abstraction, characterize several of the personifications. Some create visual effects as well: "Gigantick," characterizing the moral nature of pride and the physical nature of its imagined realization; "pale," evoking the effect of terror as well as its appearance. Such actions as mourning, roaring, biting, and thirsting stress the nature more than the look of the figures. Pope conveys the chaos that Peace sequesters by his array of actions. If he sketches a picture in the passage, he more importantly comments on the emotions and impulses that compel human beings toward discord.

Pope's choice of the couplet form does not, of course, altogether account for the kind of effect he seeks. Yet the form urges him toward economy, and economy requires that he elucidate the import of his images in order to convey his political message. Couplets might, as we have seen, serve descriptive purposes as well, but when verse attempts to enforce a didactic point, couplets press toward emphasis on meaning rather than appearance.

Oliver Goldsmith, writing in couplets almost thirty years after Joseph Warton published *The Enthusiast*, like his predecessor offers an image of virtue abandoning England – an image that may, indeed, have been inspired by Warton. But the ending of *The Deserted Village* (1770) sounds very different from that of the earlier poem.

> Even now, methinks, as pondering here I stand,
> I see the rural virtues leave the land. . . .
> Downward they move a melancholy band,
> Pass from the shore, and darken all the strand.
> Contented toil, and hospitable care,
> And kind connubial tenderness, are there;
> And piety with wishes placed above,
> And steady loyalty, and faithful love.
>
> (399–400, 402–07)

Like Pope, Goldsmith emphasizes the character rather than the appearance of his personages. The only visual detail is the darkening of the beach. Although *The Deserted Village* is an expansive poem, developing at length its portrayal of idyllic village life, it too shows on occasion the couplet's pressure.

Boswell reports an episode in which Dr. Johnson read aloud, to the enjoyment of the assembled company, from Thomson's *The Seasons*. After he completed his reading and the group expressed its admiration, he revealed that he had read only every other line. One may suspect that he cheated a bit, but he makes a critical point: blank verse not only allows but encourages looseness. Such looseness may constitute a poetic virtue: perhaps the most attractive aspect of Joseph Warton's verse is its meditative movement among subjects. The shift toward blank verse in the middle of the eighteenth century, like the turn to the many varieties of ode, speaks of an impulse toward new kinds of expressiveness.

# 9

# Old Poetry, Old Language: Imitation and Fraud

One of the most important books of poetry published in the eighteenth century contained few eighteenth-century poems. Bishop Thomas Percy's compilation, *Reliques of Ancient English Poetry*, published in 1765, consisted mainly of old English ballads, some of them edited in accord with contemporary taste, but many left essentially in their original form. In order to illustrate the continuing presence of ballads in poetic tradition, Percy also included some poems of recent composition. He explicitly claimed the power of a specifically English tradition: one need not turn to the classics, he suggested, to find poetic authority.

Percy was not the first to make this point: others before him had drawn on Spenser and Milton for authority, and others had perceived the virtues of the folk ballad. *Reliques*, however, which included Percy's learned essays on such matters as verse alliteration and medieval metrical romance, as well as on the ballad tradition, appeared at the right moment to capture popular attention. It won wide readership, made the ballad respectable, and influenced subsequent poetry and scholarship alike.

In transcribing old ballads, from the original Percy manuscript and from later finds along the Scottish borders, Percy not only tactfully edited them; he also composed some of his offerings himself, although not in the voice of an eighteenth-century bishop. *The Friar of Orders Gray*, for instance, probably his best-known composition, combines, Percy explains, some of the "little fragments of ancient ballads" that he has found "dispersed through Shakespeare's plays," "with a few supplemental stanzas to connect them together and form them into a little TALE." The 108-line ballad indeed incorporates Ophelia's mad songs and, more surprisingly, the first stanza of a song from *Much Ado About Nothing*: "Sigh no more, lady, sigh no more, / Men were deceivers ever." It transforms the emotional weight of such excerpts. The "Sigh no more" stanza, in Shakespeare's play a lyric of playful cynicism, becomes for Percy an inlet to sentiment, and Ophelia's foreboding fragments foretell only a happy ending. In the "little TALE" Percy composes, a young woman questions a friar in an effort to discover what has become of her lover, only to be told,

> O lady, he is dead and gone!
> Lady, he's dead and gone!
> And at his head a green grass turfe,
> And at his heels a stone.
>
> (17–20)

Undiscouraged, she continues her interrogation. At a later stage of it, the friar suggests, in response to the lady's expressions of grief, that she is well off without her lover, given that "Men were deceivers ever." Her "much-lov'd youth," she responds (77), always remained true. After several such exchanges, the friar reveals that he himself is in fact the beloved youth, and that since he has not passed his year's probationary period, he is free to rejoin the woman he loves. The ballad concludes, in the woman's voice,

> Now farewell grief, and welcome joy
> Once more unto my heart:
> For since I have found thee, lovely youth,
> We never more will part.
>
> (105–08)

Like the old ballads, this one tells a tale, but one unmarked by the anguish that often characterizes the ancient stories. Pathos replaces tragedy; a pretended death substitutes for the real thing. The kind of emotion summoned by the dialogue of friar and lady perhaps bears a closer relation than that of old ballads to the actual experience of most of its readers, as well as to the sort of feeling evoked by many mid-eighteenth-century novels. Percy writes for his audience. He skillfully employs the typical understatement of older ballads, suggesting by the young man's extended duplicity his lingering resentment of possible arrogance in the woman – arrogance never narrated, only hinted by the report that the lover complained of the lady's pride. An expert piece of compilation and composition, the ballad both preserves old techniques and appeals to new readerships.

The language of Percy's ballad deviates relatively little from eighteenth-century norms. We find an occasional archaism – "a pil-grime's weedes," "eyne" for "eyes," "kirk-yard" – but typically the diction is straightforward and simple, even at the risk of flatness:

> Now say not so, thou holy friar,
> I pray thee say not soe:
> My love he had the truest heart:
> O he was ever true!
>
> (73–77)

The use of such a vocabulary, justified by the effort to imitate an ancient mode, tacitly argues for the possibility of new poetic procedures in the eighteenth-century present. If emotional effect could be achieved without reliance on poetic diction, the fact suggested fresh resources for those striving to elicit feeling from readers. Wordsworth would articulate the full implications of the possibility now announced.

Percy's turn to ballads, with its implicit assertion of English poetic tradition, fitted in with isolated efforts by other poets of his time. We have already encountered Thomson's use of Spenserian verse in *The Castle of Indolence*, without commenting on its implications. Like William Shenstone's popular poem, *The School-Mistress* (1742), Thomson's poem both burlesques and celebrates a poetic mode of the past. The burlesque emerges in characterizations of residents in Indolence's realm; the celebration pervades much of the poem. One feels the poet's pleasure in a vocabulary belonging to bygone times. Often a stanza's effect turns on a word or two, unidiomatic in the eighteenth century, but recalling Spenser's realm of enchantment. Consider, for example, these lines from the opening narrative of the castle and its inhabitants:

> Thus easy rob'd, they to the fountain sped,
> That in the middle of the court up-threw
> A stream, high spouting from its liquid bed,
> And falling back again in drizzly dew:
> There each deep draughts, as deep he thirsted, drew;
> It was a fountain of *Nepenthe* rare:
> Whence, as Dan HOMER sings, huge pleasaunce grew,
> And sweet oblivion of vile earthly care;
> Fair gladsome waking thoughts, and joyous dreams more fair.
>
> (1.27. 235–43)

*Pleasure* would work metrically here as well as its archaic equivalent, *pleasaunce*, but the Spenserian word by its very unfamiliarity carries extra emphasis. Its unfamiliarity also allows it to accrue virtually physical weight, "huge" and growing like a solid thing out of the fountain. Similarly, the "gladsome" thoughts of waking, given their fairness, become themselves dreamlike images. The vocabulary associated with enchantment by its most conspicuous earlier use helps to evoke an enchanted place.

Thomson employs Spenserian diction for other purposes as well. Here is a stanza from later in Canto I, describing the Mirror of Vanity:

> *Of vanity the mirror* This was call'd.
> Here you a muckworm of the town might see,
> At his dull desk, amid his legers stall'd,
> Eat up with carking care and penurie;
> Most like to carcase parch'd on gallow-tree.
> *A penny saved is a penny got*:
> Firm to this scoundrel maxim keepeth he,
> Ne of its rigour will he bate a jot,
> Till it has quench'd his fire, and banished his pot.
> (1.50. 442–50)

The clerk here described is at once a worm, a workhorse ("stall'd" among his ledgers), and the dried out corpse of a criminal, the hanged man equated with animals by describing his body as a carcass. The exuberance of metaphor arguably derives from the freedom Thomson feels in a poetic mode that liberates him from the obligations of the literal.

Like poets of every period, Thomson and his contemporaries felt the obligation to "make it new," as Ezra Pound would put it. Paradoxically, they might rely on the old to create the effect of newness. *The Castle of Indolence*, altogether conventional in its explicit recommendation of industry over laziness, breaks fresh ground by its loving exploration of a fantasy realm in the language of a great poetic forebear. Although the poem contains entire stanzas composed in orthodox eighteenth-century diction, its exploration also of an unfamiliar linguistic mode opens it to imaginative adventure.

*The School-Mistress* employs Spenserian diction and the Spenserian stanza to very different effect. The element of burlesque is more conspicuous here, and the poet plays on the joke of using "poetic" language for trivial matters. Yet the poem also celebrates the trivial, dignifying its subject by its diction. The opening stanza makes a direct and compelling case for the value of obscure worth. Like Gray in the churchyard elegy, imagining what greatness may lie beneath the country tombstones, Shenstone imagines the possibilities in schoolchildren growing to maturity, but he also glorifies the schoolmistress as she is in the present:

> Aʜ me! full sorely is my heart forlorn,
>   To think how modest worth neglected lies;
> While partial fame doth with her blasts adorn
>   Such deeds alone, as pride and pomp disguise;
>   Deeds of ill sort, and mischievous emprise!
> Lend me thy clarion, goddess! let me try
>   To sound the praise of merit, ere it dies;
>   Such as I oft have chaunced to espy,
> Lost in the dreary shades of dull obscurity.
>
> (1–9)

"To think how modest worth neglected lies." "To sound the praise of merit, ere it dies." These are lines we might encounter in many an eighteenth-century poem. Shenstone, however, mingles his conventional language and sentiment with less familiar diction. A poem by Pope would not remark on "mischievous emprize," nor would one of Pope's spokesmen "have chaunced to espy" something. The claim of personal feeling implicit in the "forlorn" heart, the hint that praise of modest worth constitutes an important poetic endeavor, and the unfamiliar vocabulary all indicate effort at something new.

In his "Advertisement" to the poem, Shenstone explains his intentions: "What particulars in Spenser were imagined most proper for the Author's imitation on this occasion, are his language, his simplicity, his manner of description, and a peculiar tenderness of sentiment remarkable throughout his works." For Shenstone, as often for Thomson and almost always for Percy, "tenderness of sentiment" is the point. His resort to Spenserian language both justifies such tenderness, according to his reading of the earlier poet, and creates protective distancing from what might be seen as excessive feeling about someone who, after all, belongs to the lower class.

Ostensibly, the poet praises the schoolmistress for her virtue: "For she was just, and friend to virtuous lore, / And pass'd much time in truly virtuous deed" (127–28). He admires the fact that she breeds her own sheep and cards her own wool and makes her own "russet kirtle" (65). He observes the good discipline she keeps, and urges its necessity. The poem's central action – its only action, really – is the whipping of a naughty schoolboy, with its after-effects. The episode allows for a wide distribution of authorial sympathy: to the victim's little sister, who witnesses and suffers from his punishment; to the other children, fearful about their own fates; and to the victim himself. It also gives Shenstone scope for elaborate Spenserian description and reflection:

> His face besprent with liquid crystal shines,
> His blooming face that seems a purple flow'r,
> Which low to earth its drooping head declines,
> All smear'd and sully'd by a vernal show'r.
> O the hard bosoms of despotic pow'r!
> All, all, but she, the author of his shame,
> All, all, but she, regret this mournful hour:
> Yet hence the youth, and hence the flow'r, shall claim,
> If so I deem aright, transcending worth and fame.
>
> (217–25)

The Spenserian precedent allows expansiveness – not the looseness of blank verse, but encouragement to explore the implications of imagery, as Shenstone draws out the analogy between the child's tear-marked face and the flower smeared by rain, and to value the decorative. The poet luxuriates in description of garden flowers and of the good things available at "the huxter's sav'ry cottage" (287), including the abundant cherries that

> With thread so white in tempting posies ty'd,
> Scatt'ring like blooming maid their glances round,
> With pamper'd look draw little eyes aside.
>
> (299–301)

He makes his evocation of the rural schoolmistress an exercise not only in nostalgia but in poetic inventiveness.

Less poetically elegant predecessors than Spenser also attracted the attention of mid-century poets. Thomas Gray celebrated the traditions of Welsh oral poetry in *The Bard* but used the techniques of the Greek Pindar as his model for the poem. In other works, however, he drew on Old Icelandic poems for form as well as content; in at least one instance, he imitated an ancient Welsh form. An "Advertisement" to three odes (two paraphrasing Icelandic models; one imitating Welsh) written for their first publication in 1768 explains that he had once thought of writing a history of English poetry. In pursuit of that project, he wished to offer "specimens of the Style that reigned in ancient times among the neighbouring nations"; these odes belonged to that enterprise.

In his knowledge of relatively obscure ancient languages, his awareness of the complex influences on the development of the English language, and his eagerness for poetic experiment, Gray was unusual among his contemporaries. His odes, however, played their part in responding to and developing a more widespread taste for poetry based on old traditions. The poetic appeal of Gray's models lay not in their expansiveness, not in any equivalent for the Spenserian mode, but in their economy and energy. *The Fatal Sisters*, sixty-four lines long, employs the collective voices of its characters, singing a song about who will live and die in a forthcoming battle. The sisters are, Gray's note explains, "female Divinities. . . . Their name signifies *Chusers of the slain*." Four stanzas will suggest the poem's tone and method:

> Ere the ruddy sun be set,
> Pikes must shiver, javelins sing,
> Blade with clattering buckler meet,
> Hauberk crash, and helmet ring.
>
> (Weave the crimson web of war)
> Let us go, and let us fly,
> Where our Friends the conflict share,
> Where they triumph, where they die.
>
> As the paths of fate we tread,
> Wading thro' th' ensanguin'd field:
> *Gondula*, and *Geira*, spread
> O'er the youthful King your shield.
>
> We the reins to slaughter give,
> Ours to kill, and ours to spare:
> Spite of danger he shall live.
> (Weave the crimson web of war.)
>
> (21–36)

Most of the eighteenth-century poetry we have encountered so far makes heavy use of adjective–noun combinations, relying on adjectives for defining as well as decorative power. Gray, in his Icelandic imitations, does not eschew adjectives, but he uses them sparingly and to striking effect. The last stanza quoted above, for instance, contains a single adjective: *crimson*. Against the bareness of the other lines; the pattern of strong, threatening nouns – *slaughter, danger, war*; and the uncompromising energy of *kill* and *spare*, the sudden burst of color (which duplicates the color of the only emphatic adjective in the previous stanza, *ensanguin'd*, and recalls the crimson web in the stanza before that and even the ruddy sun of the first quoted stanza) carries powerful impact.

Bareness marks most of Gray's efforts to convey the effects of early Scandinavian verse, with an effect especially marked in contrast to the elaboration characteristic of much of his peers' work (and much of his own), including, of course, the Spenserian imitations. Like some of the ballads that Percy collected, this poetry uses on the whole a simple, familiar vocabulary, relying heavily on one-syllable words. It offers, unlike many contemporaneous works, a poetry of subtraction rather than addition. So different is it from the period's prevalent modes that it seems brilliantly, excitingly new – although some of its potential for excitement comes from the fact that its models are actually very old.

Improbably enough, an Edinburgh schoolmaster and a boy who committed suicide at the age of seventeen proved most influential among the poets who turned to a distant British past. The schoolmaster, James Macpherson, sought ancient Gaelic songs and stories in the Highlands of Scotland and published "translations" of them to general applause. The "marvelous boy," as Wordsworth would call him, Thomas Chatterton, likewise claimed to have discovered old manuscripts, from which he published poems that caused considerable stir. Both these discoveries of ancient sources soon came under suspicion. Old Scottish manuscripts were found actually to exist, and oral tradition certainly survived, but it eventually became clear that Macpherson had essentially composed most of the works he published as ancient, even though he typically based them on poems he had found and that Chatterton's "medieval" English poems issued entirely from his invention.

From the point of view of a literary historian looking back to the eighteenth century, the fact that two poets would have thought it worthwhile to claim ancient provenance for their compositions, coupled with the fact that both won lavish public attention for their work, emphasizes the new directions of mid-eighteenth-century verse. Both men, conscious of the importance of cultural tradition, wished to celebrate the past partly as a way to comment on the present. They valued the imaginative distance they achieved by writing in the voices of bygone poets. The public, too, found such voices appealing, both because of the values they communicated and because of the language in which they transmitted those values.

Macpherson employed what we would now call "prose poetry" for his adaptations of what he had heard in the Highlands. He claimed epic structure and importance for the works he presented. *Fingal*, for instance, centers on battles and the exploits of heroes, although it includes many brief stories of romance – brief because they usually end quickly in the deaths of one or both protagonists. The heroes boast about their exploits and proclaim their ideals (the main one being "victory or death"). Ghosts partially fill the place of gods in Greek and Latin epics, lacking the power to affect events, but capable of prophesying. The natural world provides a steady point of reference, the main source for metaphors and similes and a frequently acknowledged environmental power.

A representative passage from Book I of *Fingal* will suggest the kinds of effect Macpherson achieves:

Bright are the chiefs of battle, in the armour of their fathers. – Gloomy and dark their heroes followed, like the gathering of the rainy clouds behind the red meteors of heaven. – The sounds of crashing arms ascend. The gray dogs howl between. – Unequally bursts the song of battle; and rocking Cromla echoes round. On Lena's dusky heath they stood, like mist that shades the hills of autumn: when broken and dark it settles high, and lifts its head to heaven!

Hail, said Cuchullin, sons of the narrow vales, hail ye hunters of the deer. Another sport is drawing near: it is like the dark rolling of that wave on the coast. Or shall we fight, ye sons of war! or yield green Innisfail to Lochlin! O Connal speak, thou first of men! thou breaker of the shields! thou hast often fought with Lochlin: shalt thou lift up thy father's spear?

Cuchullin! calm the chief replied, the spear of Connal is keen. It delights to shine in battle, and to mix with the blood of thousands. But tho' my hand is bent on war, my heart is for the peace of Erin. Behold, thou first in Cormac's war, the sable fleet of Swaran. His masts are as numerous on our coasts as reeds on the lake of Lego. His ships are like forests cloathed with mists, when the trees yield by turns to the squally wind. Many are his chiefs in battle. Connal is for peace. – Fingal would shun his arm the first of mortal men: Fingal that scatters the mighty, as stormy winds the heath; when the streams roar thro' echoing Cona: and night settles with all her clouds on the hill.

The vocabulary of this passage – and of all Macpherson's poems – is almost as simple as that of the ballads and of Gray's Icelandic imitations. Here, too, adjectives play a far less important part than they do in most eighteenth-century verse. One-syllable words figure heavily and emphatically.

The effect of the Ossian poems (the name alluding to an ancient bard), however, differs dramatically from that of Gray or the ballads. In the first place, the omnipresent allusions to nature, as literal reality and as point of metaphoric reference, create the compelling atmosphere of a unified world. Although the vocabulary is not archaic, the faintly archaic patterns of speech lend distance to the scene. The generally short sentences accumulate a strong rhythmic beat, not metrical, but musical nonetheless. Cuthullin alludes to war as "sport," but Connal's immediately following speech, although it includes a claim of the speaker's delight in battle, creates an ominous counterweight. The ambiguity thus established helps to create a sense of slow movement toward a fated conflict – a pace dramatically different from that of the speedy ballads.

Most important is the pervasive atmosphere of melancholy, even in a passage like this one, which partially celebrates war. Gray dogs, mist, the pessimistic undertone of Connal's speech: all suggest more sorrow than joy. The same atmosphere pervades *Fragments of Ancient Poetry* (1760), Macpherson's first public effort at imitating the ancient mode. The allegedly fragmentary nature of the poems included here demands more condensation than do the longer, "epic" works. Thus, Fragment 7 recounts in relatively few lines a tragic tale of love and death. Two men, close friends, love the same woman; they fight over her; the man killed is the object of the woman's love; she kills his slayer and then herself; all three are buried together. The poem's speaker, Ossian, mourns the death of his son, the first man killed.

He fell as the moon in a storm, as the sun from the midst of his course, when clouds rise from the waste of the waves, when the blackness of the storm inwraps the rocks of Ardannider. I, like an ancient oak on Morven, I moulder alone in my place. The blast hath lopped my branches away; and I tremble at the wings of the north. Prince of the warriors, Oscur my son! shall I see thee no more!

We can recognize the same devices deployed in *Fingal*: metaphorical references to nature, incantatory place names, rhythmic prose. All contribute to the melancholy tone permeating the whole.

Much of this period's poetry, as we have seen, involves new stress on feeling. Macpherson's verse, different though it seems from that of his contemporaries, supports the interest in emotion, both by evoking emotion in the reader through atmospherics and plot and by making his characters on occasion articulate it. Fragment 7, despite its insistence on metaphor, tells a story almost as rapidly as one of Percy's ballads might. The impact of the multiplied, senseless deaths combines with the father's understated grief ("My eyes are blind with tears; but memory beams on my heart.") to assert the sadness of life, which often presents itself as the central theme of the Ossian poems. Fragment 8, also spoken by Ossian, contains reminiscences of battle and death but dwells mainly on his melancholy as sole survivor: "Sightless I sit by thy tomb. I hear the wind in the wood; but no more I hear my friends. The cry of the hunter is over. The voice of war is ceased." Like the speaker in Gray's *The Bard*, this blind poet finds himself alone. Unlike Gray's bard, he concerns himself more heavily with evoking his pain than with declaring his power.

The world of the past that Macpherson tries to recreate – a dark natural world of mountains, water, and mist, populated by warriors and beautiful maidens – combines the harshness of constant battle with the softness of constant sadness. Love and courage are its highest values, although courage can take unexpected forms: Macpherson represents a warrior whose courage shows itself in willingness to argue the heroism of avoiding certain defeat. This bygone world (one may perhaps doubt if it ever existed) has little obvious relevance to the eighteenth-century British public – yet that public, perhaps troubled by the increasing dominance of commerce in the society they actually inhabited, found it appealing.

Chatterton wrote in many of his period's conventional modes, showing himself, for instance, expert in deploying the heroic couplet and ferocious as a satirist. His originality emerged most clearly, however, in the medieval imitations, which also caused the greatest excitement among his contemporaries. He had imagined for himself an entire medieval world; his poems in that world's various voices contributed to a large picture. Although many have narrative content or context, they also reveal intense lyricism. *The Mynstrelles Songe* from the tragedy of *Ælla*, for example, tells by implication the kind of story that might provide the substance of a ballad. A young man has died; a young woman (the imagined speaker of all but the final line) mourns him; after announcing her intention of dying on his grave, she does so. The maiden evokes her grief by using details from nature and her sharp memory of the man:

> Swote hys tyngue as the throstles note,
> Quycke ynn daunce as thoughtes canne bee,
> Defte hys taboure, codgelle stote,
> O! hee lyes bie the wyllowe tree:
> > Mie love ys dedde,
> > Gonne to hys deathe-bedde,
> > Al under the wyllowe tree.

> (15–21)

Chatterton glosses "Swote" as meaning "sweet"; modern editors might also explain "taboure" (a small drum) and possibly "codgelle stote" (stout cudgel or club). The language, however, hardly needs explanation. If one enters imaginatively into the world of the poem, it becomes easy enough to grasp at least the general import of most of the unfamiliar (ancient or invented) language.

To compare the beloved youth's voice to a bird song is fairly conventional. More startling is the further account of his tongue as "Qycke ynn daunce as thoughtes canne bee," in which the vehicle for the simile becomes abstract thoughts rather than the substance of the external world. Thoughts can dance; so can tongues. Indeed, the dancing of a tongue often emanates from the liveliness of the thoughts that produce speech. Both dances are of course metaphorical, but because the "as" links tongue and thoughts, the dance has almost literal force.

The stanza's first three lines emphasize the aliveness, the energy, of the remembered man. The last four lines, three of them constituting a refrain reiterated in every stanza but the final one, stress the horrifying contrast of his deadness and his burial, near the willow tree, yet forever cut off from the vitality of living nature. Various versions of the same contrast, the incomprehensible difference between life and death, recur throughout the poem. Once the young man's eyes were black, his skin white, his face ruddy; now the only color associated with him is the whiteness of his shroud – whiter than the moon, the morning sky, or the evening cloud. But the shroud's whiteness, unlike the color of skin or eyes, gives pleasure to no one.

By the time the young woman declares her intention of dying, her death has come to seem inevitable and desirable, associated not only with the company of her lover but with the friendly ministrations of fairies. "I die; I comme; mie true love waytes," the "damselle" says (58), in the poem's satisfying conclusion. Chatterton arouses pity in his readers, but he also perhaps persuades them that death sometimes provides the only acceptable resolution for grief.

How important is the poet's curious language to his effects? The maiden's lament, with its touching concrete particulars, would carry emotional weight also if couched in more familiar diction. Even in modern English, the refrain could create its effect by reiterating the physical fact of deadness. Yet the unfamiliar language contributes to the impression the poem makes by generating an alienation effect: insisting that this story belongs to a distant, finally unknowable, past. The tale of love and death speaks of issues relevant to any era, but its language, like its serious allusions to fairies, tells us that we read across a great gap. The strange vocabulary's demand on readers' attention intensifies the experience of the poem.

The point becomes more complicated in what is probably Chatterton's best-known poem, *An Excelente Balade of Charitie: As wroten bie the gode Prieste Thomas Rowley, 1464*. A narrative poem composed in rhyme royal, a seven-line form invented by Chaucer, it tells a little story about a man in desperate need, caught in a terrible storm, who begs for help from a prosperous abbot, only to be rebuffed. A poor friar, however, shares with him not only a small coin but his cloak, provoking the poem's pointed conclusion:

> Virgynne and hallie Seyncte, who sitte yn gloure,
> Or give the mittee will, or give the gode man power.
> (90–91)

Versions of this story have appeared in many times and places. It is essentially the tale of the Good Samaritan, although Chatterton's account stresses the poor man's suffering more than the monk's rescue of him. It also dwells on the abbot's splendor and high self-regard as well as his rejection of human need:

> His cope was all of Lyncolne clothe so fine,
> With a gold button fasten'd neere his chynne;
> His autremete was edged with golden twynne,
> And his shoone pyke [shoe laces] a loverds [lord's] mighte
>     have binne;
> Full well it shewn he thoughten coste no sinne:
> The trammels of the palfrey pleased his sighte,
> For the horse-millanare [milliner] his head with roses dighte.
>
> (50–56)

As in his ventriloquizing of a young woman's mourning, Chatterton here demonstrates his fine sense of detail: not only a horse that has been decked with roses by a horse-milliner, but a rider who takes particular pleasure in the fact, as he apparently takes pleasure in all the lavish details of his dress, from gold button to shoe laces.

Such details, along with a rich account of the storm and its effects, lend energy and interest to a fairly predictable narrative. Chatterton keeps his reader's attention by surprising him with minutiae: the fields "smoking" as a result of the rain, the rattling of the thunder, the elm tree swinging in the tempest, the Abbot's fancy "girdle" meeting "with mickle shame" as it becomes drenched (46). The Abbot's speech of rejection sounds authentically arrogant:

> Varlet, replyd the Abbatte, cease your dinne;
> This is no season almes and prayers to give;
> Mie porter never lets a faitour [beggar] in;
> None touch mie rynge who not in honour live.
>
> (64–67)

The self-focused notion that one doesn't bestow alms in bad weather, the proud allusions to his porter and to the ring signifying ecclesiastical power, the self-important assumption that he has the capacity to judge who lives "in honour": such details delineate the abbot.

Specificity about external nature and human nature alike makes both the inanimate world and the characters of the poem recognizable and convincing. Consequently, the "medieval" language works in a somewhat more complicated way than it does in the story of the dead lover. The effect I characterized earlier as approximating alienation may slightly disturb a reader who recognizes the actions and appearances of the described world as resembling those encountered every day. At any rate, tension exists between the immediacy of detail and the distance of language – tension calculated to make the reader aware that uncharitable people in high places do not belong only to the Middle Ages. Chatterton comments on his own society in the guise of telling a simple story from the past.

The poets considered in this chapter adopt varying strategies that serve various purposes, but all demonstrate their awareness that past traditions less familiar than those of Greece and Rome can provide new resources for the eighteenth-century writer. The sense of enlarged possibility that they established would bear abundant fruit.

# Outliers: Mary Leapor and Christopher Smart

Mary Leapor, a kitchen maid who died of measles at the age of 23, before any of her poems had been published, and Christopher Smart, by his period's standards and probably by ours at least intermittently mad, seem unlikely representatives of the eighteenth-century poetic scene. Both wrote surprising poetry; both found enthusiastic academic audiences long after their own time. Nor were they altogether neglected in their period. Two volumes of Leapor's verse were published posthumously, by subscription, earning money to help support her impecunious father. Although Smart's *Jubilate Agno*, now widely considered his greatest poem, did not see print until the twentieth century, he won prizes at Cambridge University for his devotional verse; his hymns were popular; and for much of his adult life, he made his living by writing. The careers and the literary productions of these two writers call attention to the fact that eighteenth-century England, despite the power of literary convention, could make room for the unconventional. Leapor in all her work and Smart in most of that published in his own time employed established forms. Smart, however, used those forms in new ways, and Leapor used them on occasion to explore startling subjects.

For Leapor, her poems suggest, Pope loomed large. We know nothing of her education, although one of the early editions of her poems testifies that she owned a small collection of books. She may have gone to the local school in Brackley, Northamptonshire, where her father was a gardener. Her first employment in domestic service was at Weston Hall, where she perhaps consulted the library. Bridget Freemantle, whom Leapor celebrates as "Artemisia" in several poems, befriended her and urged her to publish her work, but Leapor apparently did not think her own verse worthy of print. Discharged from her position, she returned home to serve as housekeeper to her father, her final employment.

Like other poets who lacked conventional education, Leapor made a point of demonstrating knowledge of her predecessors in verse, with particular emphasis on Pope. In her letters and in her poetry, she often expresses a reverential attitude, but her use of Pope as a model occasionally comments on his insufficiencies: for instance, his failure adequately to consider women as a subject. Daringly, she writes *An Essay on Woman*, inviting comparison to Pope's *Essay on Man* although her work has virtually nothing in common with his aside from its use of couplets. Its divergence from Pope's model in itself conveys criticism. For Pope's grand metaphysical scheme, Leapor substitutes attention to uncomfortable particulars. She makes no great claims for women; she simply tries to expose the female situation.

Her methods are indirect and ingenious. Here are her opening couplets:

> Woman – a pleasing, but a short-lived Flow'r,
> Too soft for Business, and too weak for Pow'r.
> A Wife in bondage, or neglected Maid;
> Despis'd, if ugly; if she's fair – betray'd.

These couplets constitute two sentences, if you measure the end of sentences by the punctuation of periods. The sentences, however, lack verbs. Woman is here an object of perception, not an actor. She can be neglected, despised, betrayed, or in bondage – all presumably by men. The lines provide no evidence that she has any capacity to act. By male standards, she can be assessed as a flower, too soft and too weak for significant enterprise. She is far indeed from Pope's commanding figure of Man, dominating the created universe despite his insufficiencies of perception and speed relative to some "lower" animals.

The poem goes on to articulate a grotesque blazon: the woman praised on the basis of her possessions, here bizarrely merged with her appearance.

> 'Tis Wealth alone inspires ev'ry Grace,
> And calls the Raptures to her plenteous Face.
> What Numbers for those charming Features pine,
> If blooming Acres round her Temples twine?
>
> (5–8)

Her "plenteous" face declares the plenty of her belongings, as the blooming acres twine around her temples. It is impossible really to conceive, on the basis of what purports to be a description, what this woman looks like: her appearance, after all, is irrelevant. Her charms exist only so long as her money remains the object of desire. Once a husband possesses her and her fortune, her putative charms – though presumably not those of her wealth – disappear. The advent of Hymen, god of marriage, "Dissolves her Triumphs, sweeps her charms away, / And turns the Goddess to her native Clay" (17–18). The imagined male point of view has continued to control the perceptions recorded in the poem thus far.

At line 19, the point of view shifts sharply, as the poem's speaker begins to "sing / What small Advantage Wealth and Beauties bring" (19–20). In Popean fashion, she offers two exempla, the case of Sylvia, a beauty, and of Pamphilia, a wit. Sylvia's beauty bores her husband. Everyone fears Pamphilia's wit; "The men are vex'd to find a Nymph so wise" (30); and her high intelligence only causes her to feel more intensely the censure of the world. As for wealth, the case of Cordia, who frightens away beggars and lives in filth, indicates that money does not bring happiness. The poet herself, she says, wants only a fire and a friend, indolence and ease.

This *Essay* concludes with telling summary of the female situation, both as the poem has previously sketched it and more inclusively. First we are reminded that neither avarice nor pride, neither wit nor idiocy, protects women from the bad opinion of others. Then the poet, surprisingly, acknowledges categorical female faults:

> Tho' Nature arm'd us for the growing Ill
> With fraudful Cunning, and a headstrong Will;
> Yet, with ten thousand Follies to her Charge,
> Unhappy Woman's but a Slave at large.
>
> (57–60)

The accusation of women's cunning and willfulness may sound like a male judgment, but the context shifts its effect: cunning and will only serve as protections against "the growing ill" that defines a woman's life, regardless of her capacities. The ten thousand follies sum up the charges against her – not her true nature. The poem's final line devastatingly encapsulates the message of the whole: woman may be left "at large," given apparent scope, but slavery remains her essential state.

The power of *An Essay on Woman* derives partly from its refusal of the personal. Whereas Sarah Fyge Egerton, for instance, expressed her outrage at social restrictions on women by insisting on her own feelings, Leapor here purports mainly to make statements about the nature of things. Speaking of herself in the third person, as "Mira," she acknowledges a desire for indolence and ease; otherwise she does not specifically implicate herself in the female situation. One may suspect that her dwelling on the difficulties of Pamphilia, despised for her wit, has personal relevance, but she never says so. Instead, she claims the stance of an objective observer, conscious of suffering ("The keen Sensation of superior Woe"; 32), but not involved in it. Even when she speaks finally of "unhappy Woman," she does not remind the reader that she herself belongs to the unhappy sex.

Yet the poem generates emotional force, partly by eliciting uneasiness. The opening sequence, with its shifting tone, its unconventional syntax, and its array of images creating cognitive dissonance, leaves the reader no comfortable position. Although male desire for money from marriage provides a target for its satire, the subject, after all, is "woman," and Leapor's lines make it unclear how we should feel about this soft pleasing flower with no ability to act. Shall we sympathize or condemn? After all, if women are altogether passive creatures, men can hardly be blamed for wanting money to accompany them in marriage. The gross male flattery implied by the early imagery becomes less blameworthy if women are willing to accept it.

The vignettes that compose the poem's middle section sound more predictable, often drawing from Pope, relatively direct in claiming response, not unduly intense. The concluding line, however, with its revelation of woman's slavery, once more leaves the reader off balance. Since the preceding couplet has apparently concurred in the male judgment of female flaws, we are unprepared for the unequivocal statement of woman's ultimate victimization. Now we know what we are supposed to feel; now the speaker's outrage is apparent. Yet the clear statement does not erase earlier ambiguities; the poem leaves its residue of unease.

Leapor's poem does not claim the ambition of Pope's *Essay on Man*. Its comparative modesty of statement and its refusal to venture into the metaphysical perhaps imply a lack of presumption that marks women as compared to men, but it openly criticizes only Pope's omission of woman as a category – at the same time that it suggests reasons why such omission might occur. Yet the poet's boldness in inviting comparison with Pope, along with her boldness of statement and suggestion in the poem itself, declare an unexpected degree of self-confidence in a young servant girl. Both assertive and inventive, she makes a powerful statement in a short poem.

Her varied manipulations of her poetic persona display Leapor's expertise. By no means does she always refrain from claiming direct emotional involvement in her subject. On the contrary, she can use her own situation and assert her own feelings to great effect. Thus *An Epistle to a Lady* (which does not in any obvious way allude to Pope's poem with a similar title) begins in the third person, with an account of "Mira," a name that Leapor often uses to refer to herself. Although it announces a theme of misfortune ("In vain, dear Madam, yes in vain you strive, / Alas! to make your luckless *Mira* thrive"; 1–2), its tone is light-hearted, its metrical movement rapid and jaunty. Still in the third person, the poem recounts Mira's dream of books and pictures and painted parlors, and her wakening:

> Convinc'd too soon, her Eye unwilling falls
> On the blue Curtains and the dusty Walls:
> She wakes, alas! to Business and to Woes,
> To sweep her Kitchen, and to mend her Clothes.
> (28–31)

Dusty walls are an unusual detail for an eighteenth-century poem, and such obligations as sweeping and mending are rarely alluded to. Still, as an apparent example of "Woes," sweeping the kitchen seems comically disproportionate.

The poem moves quickly, however, to a new subject, a new tone, and a new voice. Sickness arrives, "At whose Appearance all Delusion flies" (33). The next pronoun is "mine," as the poet abandons the distance of the third person. She abandons also any pretense of jauntiness. Now books and paintings no longer appeal to her; she narrates a contemplation of death. First she thinks of her mother's death, then of her own; finally, as she imagines herself dying, she suddenly returns to the third person and broadens her perspective. She says that she will

> fall resign'd beneath the mighty Blow.
> Nor I alone – for through the spacious Ball,

With me will Numbers of all Ages fall:
And the same Day that *Mira* yields her Breath,
Thousands may enter through the Gates of Death.

(62–66)

"I" gives way to "*Mira*" as the speaker thinks of herself as only one in a universe full of souls. The thought concludes, and in a sense resolves, the poem, inasmuch as it provides a way of viewing the self that makes irrelevant the earlier complaints about sweeping and mending and, more inclusively, the general claim of lucklessness. After sixty-odd lines focused on the situation of a single individual, the poem forces its reader at least briefly to ponder an individual's significance.

In her engaging account of *Man the Monarch*, Leapor employs an authoritative tone for a playful yet moving narrative of creation. She economically recounts the fates of various animals after the Fall:

To cragged Rocks destructive Serpents glide,
Whose mossy Crannies hide their speckled Pride:
And monstrous Whales on foamy Billows ride.
Then joyful Birds ascend their native Sky:
But where! ah! where, shall helpless Woman fly?

(19–23)

Woman's problem stems from the fact that Nature (no God appears in this version of the story) formed her as beautiful but weak, unable to labor hard or to participate in battle. Fear and grief destroy her beauty. She tries to use her wisdom to her advantage, but no one pays attention: "'Tis all Delirium from a wrinkled Maid" (49).

At this point Leapor uses an effective device that recurs frequently in her work, a sudden shift of direction and tone. The introduction of a new character provides an explanation if not a resolution for the story of Woman:

A tattling Dame, no matter where, or who;
Me it concerns not – and it need not you;
Once told this Story to the listening Muse,
Which we, as now it serves our Turn, shall use.

(50–53)

The stereotypical "tattling" woman, whose nature has been long bemoaned by men, tells of Man's greed for power. As he named the birds, he enjoyed the homage of the animal creation and worried about Woman's possible desire to share dominion with him. Therefore he, "better to secure his doubtful Rule, / Roll'd his wise Eye-balls, and pronounc'd her *Fool*" (59–60). Thus Man names Woman – names her "*Fool*." The impulse behind that naming, the story says, has passed down through the ages:

> Sires, Brothers, Husbands, and commanding Sons,
> The Sceptre claim; and ev'ry Cottage brings
> A long Succession of Domestic Kings.
>
> (63–65)

This poem, too, illustrates Leapor's originality. Her daring in reimagining the Genesis story, her adoption of a playful tone for an iconoclastic assertion, and her refusal, once more, to express emotional involvement in her subject: all these aspects of her verse signal her refusal to write in a merely conventional mode. She succeeds in providing amusement and insight simultaneously, offering gentle protest of the female situation in the guise of explanation.

Leapor's best-known work is *Crumble-Hall*, which gestures toward the long English tradition of "country-house poems" while providing radically new perspectives on the country house. Like earlier poems in the tradition, Leapor's offers celebration – but not of the luxuries of the rich.

The three introductory couplets, framing the poem, immediately suggest new purpose for the subgenre:

> When Friends or Fortune frown on *Mira*'s Lay,
> Or gloomy Vapours hide the Lamp of Day;
> With low'ring Forehead, and with aching Limbs,
> Oppress'd with Head-ach, and eternal Whims,
> Sad *Mira* vows to quit the darling Crime:
> Yet takes her Farewel, and repents, in Rhyme.
>
> (1–6)

Not landscape or architecture but the writing of poetry provides the ostensible subject. Moreover, unlike most country-house poems, this one begins with personal emphasis: the poet suffers from negative criticism of her verse and from gloomy weather; headache oppresses her, but so do the demanding whims of others; she thinks of her writing as a "darling Crime" – because she's a woman? or because she's a servant? – but remains unable to avoid it.

Given returning sunshine, the poet, now speaking of herself in the first person, and her Muse alike find themselves in "frolick" mood (9) and therefore begin to sing of Crumble-Hall. Their "song" begins, as its seventeenth-century forebears might, with praise of the house's hospitality. The praise includes many specific details of food and drink – beef and pies, pork, peas, and bacon, venison and rabbit, beer, wine, and ale. It also includes a rather startling comment on the visitors' greed: "the Guests ravag'd on the smoking Store, / Till their stretch'd Girdles would contain no more" (26–27).

When the poem turns to the house's architectural features, it does not avoid unattractive aspects: the spider webs developing on the ceiling, with no prospect of being swept away; the dark passage with mice running through it, where the stranger must feel his way along the wall; the greasy kitchen floor; awkward figures on a tapestry; a dead end in the hallway. The pronoun "we" recurs: the poet imagines herself conducting a stranger through the building. Then a "you" appears, also to be repeated, as the tone becomes increasingly intimate. The speaker reveals, for instance, that the man sleeping in one room, surrounded by books, is not, as "you" might guess, a student; he doesn't read the books that envelop him. She confides that the steep stairs might cause "you" to "break your Head" against a ceiling (97). In a high room, she points out

> Old Shoes, and Sheep-ticks bred in Stacks of Wool;
> Grey *Dobbin*'s Gears, and Drenching-Horns enow;
> Wheel-spokes – the Irons of a tatter'd Plough.
> (99–101)

The stranger begs off – he's gone high enough, he says. The poet, however, insists on leading him out to the roof, where "the ravish'd Eye" (105) sees an enticing prospect of fields and groves. Then comes another surprise:

> From hence the Muse precipitant is hurl'd,
> And drags down *Mira* to the nether World.
> (107–08)

The incongruity of the Muse's sudden physicality may recall other unexpected and odd physical allusions in Leapor's verse: Man rolling his "wise Eye-balls" in *Man the Monarch* (61), or the "magic toe" of the rich maiden in *An Essay on Woman* (13), or the acres winding round a woman's temples, for instance. One may find it difficult to imagine the scene in which Muse and Mira, hand in hand, are "hurl'd" downward by an unspecified assailant. And what are we to make of "the nether World," which suggests a vague equation between the world below the house top and hell?

Such jarring moments in Leapor arouse the reader's attention, typically at an important juncture. The specific transition signaled by the hurtling downward of Mira and her Muse brings them to the kitchen, where the poem pays close attention to the appearance and behavior of the culinary staff and to the multifarious productive actions demanded to prepare a meal for the gentry. The kitchen workers bring skill and attention to their tasks. Roger, however, who has over-eaten, lies snoring on the table, his unconsciousness duly mourned by his fellow servant, Ursula, who in parodic pastoral fashion lists her attentions to him ("For you my Pigs resign their Morning Due: / My hungry Chickens lose their Meat for you"; 142–43). When her dish kettle begins boiling, though, she abandons her grief for the sake of the immediate task.

The poem offers no didactic commentary on the kitchen scene or on its relation to the tour through the other parts of the great house. With another sudden transition, it changes locale again: "Now to those Meads let frolick Fancy rove" (156). The outdoors seems idyllic, but its peace is suddenly interrupted:

> But, hark! what Scream the wond'ring Ear invades!
> The *Dryads* howling for their threaten'd Shades:
> Round the dear Grove each Nymph distracted flies
> (Tho' not discover'd but with Poet's Eyes).
>
> (165–68)

The allusions to frolic fancy and to poet's eyes make a single point – one that will be reiterated: not the house, but what the poet has made of it matters here.

The poem never resolves its disjunctions. The house remains a place of decayed grandeur, with its specified occupants – greedy guests and sleeper surrounded by books – far from impressive. The kitchen remains a place of hard work and productivity, but also of grotesque lament and clumsy people. The meads are lovely, but the scream of the dryads and the running of distracted nymphs, seen only by the poet, foretell the destruction of beauty. In the final section of *Crumble-Hall*, the poet foresees the razing of the house and the clearing of its surrounding trees. She prophesies that "injur'd Nymphs" will haunt the "ravag'd Plain" (180), that strange sights and sounds will ensue, that Ursula will see elves, and that the new-built house will suffer echoes and crickets. All this will happen, she says, "or the Muse for Vengeance calls in vain" (179).

Thus the poem that began with the speaker's sense of guilt over writing poetry concludes with another reminder of the poet's power – but an uneasy reminder, which leaves open the possibility that the Muse's call might indeed prove vain. *Crumble-Hall* itself, one might assume, issues from the inspiration of the Muse it invokes. If so, it testifies to rather limited power. The poem has organized a mass of details about house and grounds. It has evoked emotions ranging from amusement to admiration. But it has not succeeded in making sense of the discrepancies between house and inhabitants, between present and past, between masters and servants. Setting forth those discrepancies, it suggests that they belong to the nature of things, not changeable in the existing state of society and not subject to transformation even by the Muse. That Muse constitutes an important resource for a servant girl, a mode of exerting force over her circumstances by clarifying them, but not one likely to, or expected to, change her lot.

Much of Leapor's verse, then, suggests at least vague social protest, against the condition of women and of servants. The young woman's methods for registering that protest rely heavily on startling the reader by unexpected shifts of locale, tone, or reference – a series of devices that emphasize the poet's sense of the incongruities society offers. She establishes an idiosyncratic voice and a special perspective that both mark her poetry's distinction and suggest her status on the edge of her poetic scene.

Christopher Smart, Leapor's contemporary, had a sharply different personal history. Not only was he a man (a fact of fundamental importance); he also came from higher in the social scale. Son of the steward of a large estate, he attended Cambridge University, where he first distinguished himself as a poet, winning five prizes for poems on the attributes of the Supreme Being. The interest in religious matters suggested by this achievement remained apparent in much of his subsequently published poetry. After being imprisoned for debt in Cambridge, Smart went to London to make his living as a writer, working for several years for the bookseller John Newbery, whose stepdaughter he married. His first confinement for madness – its main symptom a compulsion to pray in public – occurred in 1757. Neither madness nor hospitalization for it, however, interfered with his literary productivity in many modes.

Smart recurrently in his work revealed a desire to make Christian tradition widely available. He produced metrical versions of *Psalms*, wrote hymns for children and for adults, as well as an oratorio, and in *A Song to David* and *Jubilate Agno* he innovated new methods for communicating his faith. He also composed expert secular verse, published in three collections, as well as translations of Horace and Phaedrus.

*A Song to David* (1763) is the most accessible of Smart's incontestably important works. It aroused controversy at its first publication: the poet William Mason declared that it showed Smart to be as mad as ever; others complained that as a song *to* rather than *about* David, it partook of idolatry. Like Leapor, though for different reasons, Smart seemed an outsider, despite his full participation in the commercial literary scene. In *A Song to David*, he devised an intricate poetic structure through which to dramatize the poet's power to praise God. In this work, as in many others, he demonstrated, as Leapor did, the force of a distinctive poetic voice.

In this instance, the distinction derives partly from the interplay the poem establishes between abstract and concrete. In the fourth stanza, for example, Smart lists twelve abstract qualities that he attributes to David:

> Great, valiant, pious, good, and clean,
> Sublime, contemplative, serene,
> Strong, constant, pleasant, wise!
> (19–21)

He then devotes each of the subsequent twelve stanzas to exegesis of a single quality – exegesis consisting of a list of exemplary actions. Here he "explains" *clean*:

> Clean – if perpetual prayer be pure,
> And love, which could itself innure
>   To fasting and to fear –
> Clean in his gestures, hands, and feet,
> To smite the lyre, the dance compleat,
>   To play the sword and spear.
>
>                          (49–54)

The elucidation, by no means transparent, consists in examples that make the reader ponder the import of cleanliness. Is perpetual prayer a way of being clean? Smart himself suggests, by his "if," that some question exists. His next lines, however, help to answer that question, by indicating that the "cleanliness" of love consists in its capacity to purify itself through fasting and through fear (presumably of God). Thus the stanza's first half dwells on the essential identity of purity, associated with religious dedication, and cleanliness, ordinarily considered a more trivial quality.

The second half stanza radically shifts approach, to link cleanliness with action of various kinds. In the three lines, each verb pairs oddly with the noun it relates to. David smites the lyre, as he might smite an enemy, but plays the sword and spear, as he might play an instrument. He completes the dance instead of performing it. The cleanliness of his gestures and his hands and feet – or of the gestures of his hands and feet: the syntax allows either meaning – is comparatively comprehensible; why the forms of energy exemplified in the final lines embody cleanliness may leave one baffled.

As a whole, the lines suggest some equation between cleanliness and integrity: a wholeness of personality that absorbs into it all activity and all physicality. As he elaborates each of the qualities he has attributed to David, Smart redefines it, forcing his readers at least to try to think about familiar ideas in fresh ways. The sequence of meditation on qualities of character, meditation taking the form of embodiment, has almost incantatory force, as examples multiply. Inasmuch as new ideas and images rarely depend on those that have preceded them, the poem does not demand that the reader grasp in detail the import of its redefinitions. It only requires that we allow each idea its immediate force and let ourselves be absorbed into the poem's rhapsodic movement.

The fundamental enterprise of *A Song to David* becomes clearest in the twenty-one stanzas (51–71) organized around the word "ADORATION."

An elaborate account of God's original creation of the universe and an extended meditation on the Ten Commandments have preceded this sequence; fifteen stanzas on David's surpassing attributes and finally on Christ's promise of salvation follow it. The adoration stanzas, however, make apparent the function of the poem as a whole: that of praise to God, direct and indirect. These stanzas also call attention to Smart's uses of specificity, often in unexpected juxtaposition with abstraction. Two examples will suggest the many kinds of pattern the poem establishes. Here is the first:

> For ADORATION seasons change,
> And order, truth, and beauty range,
>   Adjust, attract, and fill:
> The grass the polyanthus cheques;
> And polish'd porphyry reflects,
>   By the descending rill.
> (307–13)

One might expect a poetic allusion to the changing of seasons to introduce reminders of, say, the shifting colors of various times of year. Instead, reference to seasonal change introduces three abstractions attached to verbs that make them seem concrete. Order, truth, and beauty become forces that organize the aesthetic effect of the seasons. The subsequent specific details – grass, flowers, stone, water – demonstrate how they work. The polyanthus, a tiny flower, both "fills" and "adjusts" the grass: it checkers the lawn (thus "attracting" the observer) and it checks the spreading of the grass, creating a double kind of order. The reflections created by the polished stone generate new forms of beauty and of order for the observer. The movement of the water contrasts with the immobility of stone and presumably aids in creating the varying reflections.

Two stanzas later, we find this:

> The spotted ounce and playsome cubs
> Run rustling 'mongst the flow'ring shrubs,
>   And lizards feed the moss;
> For ADORATION beasts embark,
> While waves upholding halcyon's ark
>   No longer roar and toss.
> (325–30)

The ounce, or cheetah, belongs to a non-English landscape, although the flowering shrubs may suggest England. One rarely contemplates a cheetah and a lizard in conjunction, but Smart's imagination insists on uncommon juxtapositions that emphasize the scope of God's creation. Every creature performs its assigned function: wildcats run; cubs play; lizards eat moss; beasts embark on Noah's ark; the halcyon, or kingfisher, floats on its own ark, or nest. Different times – the Biblical past and a possible present – as well as different places come together. And all creation serves the purpose of adoration: the very existence of diverse wonders praises God, as does the recognition of such existence.

The twenty-one stanzas adopt many techniques for making this point, which becomes powerful through its sheer insistence. To perceive the beauties of the universe is an act of worship. To record them intensifies and potentially multiplies the act. David, as Psalmist, himself exemplified the importance of praise. Smart imitates him.

It is not surprising, then, that the poem concludes with reference to its own writing. The final stanzas build to a crescendo, as the series of adjectives (*sweet, strong, beauteous, precious*), all applied to various aspects of the human and nonhuman world and finally to David himself, concludes with *glorious*. The northern lights, the "hosanna from the den [in which Daniel was confined with lions]" (508), the "catholic amen" (509), and the martyr's gore are all glorious; and "Glorious the song, when God's the theme" (506). Then the last stanza:

> Glorious – more glorious is the crown
> Of Him that brought salvation down
>     By meekness, call'd thy Son;
> Thou at stupendous truth believ'd,
> And now the matchless deed's atchiev'd,
>     DETERMIN'D, DAR'D, and DONE.
>                                  (511–16)

The attribution of glory to Christ, by Biblical tradition considered the "son of David," makes an appropriate climax for this poem of praise. The last two lines, however, introduce a new element. "Now" is a tricky word in a poem that often seems to consider all recorded history, religious and secular, part of an eternal present. The "matchless deed" may be Christ's sacrifice. Taking "now" literally, however, that deed becomes the poem itself, a recapitulation and transformation of the religious tradition of worship through praise. The poet assimilates himself to David as maker of music glorifying God. He calls attention to his daring in writing a "song" unlike its predecessors in the English canon. He hints that divine inspiration, the product of his own belief in "stupendous truth," must account for the poem's achievement as a "matchless" paean.

Smart found other modes of originality as well for religious poetry. His *Hymns for the Amusement of Children* provide vivid examples of his ability to devise fresh means of appeal. *For Saturday*, one of the shortest hymns, illustrates the point:

> Now's the time for mirth and play,
> Saturday's an holyday;
> Praise to heav'n unceasing yield,
> I've found a lark's nest in the field.
>
> A lark's nest, then your play-mate begs
> You'd spare herself and speckled eggs;
> Soon she shall ascend and sing
> Your praises to th' eternal King.

In two quatrains, the poem tells a story, makes a didactic point, and conveys delight in the natural world. The first stanza initially seems a complete little story in itself, at once exuberant and pious, but the second stanza shifts its meaning, working partly through manipulation of pronouns. The "I" that finds the nest, and that sees the finding as occasion for praise to heaven, becomes "you" in the second stanza, signaling the radical shift of perspective that creates the poem's moral insight. The feminine pronoun assigned to the lark (who by virtue of the pronoun gets oddly assimilated with the "play-mate") personalizes the bird. The theme of praise continues, transformed in the second stanza as the lark sings praises of the child who spares the eggs, her song more intimate and more grand by virtue of her ascent than is the child's initial praise. Finding the nest is cause for praise; leaving the nest alone justifies greater praise. Saturday, a holiday, becomes "an holyday" indeed because of an act of grace. "Mirth and play" allow for both finding and sparing. A complicated lesson emerges in simple terms.

Rarely in his maturity did Smart write purely secular verse, except for his translations of Latin originals. Whether he praised flowers or admirals, whether he produced fables or allegorical investigations of such subjects as "Munificence and Modesty," he customarily turned toward a subject's religious ramifications. He re-translated the Psalms, hoping to make them more accessible to English audiences; he wrote hymns for adults as well as for children. Religious preoccupations permeated his life.

The fragments of *Jubilate Agno*, a complicated religious work not assembled into plausible poetic structure until 1954, issued from a period of Smart's confinement in a madhouse. The poem remains obscure in some of its details, although comprehensible in many sequences and patterns. The section on "My Cat Geoffrey" appears most often in anthologies, because of its immediacy and charm. Other parts of the poem, however, provide fuller insight into the poet's preoccupations and his gifts.

Smart's concern with language – with the sounds and meanings of words, and with words as entities – emerges often. The poet ponders the sounds of individual letters, the relation between the sounds of words and of musical instruments, and the connections of words to one another. "For every word has its marrow in the English tongue for order and for delight," he concludes (B, 595). He speaks of the language of flowers:

> For there is a language of flowers.
> For there is a sound reasoning upon all flowers.
> For elegant phrases are nothing but flowers.
> For flowers are peculiarly the poetry of Christ.
> For flowers are medicinal.
> For flowers are musical in ocular harmony.
> For the right names of flowers are yet in heaven. God make
>     gard'ners better nomenclators.
>
> (B, 503–09)

No passage in so eccentric a work as *Jubilate Agno* can be termed typical, but this sequence exemplifies some of Smart's characteristic moves. As in *A Song to David*, he tries to expose, or at least to assert, connections among apparently disparate phenomena: flowers and phrases, flowers and Christ (a link he frequently explores in his poems), flowers and music and medicine. Language recurs as an issue: flowers have their own means of communication, but the communications of men and women, if sufficiently elegant, belong also to the realm of flowers. The matter of "right names" naturally concerns a poet. Gardeners, like Adam, have the power of naming; Smart prays that they might use that power better.

The repetition of the introductory "For" and of "flowers" creates much of the rhythmic effect here. Smart eschews conventional patterns of meter and rhyme to create his own kind of free verse, modeled loosely on Hebrew tradition. Antiphonal patterns characterize verse in that tradition, and *Jubilate Agno* was almost certainly composed antiphonally, with lines beginning "For" responding to lines beginning "Let." Unfortunately, only a few pages remain that exemplify the pattern. At least as important as the verse pattern, though, is Smart's highly personal use of language. As he explains earlier in Fragment B, "For my talent is to give an impression upon words by punching, that when the reader casts his eye upon 'em, he takes up the image from the mould which I have made" (404). The verbal repetitions, the recurrence of themes and images, the insistence of such sequences as the one about flowers: these devices indeed have the effect of "punching," of a forcible demand for attention to new ways of thinking and feeling, and new ways of using language.

The "Let" verses often employ Biblical proper names, placed in conjunction with animal names. Thus: "Let Libni rejoice with the Redshank, who migrates not but is translated to the upper regions." The "For" verse corresponding to this one reads, "For I have translated in the charity, which makes things better and I shall be translated myself at the last" (B, 11). The paired lines suggest three different senses of the verb *translate*, and hint at yet another meaning. In Smart's mythology (which he may have thought natural history), the redshank (a European sandpiper with red legs and feet) does not travel long distances by its own volition but is mysteriously carried from one place to another: *translated* meaning *transferred*. When the poet speaks of himself having translated, he means, in the first instance, that he has converted the language of poets like Horace from Latin to English. Imagining himself as translated at the last, he thinks of being carried to heaven without dying first. A vaguer meaning hovers around the idea of translating "in the charity." The phrase hints the possibility that all poetry can be understood as a form of translation, the poet's purpose in writing affecting his means of conveying meaning. Smart looks at the world and "translates" it into language with the purpose of glorifying God and illuminating his readers: thus the charity.

The density of meaning in a single pair of lines – and my comments have by no means exhausted the meanings – suggests why *Jubilate Agno* makes high demands on its readers. The poem also possesses the capacity, however, simply to delight the reader, especially by its comments on animals and on language – often in conjunction. A long sequence connects animals with languages (cats with Greek, mouse with Latin, bull and dog with English) and with individual words. Smart attends lovingly to even unlikely animals:

> For the Mouse is a creature of great personal valour.
> For – this is a true case – Cat takes female mouse from the
>     company of male – male mouse will not depart, but
>     stands threatning and daring.
> For this is as much as to challenge, if you will let her go, I will
>     engage you, as prodigious a creature as you are.
> For the Mouse is of an hospitable disposition.
> For bravery and hospitality were said and done by the
>     Romans rather than others.
>
> (B, 638–42)

The final line supports the poem's view that "the Mouse (Mus) prevails in the Latin" (636): not only does *mus* form an ending for Latin words, but the mouse as creature exemplifies Roman virtues.

The qualities that we discovered in Leapor's poetry – such virtues as daring, originality, a predilection for the unexpected – appear also in Smart's, in different keys. Leapor's daring manifests itself most often in choice of subject: a challenge to Pope, or to the natural superiority of males, or to conventions governing women. Smart, in contrast, picks the apparently conventional subject of the human obligation to God, for instance, and treats it in startlingly new ways. Both poets, in their best work, adopt strong, distinctive voices. Both can eschew display of personal emotion – as Smart does, for example, in the passage about the mouse – but both prove capable of passionate utterance. To go beyond such general characterizations to the particularities of the two poets' works is to discover vast differences between them. Indeed, they might seem to have nothing in common – nothing beyond the unpredictability of their approaches. Leapor's couplets and Smart's piety strike familiar notes, but they use their raw materials in unfamiliar ways – reminding us yet again of the vast range of poetic possibility in eighteenth-century Britain.

The unexpectedness that characterizes Leapor's verse and Smart's may cause us to look back at the other poetry we have considered from the second third of the century and to realize that much of it, too, has strikingly unexpected aspects. An ode in which God and Fancy copulate? A ballad in imitation-medieval language by an eighteenth-century writer? Furies discussing a scene of battle? Poetry written in lines that look like prose, recapitulating scenes from an imagined distant past? An epic poem on Dullness? Poetry about their work by a thresher and a female laborer?

In form and in content, much mid-century verse violates conventions that had seemed firmly established. Pope, toward the end of his career, continues to write in heroic couplets, but he has enlarged his theater of action and intensified the daring of his imagery. Collins and Gray purport to imitate classic forms, but for modern purposes. Even Gray's unpretentious stanzas in the churchyard elegy take his readers to unexpected places, as the poet challenges assumptions about identity. Macpherson and Chatterton, passing off their carefully constructed imitations as ancient creations, force attention on what the non-classical past has to offer eighteenth-century readers, as does Bishop Percy, with his imitations and his restorations. Duck and Collier, deploying classic references to sing of hard labor, are as startling as Gray, who plays with the Muse instead of taking her seriously (*Ode on the Spring*) or openly questions the emotional force of conventional allusion (*Sonnet on the Death of Richard West*).

Leapor and Smart appear to take little for granted about the writing of poetry, except for the fact that poetry matters. Even as Leapor imitates Pope in form, she twists the form to new uses. Their contemporaries, too, though – including Pope – now employ convention adventurously and abandon it at will. Their poetry does not sound like that of the nineteenth or twentieth or twenty-first century, but neither does it sound like Ben Jonson or Dryden – or, for that matter, Pomfret, at the beginning of their own century.

# 11

# How to Live: Poetry and Politics

The testimony of poetry would suggest that notions of how to live changed radically between 1700 and 1770. Although Pomfret's ideal of prosperous rural seclusion might still appeal to some, those who espoused it now proved more likely to comment on its political implications. Pomfret, in *The Choice*, observed in passing the corruption of courts, in order to emphasize his own good fortune in avoiding it. The most famous poem of 1770, Oliver Goldsmith's *The Deserted Village*, noted in detail how the greed and careless power of the rich made it impossible to preserve an idyllic village community – and the mere notion of idyllic possibility seemed fatuous to some commentators on Goldsmith's poem.

As Goldsmith's endeavor in *The Deserted Village* indicates, poetry retained its authority as a mode of social and philosophic commentary. The mid-century interest in openly expressed feeling, however, also remained powerful, and poets frequently deployed sensibility as a basis for judgment. Thus *The Deserted Village* in its opening line describes Auburn as "Sweet" and as the "loveliest" of villages, using language more customarily applied to women. The village, which provides "Dear lovely bowers of innocence and ease" (5), is described as a spot "Where humble happiness endeared each scene" (8). Such emotive language (note the repetition of "lovely" and "dear" within the first eight lines) both insists on and defines the value this vanished village holds.

Equally emotive is the diction that evokes the forces destroying the idyll.

> But times are altered; trade's unfeeling train
> Usurp the land and dispossess the swain;
> Along the lawn, where scattered hamlets rose,

> Unwieldy wealth, and cumbrous pomp repose;
> And every want to luxury allied,
> And every pang that folly pays to pride.
>
> (63–68)

The followers of trade are "unfeeling," meaning that, devoid of "sympathy," they do not feel for others. Such an indictment declares them virtually nonhuman. As for the wealthy, they both cause and experience suffering, feeling the pain that results from their own "folly." Wealth and pomp, clumsy and excessive, create wants and pangs in those who possess them, as well as corollary pangs in those whom they exclude.

In expressing his anger against "trade" and "wealth," Goldsmith alludes to the causes and consequences of the enclosure movement as he saw it. Enclosure sounds innocent enough: it means bringing together separate strips of land within fences or hedges. Practiced to a degree at least since the sixteenth century, enclosure had become markedly more prevalent around 1760. It created great advantages for already prosperous farmers, enabling large-scale fertilization and crop experimentation, establishing capitalistic principles for agriculture, and generating wealth. Its effects on the poor, however, were often disastrous. Those without clear title to their small plots of land and those who had subsisted by using the resources of common land found themselves effectively evicted from their homes. Poor country people streamed to the cities in search of work. Their exodus created the depopulation that Goldsmith mourns.

Nor does the poet value the wealth created for some by the misery of others. *The Deserted Village*, partly an exercise in nostalgia, emphasizes throughout the emotional weight of the "lovely" past and the "forlorn" (76) present. It uses the first-person pronoun strategically to underline the personal feeling that exemplifies the observer's suffering as well as that of the dispossessed. The observer suffers his own kind of dispossession: he had always imagined, he says, retiring to the harmonious community he remembers.

> In all my wanderings round this world of care,
> In all my griefs – and GOD has given my share –
> I still had hopes my latest hours to crown,
> Amidst these humble bowers to lay me down.
>
> (885–88)

Describing himself as a man of feeling, he embodies the misery of wealth's impact on poverty. He endures also the pain of loss intensified by memory. In a series of sentimental vignettes, he describes the people of the village in their communal functioning – all now gone. Only in the poem's final lines does he move away from verse manifestly controlled by feeling, to praise the power of poetry itself and, in an address to that power ("Thou source of all my bliss, and all my woe"; 415: an emotional force in itself), urges poetry to "Teach erring man" (426) to eschew wealth for virtue. Although the choice of how to live no longer allows the peace of bygone rural communities, it can still embody such community's virtues.

*The Deserted Village* is an important poem in its political outrage and its sentimental method. Goldsmith reacts to immediate social actualities – but he reacts by looking backward, seeking answers in the past. Inasmuch as he implies recommendations about how to live, he advocates the impossible course of returning to pre-capitalist ways. As one might expect, such a poem generated wide readership and vigorous response. Most extensive and most deft among the reactions was George Crabbe's *The Village* (1783), which, seeking to expose realities that Goldsmith had glossed over, reveals a new kind of sensibility, a new way of responding to the external world. Its recommendations about how to live, however, also – rather surprisingly – look backward.

The opening lines of *The Village* suggest its program:

> The village life, and every care that reigns
> O'er youthful peasants and declining swains;
> What labour yields, and what, that labour past,
> Age, in its hour of languor, finds at last;
> What forms the real picture of the poor,
> Demands a song – The Muse can give no more.
> (1–6)

Writing, as Goldsmith had done, in the heroic couplet strongly associated with poetry of the early century, Crabbe announces a new project for the Muse: to expose reality rather than represent idealized versions of existence. Moreover, he claims such exposure as the Muse's most essential function: she can give no more.

Reflecting on traditions of pastoral poetry, the poem goes on to assert that writers continue to work in these traditions because "They ask no thought, require no deep design, / But swell the song, and liquefy the line" (33–34). Fields and flocks appeal, Crabbe points out, to "him that gazes or [to] him that farms [that is, to one who owns a farm]" (40) – not to "The poor laborious natives of the place" (42) who suffer the real hardships of rural existence. The poet believes that his stress on poetry's truth-telling function constitutes a new departure. Poetry has hitherto existed, he suggests, to flatter or to soothe: not to expose.

Unlike Goldsmith, Crabbe indicates no faith in poetry's power to educate or to inspire: his Muse can do no more than describe. He points out that laborers, hungry and exhausted, have neither time nor energy to respond to verse. Goldsmith rhapsodized over village games; Crabbe reveals that erstwhile athletes now deploy their strength in smuggling. Crabbe too places himself in the rural scene by means of the first-person pronoun, only to find himself cut off from happiness in the past as well as the imagined future by the corruption not of the rich but of the poor.

> Here wand'ring long amid these frowning fields,
> I sought the simple life that Nature yields;
> Rapine and Wrong and Fear usurp'd her place,
> And a bold, artful, surly, savage race.
>
> (1: 109–12)

The activities of that "race," as he explains, include fishing, but also the acceptance of bribes for votes and the plundering of shipwrecked vessels.

*The Village* grows fiercer as it continues, its increasing intensity marked by the introduction of the second-person pronoun. The poem's "you" appears to have been taken in by the sentimentalities of previous poets. When the speaker acknowledges that the poverty and vice he has described may be products of niggardly nature in an unfertile region and turns his attention to richer soil, he points out that only a few enjoy the advantages of natural productivity; the laborer must still labor. "You," he speculates, may think that the laborer enjoys the advantages of health, which "languishes with Wealth" (1: 142). (Samuel Johnson, we may recall, suggests this point in *The Vanity of Human Wishes*.) "You" would be wrong: hard work in all weathers produces ailments that may bring life to a premature close. "You," it turns out, belong to the idle rich, who profit from the labor that they fail fully to acknowledge. "Then own," he urges us, "that labour may as fatal be / To these thy slaves, as luxury to thee" (1: 154–55). "You" are too dainty to touch such stinted meals as laborers welcome; "you" dream of rural ease, pleased alike by smooth streams and smooth verses.

The implicitly antagonistic relation between the poem's speaker and his imagined reader underlines the issues of class that provide a political framework for *The Village*. Class barriers, in the poem's logic, raise insuperable obstacles to understanding. The prosperous man or woman who believes Goldsmith to provide a picture of life can hardly grasp the actualities Crabbe claims to reveal, of careless, contemptuous doctors, uninterested clergymen, and unrelieved suffering for the poor. The poem's first book ends with the death of an old man, neglected alike by doctor and pastor, and mourned only by the children he befriended.

The second, and last, book begins with a reminder of the view of poetry promulgated by the earlier part of the poem. The poet who has claimed that poetry disguises truth now boasts that he has fulfilled his purpose of converting verse into a medium for truth. He has, he says, told the truth about the village:

> No longer truth, though shown in verse, disdain,
> But own the village life a life of pain.
>
> (2: 1–2)

Given the conviction that he has persuaded his audience, he can now relax his insistence for long enough to narrate the "gleams of transient mirth and hours of sweet repose" that occur in the midst of the woes he has described (2: 3).

The more positive view of village life, however, proves fleeting. Soon Crabbe begins to demonstrate not just the pain but also the vice of villagers, exemplified by a burly man striking his pregnant wife on her naked breast. It turns out, too, that the rich share the vices of the poor: the judge has a mistress who feels grateful not to be in the situation of the disgraced working-class girl; the rural trollop acquires a venereal disease from an aristocratic lover and passes it in turn to a country swain.

> In his luxurious lord the servant [shall] find
> His own low pleasures and degenerate mind;
> And each in all the kindred vices trace
> Of a poor, blind, bewilder'd, erring race;
> Who, a short time in varied fortune past,
> Die, and are equal in the dust at last.
>
> (2: 95–100)

Having reached this eloquent conclusion, Crabbe shifts direction. Virtually the entire second half of Book 2 concerns the death of Lord Robert Manners, second son of John Manners, Marquess of Granby, and Lady Frances Seymour, a naval officer who died at sea in 1782 as a result of wounds sustained in battle. Devoting nearly 100 lines to the young man's virtues, his death, and the responses of his survivors, Crabbe makes Manners into the type of selfless heroism.

Our poor, blind, bewildered, erring race, then, embodies also possibilities of courage, integrity, and discipline. Perhaps Lord Robert Manners provides a model of "how to live." Yet his appropriateness for the poetic enterprise of *The Village* does not seem self-evident, and awareness that his father was Crabbe's employer (ordained in 1782, Crabbe served as chaplain to John Manners, who would become Duke of Rutland) may induce a certain cynicism about why the poet expended so many lines in his praise.

Postponing further consideration of Lord Robert Manners as a figure in Crabbe's poems, we might ponder how *The Village* differs from earlier attempts to tell the truth about the working poor: such poems, for example, as those by Stephen Duck and Mary Collier, on the thresher's labor and on the work of poor women. *The Thresher's Labour* opens with direct acknowledgment of Duck's patron:

> The grateful Tribute of these rural Lays,
> Which to her Patron's Hand the Muse conveys,
> Deign to accept; 'tis just She Tribute bring
> To Him whose Bounty gives her Life to sing.
>
> (1–4)

The poem's speaker positions himself from the beginning as deferential to those above him in rank. He writes always as an insider, a participant in the labor he describes. Although he stresses the hardship of the worker's life, he suggests no vice: both the workers and their social betters behave appropriately for their stations. Collier betrays more sense of injustice than Duck does; she indicates her anger at Duck himself and hints outrage at her employers' thoughtlessness. Thoughtlessness, though, is the worst crime she accuses them of. Her own participation in the drudgery she describes supplies her authority for verse.

Crabbe writes from a different aesthetic, moral, and social position. Newly secure as a clergyman (he had previously struggled to make a living as a writer in London), he thus belonged to the gentry. He observes the village as an outsider, with a perspective from which he might criticize working class and aristocracy alike. His claim to tell the truth constitutes his justification for poetry, not only his immediate pretext. He feels himself to be doing something new, not just because he reveals previously obscure aspects of village life, but because he makes factual rather than moral truth poetry's foundation.

And his poetry indeed accomplishes something new. Exposure of lower-class and upper-class vice already existed; the fact that the poor often worked hard was known, although never previously expounded in verse like Crabbe's. More revolutionary was the poet's attention to the truth of appearances. Thus he describes the heath just beyond the village:

> From thence a length of burning sand appears,
> Where the thin harvest waves its wither'd ears;
> Rank weeds, that every art and care defy,
> Reign o'er the land and rob the blighted rye:
> There thistles stretch their prickly arms afar,
> And to the ragged infant threaten war;
> There poppies nodding, mock the hope of toil,
> There the blue bugloss paints the sterile soil;
> Hard and high, above the slender sheaf,
> The slimy mallow waves her silky leaf.
>
> (1: 66–75)

Stephen Duck, describing the mowers at work, describes also a fairly conventional pastoral scene, which the laborers are too tired to respond to. Crabbe takes no such simple recourse. Instead, he sketches a scene of barrenness – out of which he conjures both beauty and drama. The thistles with prickly arms threatening war (and of course they do in fact menace a poorly-clothed child) and the poppies that "mock the hope of toil" suggest a landscape at odds with its human inhabitants. But the bright blue bugloss, another prickly weed, remains blue and radiant, even as it signals the soil's uselessness for agricultural pursuits, and the mallow in all its sliminess can yet display a "silky leaf." The poet sees it all: he can, as he claims, "paint the cot, / As truth will paint it, and as bards will not" (1: 53–54). Exposing truth of appearance as well as of substance, he invites new kinds of emotional response, asking his readers simultaneously to appreciate and to deplore, not to moralize.

To realize the newness of Crabbe's vision and the fresh accomplishment of his verse makes it all the more difficult to understand why the poet spends almost 100 lines glorifying Lord Robert Manners. The introduction to the sequence epitomizes the sudden flatness that overtakes the poem:

> And you, ye poor, who still lament your fate,
> Forbear to envy those you reckon great;
> And know, amid those blessings they possess,
> They are, like you, the victims of distress.
>
> (2: 101–04)

The transition to the concerns of the Manners family seems too easy for effectiveness, and the poet himself betrays self-doubt in his comments about his craft. Hitherto, his assertions about poetry have focused on the falsity of conventional verse that prettifies the country and on the commitment to truth inherent in his own kind of poetry. Now, addressing Manners, he writes, "Belov'd of Heav'n! these humble lines forgive, / That sing of thee, and thus aspire to live" (2: 117–18). Later, he inquires, "What verse can praise thee?" (2: 138). Yet more emphatically:

> 'Tis not, I know, the chiming of a song,
> Nor all the powers that to the Muse belong;
> Words aptly cull'd, and meanings well exprest,
> Can calm the sorrows of a wounded breast.
>
> (2: 157–60)

Such conventional demurs fit with the extravagant praise lavished on the dead hero, but they may raise questions about what has happened to the poet's commitment to "truth" and to his poetic self-assurance. This is, at any rate, a different kind of truth from that of weeds and rags. The lines belong to a long tradition of elegiac verse glorifying heroes of the upper class. Although the virtues here celebrated – reason, courage, "The noble spirit" (2: 179) – might belong to peasants as well as peers, the noble spirit more typically inheres in members of the nobility. Crabbe has radically changed his poetic emphasis.

Anthologies often print Book 1 of *The Village* alone. It plausibly stands by itself as a sketch of harsh realities, and it demonstrates vividly the power of Crabbe's innovations. The dramatic shift of direction in Book

2, however, reveals something else of importance: it illustrates the strain of the new. As a literary man in London, Crabbe might feel freer than he felt as a beneficiary of patronage to commit himself fully to experiment. However sincere his grief for the dead naval officer, his position in the household surely urged him toward public statement of that grief, and the weight of tradition dictated the form his statement would take. Reading audiences might welcome the new (Crabbe's later career, extending well into the nineteenth century, demonstrated his innovations' acceptability), but newness could go only so far when the poet faced emotionally fraught situations that had inspired generations of his predecessors. Crabbe's falling back on convention demonstrates convention's appeal and its power. The poet deploys it to say what he wants to say: not something new, but something familiar.

"The strain of the new," however, refers to more than poetic technique. The new circumstances of the eighteenth century's final third imposed their own strains on poets, as on the rest of the populace. Robert Manners died in a battle of the American Revolution, between the British and the French, who had allied themselves with the colonies. In 1782, when he was killed, the war had not yet come to an end (the Peace of Paris a year later officially ended it), but the British had suffered two major military defeats that made the eventual outcome predictable. A triumph by a colony over the growing empire that had believed itself supreme could only be profoundly unsettling. The unease created by this war joined with concerns over growing industrialization, over the exodus from the country to the city that Goldsmith had deplored, over the dominance of trade and the power of money, and, increasingly, over the horrors of slavery and the condition of prisons. From time to time poets treated such subjects, as we shall see. One poetic reaction to them, however, was intensifying retreat to the personal.

Crabbe, in using the imagined virtues of a hero dead in futile battle as a pattern for behavior, avoids the political and social problems of considering the inception or conduct of the war – at the cost, perhaps, of a certain hollowness. He finds virtue in an individual. His poem's recommendations about "how to live" appear only in the section on Manners, which advocates the qualities the hero exemplified and sets down rules for appropriate mourning (governed by reason as well as affection). The more striking sections on country life show how people actually live rather than how they might wish to. Unlike the satiric presentations that had abounded earlier in the century, *The Village* neither explicitly nor implicitly provides any prescriptions for remedying the situation it describes. Its endorsement of Manners's virtues does not bear directly on the problems represented by a corrupt rural community. Crabbe reveals his own nostalgia in reverting to praise of the upper class as embodying the positive traits that he fails to find in the village. His brilliant evocation of life as it is for the poor offers no moral satisfactions; Book II of *The Village* gestures at providing them – despite the claim that poetry's function, as the poem repeatedly states, is only to tell the truth: not to instruct its readers about alternatives.

Most poets did not share Crabbe's professed view on this point. William Cowper in *The Task* exemplifies a tactic employed also by others who offered verse recommendations about how to live: he uses a version of his personal situation as a starting point for reflection on social actualities and individual responsibilities. (For a fuller treatment of *The Task*, see Chapter 15.) Having retreated from London, site of his first disastrous mental breakdown, to the country, he could write passionately of the evils he had left behind:

> The law by which all creatures else are bound,
> Binds man the lord of all. Himself derives
> No mean advantage from a kindred cause,
> From strenuous toil his hours of sweetest ease.
> The sedentary stretch their lazy length
> When custom bids, but no refreshment find,
> For none they need: the languid eye, the cheek
> Deserted of its bloom, the flaccid, shrunk
> And wither'd muscle, and the vapid soul,
> Reproach their owner with that love of rest
> To which he forfeits ev'n the rest he loves.
> Not such th'alert and active. Measure life
> By its true worth, the comforts it affords,
> And theirs alone seems worthy of the name.
>
> (1: 385–98)

Cowper had called his poem *The Task* because it originated in a task set for him by a friend as a means of alleviating his depression: the task of writing a poem about the sofa. The sofa, as he points out in his opening lines, provides an opportunity for rest, which seems at the beginning to be an object of celebration. The idea of a task, however, holds far more power for the poet. The saving power of activity provides a recurrent theme of *The Task*. To recommend it for others, as it had been recommended to Cowper himself, rouses the poet's didactic energy.

The method of the passage above also recurs. Cowper deplores inactivity by making its practitioner seem both physically and morally repellent, with withered muscle and vapid soul. The active, in contrast, receive immediate reward – not only the capacity for genuine rest, but a whole series of "comforts," which the poem goes on to specify. Not only in the hereafter but also in the immediate present are appropriate rewards and punishments meted out. By insisting on this point, Cowper enforces a vision of a morally coherent universe. He writes not only of how one *should* live but of how one *must* live in order to have any chance of happiness.

A particularly striking example of the poet's fierce dichotomizing also appears in Book 1. Praising the glories of outdoor life, Cowper describes the sick man released from imprisoned illness into the open air: "He walks, he leaps, he runs – is wing'd with joy, / And riots in the sweets of ev'ry breeze" (1: 443–44). "The spleen is seldom felt where Flora reigns," the poet generalizes (1: 455). The obvious corollary – that spleen occurs often to those committed to indoor life – soon follows, with a compelling portrayal of urban card players.

> The paralitic who can hold her cards
> But cannot play them, borrows a friend's hand
> To deal and shuffle, to divide and sort
> Her mingled suits and sequences, and sits
> Spectatress both and spectacle, a sad
> And silent cypher, while her proxy plays.
> Others are dragg'd into the crowded room
> Between supporters; and once seated, sit
> Through downright inability to rise,
> 'Till the stout bearers lift the corpse again.
>                                         (1: 472–81)

Physical incapacity reflects its moral equivalent. The men and women physically unable to rise from their seats are dead not only in their inertness but also in their lack of awareness of their own corruption. Apparently deprived of all that makes life worth living, they yet "love life, and cling to it" (1: 482). Their love, however, is not unqualified: "They love it, and yet loath it; fear to die, / Yet scorn the purposes for which they live" (483–84). Still, they cannot relinquish those purposes: they dread solitude, fear shame, and remain compelled by their habits.

*The Task* does not provide only negative examples. It shows how one should live, as well as how one should not. Activity is by no means the only desideratum for the good life. In general, the man or woman who lives in harmonious relation to nature wins the poet's approval, but the more fundamental issue is that of Christian commitment – a more serious and demanding matter than it appeared to be for Pomfret. Toward the end of *The Task*, Cowper offers a portrait of the good man in terms that suggest a good deal about his poetic project as a whole. Toward the end of that extended portrait, the speaker addresses himself to the worldly observer who may feel contempt for his virtuous and unworldly counterpart:

> Forgive him, then, thou bustler in concerns
> Of little worth, and idler in the best,
> If author of no mischief and some good,
> He seek his proper happiness by means
> That may advance, but cannot hinder thine.
> Nor though he tread the secret path of life,
> Engage no notice, and enjoy much ease,
> Account him an incumbrance on the state,
> Receiving benefits, and rend'ring none.
> His sphere though humble, if that humble sphere
> Shine with his fair example, and though small
> His influence, if that influence all be spent
> In soothing sorrow and in quenching strife,
> In aiding helpless indigence, in works
> From which at least a grateful few derive
> Some taste of comfort in a world of woe,
> Then let the supercilious great confess
> He serves his country, recompenses well
> The state beneath the shadow of whose vine
> He sits secure, and in the scale of life
> Holds no ignoble, though a slighted, place.
>
> (6: 951–71)

The fluent blank verse conveys passionate conviction as Cowper outlines his vision of the good man: responsible to others, giving help to the poor, comforting and soothing, alleviating strife, seeking his "proper happiness" – the adjective carrying great force, here suggesting not social propriety but appropriateness to the human condition in a divinely ruled universe. The good man possesses Christian virtues, and the poet establishes a Christian context for representing them. The speaker's contempt for "the supercilious great," who fail to recognize the worth of the man characterized earlier as "the solitary saint" (948), hinges partly on that failure, but also on their idleness, their failure to perform the good works that define the proper condition of a human being.

For a poet as deeply committed to Christian conviction as Cowper, there is nothing surprising in any of this. The hints of a political subtext, however, call attention to an aspect of the verse that will recur in many late eighteenth-century works. The speaker urges his inter-locutor not to consider the good man an encumbrance on the state, someone who receives but fails to contribute. Such a man contributes in ways that may prove invisible to his social betters. His contributions possess importance nonetheless. If this inconspicuous saint profits by the support and shelter of the state, he also "serves his country" – whether or not his country recognizes or acknowledges the service.

This double awareness, of how humanity both serves and depends on God, serves and depends on secular government, characterizes much of Cowper's verse. "To smite the poor is treason against God," he writes in *Charity* (217), a poem centrally concerned with a crucial Christian virtue. The welfare of the poor was partly the responsibility of local governments; Cowper hints that the responsibility might well belong to individuals as well, and that it partakes of the human obligation to God. In much of the poem, he considers the special obligations and situation of the British. He writes of the problem of slavery and the desperate situation of Africans, of divorce, of the nature of good schools. His understanding of how to live roots itself firmly in the here and now of his world, and he knows that the world is always and everywhere political. Implicit recommendation of this awareness makes part of his program.

This is not to say that he cannot write verse of pure devotion. *The Olney Hymns*, which have made their way into Protestant hymnals, provide abundant evidence of his capacity to do exactly that, movingly and memorably. Their implied dicta about how to live are simple – though not easy. In *The Task*, though, and in many shorter poems, Cowper proves aware of Caesar's presence as well as God's – never in doubt that obligation to God takes precedence over all others; never

reluctant to criticize those too fully given over to their worldly obligations, real or fancied; but conscious that the complexities of leading a
good life include worldly as well as theological responsibilities.

Awareness of political influences and determinants expresses itself
in many ways in the period's verse. Even such a conservative writer
as Anna Laetitia Barbauld summed up her characterization of British
national spirit as "this late sickly age / (Unkindly to the tow'ring growths
of virtue)" (*Corsica*, 4–5), alluding perhaps to the alleged corruption of
the Tory government. She also praised James Boswell for his interest
in Corsican rebels, those "animated forms of patriot zeal" (27), and glorified
their leader, General Paoli, whose "large ambitious wish to save his
country" (124) marks him as the pattern of virtue. After the Corsicans'
attempt to liberate themselves from France failed, Barbauld added a
final passage expressing regret for the loss. It concludes with these lines:

> Not with the purple colouring of success
> Is virtue best adorn'd: th'attempt is praise.
> There yet remains a freedom, nobler far
> Than kings or senates can destroy or give;
> Beyond the proud oppressor's cruel grasp
> Seated secure; uninjur'd; undestroy'd;
> Worthy of Gods: The freedom of the mind.
>                                    (195–201)

Coming at the end of a long poem that celebrates the fight for literal
national freedom, the glorification of internal freedom (however worthy
of gods) seems lame. The retreat from public discontents to private
serenity, however, appealed to many poets whose consciousness of
actual and potential political upheaval confronted them with problems
offering no obvious solution.

Barbauld provides another striking example of such retreat in *The
Rights of Woman*, presumably a response to political debate during
the 1790s stimulated by such radical thinkers as Mary Wollstonecraft.
The poem begins,

> Yes, injured Woman! rise, assert thy right!
> Woman! too long degraded, scorned, opprest;
> O born to rule in partial Law's despite,
> Resume thy native empire o'er the breast!
>                                    (1–4)

Line 4 reveals the poem's argument: woman's proper sphere is dominion over male feelings. Love is her métier; she should abandon ambitious thoughts (29) because Nature teaches her "That separate rights are lost in mutual love" (32). Thus the political realm becomes irrelevant to women. Yet the impulse to write such a poem declares the writer's awareness of challenges from beyond the domestic sphere.

In poetry as well as prose, some welcomed such challenge. Thus Helen Maria Williams, painting an idyllic picture of French peasants in the fields, depicts the poor as rescued – "taught / Some self-respect, some energy of thought" (*To Dr Moore*, 39–40) – by the early stages of the French Revolution. Writing in 1791, she inquires, "Must feudal governments for ever last?" (53) and describes the work of the Revolution as "this glorious triumph of mankind" (78). She sees herself as supporting "The common cause of millions" (82) and rejoices in the process of demolishment she imagines.

One way in which increasing awareness of political facts manifested itself belongs peculiarly to this historical moment. Poets who made their reputations through verse marked by intense emotional display (see Chapter 12) on occasion used happenings in the public realm as occasions for such display. Toward the century's end, the conjunction between political commentary and emotional indulgence had special plausibility, as the French Revolution first aroused the hopes of liberal thinkers, then degenerated into horrifying violence. In England, anxiety over the possible consequences of revolutionary ideas elicited severe governmental repression on freedom of speech, press, and assembly. Nonetheless, such writers as Thomas Paine, Mary Wollstonecraft, and William Godwin produced prose tracts celebrating the principles of liberty and equality that the French revolutionaries professed and outlining the kinds of law and custom that they implied. Poets responding to their immediate cultural context found ways to suggest their own commitments to liberty, equality, and fraternity, the professed ideals of French revolutionaries.

The figure of Marie Antoinette aroused especially intense emotional response. Mary Robinson writes *Marie Antoinette's Lamentation, in Her Prison of the Temple*, dwelling in particular on the anguish of a mother concerned for the welfare of her children. The poem, purportedly a first-person meditation by the imprisoned queen, explores divergent states of feeling: despair, heroism, pleas for the children's lives, retrospective reflections. It relies heavily on visionary figurative language:

Where'er I turn, a thousand ills appear:
  Arm'd at all points, in terrible array:
Pale, hood-wink'd murder, ever lurking near,
  And coward cruelty, that shuns the day!
See, see they pierce, with many a recreant sword,
The mangled bosom of my bleeding Lord!

(67–72)

*A Fragment. Supposed to be Written Near the Temple, at Paris, on the Night Before the Execution of Louis XVI* employs similar rhetoric, in a comparable effort to convey and arouse intense feeling over events in France. Neither poem explicitly addresses the question of how one should live one's life, but their domestication of the queen suggests a desire to present her as a female model of simultaneous victimization and heroism.

A long blank verse poem called *The Progress of Liberty* appeared only after Robinson's death, but she had published parts of it under individual titles in the concluding years of the century (and of her life: she died in 1800). The poems rely heavily on monstrous personifications – Anarchy, Despotic Power, Cruelty, Vice – sometimes described, sometimes only named, to evoke the horror of all forms of opposition to Liberty, itself present in the poems only in remote figurative terms. Parades of personifications, however, may seem remote from the springs of action. What kind of effect could Robinson have wished to create? We have encountered heavy reliance on personification and extravagant language, although of a different sort, earlier, in the poetry of Collins, for example, where it's easy to grasp the poet's desire to create a new mythology around his chosen subjects. The sense of wonder he generates from one point of view supplies his poems' *raison d'être*: readers who experience that wonder in relation to an idea of fear or of the poetical character have learned a new attitude toward emotion or toward poetry. Robinson's generalization (her Marie Antoinette becomes the type of the suffering mother) and personification appeal less readily to a twenty-first-century audience, partly because our own experience of multiplying political unrest and corruption may seem to demand particularities to make it real, thus worthy of feeling.

It may come as a surprise to learn that Robinson showed herself altogether capable of particularity on a matter of public concern. In an excursion into satire, she takes aim at a hallowed ritual of the British court, the birthday ball celebrating the king's birthday. *The Birth-Day* turns on an elaborated and particularized contrast between the rich and the poor.

> Here four tall lacquies slow precede
> A painted dame, in rich array;
> There the sad shiv'ring child of need
> Steals barefoot o'er the flinty way.
> (13–16)

After a series of such conjunctions, the poem reflects on reasons for the blindness of the rich to the poor.

> But ah! how little heeded here
> The fault'ring tongue reveals its woe;
> For high-born fools, with frown austere,
> Contemn the pangs they never know.
> (37–40)

*The Birth-Day* has exactly the force, clarity, and point that we may find missing from Robinson's verse reflections on the French Revolution.

Since we know that Robinson had available to her quite different poetic resources from those she used in most of the poems we have been considering, we must conclude that her reliance on a panoply of personifications and exclamation points resulted from conscious choice, not from inability to get closer to her subject. It is worth pondering why she would make such a choice.

Eighteenth-century poets could expect of their readers kinds of interpretive activity to which we are no longer accustomed. With poetry and painting thought of as "sister arts," readers would tend to assume an emphatic pictorial element in poetry. When Robinson evoked the arrival of Liberty in the court of Despotic Power, she provided an elaborate allegorical scene: Despotic Power frowning "Terrifically" (*The Progress of Liberty*, 101) on his iron throne as the bolts of his ponderous gates crash open; his vassals trembling in chains before him; captives groaning "Beneath his feet" (105); and on the periphery a fearful group:

> Shad'wy specters dire,
> Of persecuted innocence and worth;
> Of GENIUS, bent to an untimely grave; –
> Of ETHIOPS, burnt beneath their native sun,
> Their countless wounds wide yawning for revenge,
> Rose in a mighty host, – and yell'd despair! –
> (106–11)

We must first of all imagine this scene visually, giving the undescribed characters what lineaments we will, but "seeing" them, all crowded together like personages in a vast allegorical painting. It takes effort to visualize beings like Genius and Worth, but the poem offers clues about their posture (Genius bent) or their sex (persecuted Innocence is probably female) or their color (the Ethiopian burnt to darkness by the sun). Their faces and forms hardly matter. What matters – what the imaginative eye fixes on – is their countless gaping wounds.

Unlike a painting, this scene offers aural effects: the clash of the gates, the clanking of chains, the groaning of captives, and especially the great yell of despair. And the poem offers more specific clues to meaning than most paintings would, while demanding also that the reader figure meanings out. Thus the chains binding the vassals are "Artfully twin'd with wreaths of opiate flow'rs" (99): despotic power, in other words, deadens the consciousness of its more compliant victims. The numerous wounds of those who have been reduced to mere specters – not only the abstractions of Innocence, Worth, and Genius, but the generalized figure of the African slave – both declare the endless injuries of despotism and suggest that those injuries in themselves call for revenge. The yell of despair simultaneously expresses defiance, given the new presence of Liberty.

These comments do not exhaust the implications of the scene, but they indicate how complicated the effects and the meanings of personification can be. Robinson, writing about liberty, seeks to interest her audience not in a particular situation but in a large and vital public issue. She therefore tries to establish both pictorial and emotional grounds for taking it seriously – and for recognizing its complexity. The straightforward approach of *The Birth-Day* is calculated to create a single, simple response of outrage. The long political poems attempt much more, working to move their readers both to see the individual ethical implications of political behavior and to acknowledge the large importance of public affairs.

Robinson makes her concern with politics perfectly clear. All the poems treated in this chapter, however, demonstrate a consciousness of public affairs that has become part of imagining how individuals can and should lead their lives. Goldsmith, looking backward, can offer for the moral and social losses implicit in a capitalist society no recourse beyond nostalgia. Crabbe, attacking nostalgia's falsifications, yet can only recommend traditional virtues that do not confront the corruption he depicts. Barbauld relies on traditional gender arrangements as a solution to current unrest. Cowper and Robinson, in contrast, convey the need to remediate political actualities by virtue of individual moral choices. Cowper employs a rhetoric of assurance, sometimes quiet, sometimes strident; Robinson often relies on rhetorical extravagance. The two poets speak for different programs: Cowper believes himself to be endorsing God's prescriptions for humankind. Both, however, express the same sense of a poet's mission to reform as well as describe existent society.

Increasing unease over the class system manifests itself in many of these poems. Collier and Duck, earlier in the century, had delineated the harsh lot of the working class, but displayed little resentment of the greater privilege of their employers. When Cowper speaks of "the supercilious great" (*The Task* 6: 967), he ironizes the noun *great* and conveys scorn for the pretensions of those who continue to posit an equation between merit and social rank. Although he does not make rank itself a desideratum of virtue, his distinctions between the good and the corrupt – between card players, for instance, and the man who rejoices in doing good – often appear to celebrate those belonging to a middle station in society, neither so poor as to lack all resources nor so rich as to enjoy a life of self-indulgence. Robinson's contempt for those rich folk who ignore the poor animates *The Birth-Day*. Goldsmith appears to believe that goodness belongs only to those of humble station. Such diverse indications of discomfort with prevalent assumptions about class divisions provide one more index of a growing consciousness among poets about the implications of social arrangements.

# 12

# Matters of Feeling: Emotion Celebrated

Proclamations of feeling abounded in late eighteenth-century poetry, with the causes for announced feeling varying wildly. Poets reported strong emotion about wrongs inflicted upon them, about the sufferings of others, about flowers and mountains. Often they constructed their personae to suggest identity between the literal poet and the voice of their poem in order to offer what purported to be accounts of their inner lives, thus creating precursors for twentieth-century confessional poetry. No longer did they commonly adopt techniques of indirection to convey emotion, nor did abstract emotions like Collins's Fear and Pity typically attract their attention. When Charlotte Smith wrote, in the preface to the first and second editions of her *Elegiac Sonnets and Other Poems*, "Some very melancholy moments have been beguiled by expressing in verse the sensations those moments brought," she exemplified the close connection that poets now claimed between experience and expression: not just therapy, as her sentence suggests, but often delicious indulgence.

Many, although not all, of the late eighteenth-century poets of feeling were women. *Clifton Hill*, a long poem by Ann Yearsley, illustrates some of their preoccupations and techniques. Recording the speaker's nighttime wanderings in the woods, *Clifton Hill* allows scope for reflection of many kinds. The speaker dwells, for instance, on past encounters with her mother, in which that parent attempted to reconcile her to the idea of death. Her own intense negative response to the very idea, however, remains unabated: "My aching brain now whirls, with horror fraught," she writes (76), remembering the fact of her mother's death.

> Alone I climb the craggy steep;
> My shrieking soul deserted, sullen views
> The depths below, and Hope's fond strains refuse.
>
> (88–90)

The extravagant diction – the whirling, aching brain fraught with horror, the shrieking soul – reflects the poem's insistence on its own intensity. When the wanderer encounters a flock of sheep, she observes that humans are their only foes and entreats them to dispel their fears, since "My woe-struck soul in all your troubles shares" (106). The cause for her pervasive woe never emerges, but she offers her grief as a guarantee of authenticity. Her bathetic claim to share the sheep's troubles asserts her sensitivity to all living creatures.

Nature at some times appears to encourage indulgence of the speaker's woes. At other junctures, it provides relief from pain. After evoking a scene of raucously celebrating sailors, Yearsley writes,

> Yours be the vulgar dissonance, while I
> Cross the low stream, and stretch the ardent eye,
> O'er Nature's wilds; 'tis peace, 'tis joy serene,
> The thought as pure as calm the vernal scene.
> Ah, lovely meads! my bosom lighter grows,
> Shakes off her huge oppressive weight of woes,
> And swells in guiltless rapture.
>
> (192–99)

The word *vulgar* introduces a surprising note. Yearsley has arrived at the subject of sailors by an intricate stream of consciousness: contemplating the animal tenants of the wood leads her to think of their eating weeds driven down the river; that thought produces a brief meditation on the wonders of Commerce; the global implications of commerce make her focus on the sailors whose ships enable it; she imagines the joyfulness of the sailor's return, to parents, lovers, and merchants; then the sailors celebrate their safe arrival, driven by "love and joy" (191). To have the celebration turn into "vulgar dissonance" comes as something of a shock. Yearsley's vivid awareness of social class may account for the phrase. Like Stephen Duck and Mary Collier, Yearsley belonged by origin to the working class. She was selling milk from door to door when Hannah More, the evangelical poet and educator, "discovered" her, having been shown her verse by a cook. Several of her poems consist largely in praise for her patronesses, who rescued her from poverty and volunteered to "correct" her verse. She called herself "Lactilla," in reference to the milk, and was often alluded to as "the milkmaid poet." Grasping the hope of ascending in class by means of her verse, she cultivated sentimental attitudes and poetic allusions. "Blame not my rustic lay, nor think me rude [meaning uncouth or naive]," she writes (146), with manifest anxiety about how she might be perceived. Her reminders of her "weight of woe" and her "raptures" testify to her extreme sensibility, a quality often claimed by those of elevated social class. We may recall, in this connection, that both Joseph and Thomas Warton similarly suggested their superiority: their responsiveness to nature differentiated them from those concerned with man-made splendor.

On occasion, the poem's speaker does not directly claim emotion as her own. She tells the story of Louisa, a "fair Maniac" (206) who lived near a haystack that the speaker encounters in her wanderings. Unsheltered from the weather, Louisa roamed the "wilds" (214) in storm and sunshine alike, enjoying her solitude and her musings. Once she was an innocent girl who fell in love. Persons unnamed confined her in a convent, where she lapsed into insanity. Escaping the convent, she is pursued by guilt:

> Her broken vows in wild disorder roll,
> And stick like serpents in her trembling soul;
> THOUGHT, what art thou? of thee she boasts no more,
> O'erwhelm'd, thou dy'st amid the wilder roar
> Of lawless anarchy, which sweeps the soul,
> Whilst her drown'd faculties like pebbles roll,
> Unloos'd, uptorn, by whirlwinds of despair,
> Each well-taught moral now dissolves in air,
> Dishevel'd, lo! her beauteous tresses fly,
> And the wild glance now fills the staring eye.
>
> (279–88)

The poem continues in this vein for a few more lines, then abruptly resolves itself. The wild eyes of the madwoman seek in vain for lost memories. The idea of memory, the speaker says, "fills my soul with sympathetic pain" (294). She urges herself to write no more about her lost past, and the poem forthwith ends.

In the extended sequence about Louisa, the poem seeks a double reader response. First we are invited to react with horrified sympathy to the evoked spectacle of the madwoman. The poet reaches for extreme rhetoric to move her readers: broken vows sticking like serpents, drowned faculties like pebbles tossed about – images with the kind of extravagance that often marks seventeenth-century poetry. The display of loss and suffering presumably arouses our pity. So does the sketched situation of the speaker, who, she hints, suffers from remembering just as Louisa suffers from inability to remember. Moreover, her soul filled with sympathetic pain deserves attention as much as that of the woman with whom she sympathizes. The Louisa sequence makes large claims on its readers' feelings. Its devices would recur in many of the period's poems.

The ambiguous pleasure of sympathetic pain, the desired response here, entails dwelling on the spectacle of the distracted woman, then contemplating yet another troubled female, the poem's speaker. Thus Yearsley summons a kind of voyeurism, presumably free of the guilt that real-life voyeurism might involve, but like its real-life counterpart an inlet to satisfaction.

Eighteenth-century commentators on the literature of sensibility frequently felt troubled by this aspect of such writing. The moral justification for deliberately stimulating a reader's pity and sympathy rested on the theory that these feelings would ultimately find expression in acts of benevolence toward beneficiaries in the real world. But another possibility occurred to certain critics: poems and fictions designed to stimulate their readers' tender emotions might in fact exhaust the emotion they raised. Far from stimulating benevolence, perhaps, such poetry could offer an imaginary outlet for feeling that would substitute for active concern with the world's hardships and injustices.

The account of Louisa, with its evocation of two suffering women, might conceivably stimulate a reader to try to ameliorate the misery of insanity and to be alert to the human pain that may lie concealed beneath a surface of propriety. Equally plausibly, it could merely encourage the reader to weep over the sufferings of the young woman doomed to madness and over the vaguer pain of the woman who writes about her. Nothing in the poem itself either urges or precludes wider reflection.

The late eighteenth century's poetry of intense feeling risked the charge of self-indulgence in its writers and of encouraging self-indulgence in readers. Charlotte Smith faced much criticism for her almost entirely melancholy tone; she justified herself autobiographically, claiming that her personal misery kept her from adopting anything but a gloomy voice in her writing. No longer did a poem on melancholy typically invoke a vague power infusing the landscape: now proclamations of suffering called for intense response. Smith, or her persona in the sonnets, claims her sorrows as an implicit mark of her superiority. Thus she writes a sonnet on "The sleeping woodman," describing the man who rests his "careless head" (6) on bark and moss and sinks to "momentary rest" (8). "Would I could taste, like this unthinking hind," she continues, "A sweet forgetfulness of human care" (11–12). But her characterization of the sleeping man suggests that she thinks herself made of finer stuff. Her difference supplies her inspiration and her invariable topic. The depth and grandeur of her sorrows provide her consistent theme.

Others had evoked Marie Antoinette as an emblem of suffering; it remained for Smith to suggest that her own sufferings make her uniquely able to comprehend the queen's.

> Ah! who knows,
> From sad experience, more than I, to feel
> For thy desponding spirit, as it sinks
> Beneath procrastinated fears for those
> More dear to thee than life!
> (*The Emigrants* 2: 169–73)

When she proclaims Marie Antoinette's "eminence / Of misery" (2: 173–74), it is difficult not to think that she would like to compete for the position.

For many twenty-first-century readers, as for many earlier ones, Smith's insistence may seem irritating. Yet she achieves remarkable effects as a result. Here is the octave of one of her best-known sonnets, *Written in the churchyard at Middleton in Sussex*:

> Press'd by the Moon, mute arbitress of tides,
>   While the loud equinox its power combines,
>   The sea no more its swelling surge confines,
> But o'er the shrinking land sublimely rides.
> The wild blast, rising from the Western cave,
>   Drives the huge billows from their heaving bed;
>   Tears from their grassy tombs the village dead,
> And breaks the silent sabbath of the grave!
>
> (1–8)

The lines supply a preamble to one more statement of the writer's hopelessness: the bones torn from their graves cannot be troubled by the noise of wind and water, "While I am doom'd – by life's long storm opprest, / To gaze with envy on their gloomy rest" (13–14). The storm described in the sonnet, however, evokes exhilaration rather than oppression. Its winds and waves epitomize energy. The highly charged adverb *sublimely*, connecting the scene with power, grandeur, and excitement, betrays the speaker's delight in the phenomena she evokes. A voiceless female power releases the sea from confinement. As the blast and billows tear the dead from their graves, the violation of that "sabbath," like the sea's unleashing, seems more thrilling than reprehensible. Despite her claim to envy the "gloomy rest" of the dead, the speaker clearly identifies with the violence.

Charlotte Smith's identification with power perhaps expresses itself most clearly in the act of writing the sonnets, a form of agency that she eagerly embraced, adding ever more poems to successive editions. Some of her most conventional poems (e.g., *Written at Penshurst, in autumn 1788*) recall the Renaissance tradition of celebrating poetry's power to withstand the ravages of time. In several sonnets, she discusses her own commitment to writing – often in ambivalent terms. Thus, the first of the sonnets begins, "The partial Muse has from my earliest hours / Smiled on the rugged path I'm doom'd to tread." After the opening quatrain, however, it proclaims that those "Who never learn'd her dear delusive art" (6) remain happier than the poets. To enforce this message in the concluding couplet, Smith borrows from Pope:

> Ah! then, how dear the Muse's favours cost,
> *If those paint sorrow best – who feel it most!*
> (13–14)

This sonnet suggests the nature of the poet's project as a whole. Feeling authorizes poetry, in her announced view. Sorrow, as an intense feeling, has a special claim to poetic inspiration. The Muse, intimately linked with suffering, both encourages and profits from the anguish of her devotees. The sonnet defines the relevant form of suffering with some precision: the pain of pity, of friendship, or of love. In this inaugural poem of a long series, Smith claims a sorrow devoid of self-absorption, intimately connected with others: in effect, a form of that eighteenth-century virtue, sympathy. The implications of "the rugged path I'm doom'd to tread," with its hint of self-pity, vanish or are reinterpreted by the sonnet's conclusion.

The insistence on unhappiness associated with commitment to poetry, like the deploring of the storm in the sonnet on the Middleton

churchyard, effectively emphasizes a feeling opposed to the one proclaimed. If the writing of verse entails consciousness of sorrow, it
also creates its own exhilaration and a barely concealed claim of
superiority. The final line adapted from Pope makes the point: only
the man or woman with unusual capacity for feeling can hope to achieve
the "best" poetry. The Muse's favors may cost dearly, but the sonnet
emphasizes the vital presence of those favors.

By asserting emotional sensitivity as a doom – the Muse's demand
– rather than a choice or an innate capacity, Smith defends in advance
against the charges of self-centeredness and self-gratification that would
in fact be leveled at her. In her most self-absorbed moments, she
suggests, she serves only as handmaiden to the Muse. The thorns
pierce her bosom; she'd rather smell the flowers. But her stance
differs markedly from that of Anne Finch, early in the century, or
Thomas Gray, in the middle period. Finch depicts herself as struggling
against the spleen, with its attendant sorrow; Smith embraces her
melancholy as personal and poetic destiny. Gray's self-representation
as depressed isolate occupies the peripheries, not the centers, of his
poems: the personal, he assumes, matters less to a reading audience
than does the general. Smith appears to assume just the contrary.

The position of suffering she announces in the first sonnet persists
throughout the long sequence, enabling the poet often to devise new
twists on familiar themes. Thus, in *The return of the nightingale*, she evokes
the warm breeze of spring, the song of the nightingale, the power of
hope and love – only to declare their irrelevance.

> With transport, once, sweet bird! I hail'd thy lay,
>     And bade thee welcome to our shades again,
> To charm the wandering poet's pensive way
>     And soothe the solitary lover's pain;
> But now! – such evils in my lot combine,
> As shut my languid sense – to Hope's dear voice and thine!
>
> (9–14)

Similarly, in a sonnet *To tranquillity*, the poet declares that the quality
she apostrophizes is rarely to be found: perhaps by the cradle of a sleeping infant, perhaps by a deathbed, "Where the poor languid sufferer
– hopes to die" (8). She imagines discovering tranquility herself only
after death, in a "heavenly scene" (10) where care and anguish, hope

and vain regret have vanished, "And Memory – lost in happiness serene, / [Shall] Repeat no more – that misery has been mine!" (13–14). If memory recalls happy scenes, in the 92 sonnets, the poet typically uses the recollection to contrast with her present disconsolate state. If memory reminds of past misery, it can be labeled another of the burdens on the sufferer's existence.

In the sonnets Charlotte Smith employs many metaphors to evoke the unhappiness of her situation. One notable instance has her elaborating the situation of a "captive escaped in the wilds of America" (the poem's title). He imagines horrors all around him,

> And every hollow blast that shakes the wood,
>   Speaks to his trembling heart of woe and death.
> With horror fraught, and desolate dismay,
>   On such a wanderer falls the starless night.
>
> (7–10)

This captive's role as metaphor emerges only in the final quatrain: he sees a light that guides him to "some amicable fort" (12); as he blesses the light, so the speaker of the poem blesses the "cheering light" (14) of another woman's friendship. Retrospectively, we realize that the captive's suffering provides a figure for the speaker's anguish.

The state of feeling is familiar: we may readily understand why early readers complained of tonal monotony. We may understand also, though, why they enthusiastically bought Smith's collections of verse. If her frequent exclamation points, like her diction, insist that we take the speaker's feelings seriously, the poet's varied strategies for delineating her emotional predicament enforce the message. The verbal dramatization of emotion articulated a new basis for valuing individuals. Smith's persona not only demanded attention for her misery; she also insisted that poetic inspiration required such misery. Domestic suffering – not just the anguish of unrequited love or the imaginatively charged sense of fear – merited a reader's consideration. By extension, readers might feel that their own psychic upheavals likewise deserved extended contemplation.

Despite the psychological monotony of the sonnets as a group, Smith proved adept also at evoking less dismal feelings. Her long poem, *Beachy Head*, for instance, considers memory from a complicated perspective, generating feeling by creating conjunctions of time. The poem begins with the speaker imagining herself as sitting on the "stupendous summit" of Beachy Head, a "rock sublime" (1). It emphasizes this as a locale of the imagination: such sitting is something the speaker "would" do (4, 12), not something she claims to have done. Were she in this remarkable location, she continues, "Fancy should go forth" (4) and recreate the process of divine creation that generated the earth, the sea, and the sun. The Biblical scene soon merges with an imagined local scene that in turn combines with an immediately present vision, signaled by "now" (18), in which the observer, her location unspecified, watches rising sun, rising tide, and fish-seeking wild fowl.

Although she does not directly articulate the emotion accompanying imaginary and actual contemplation of a grand natural scene, the speaker conveys calm, wonder, and awe. To gaze over the sea, meditating on cliffs and birds and sun, separates one from petty daily cares. The poem's tone becomes increasingly elevated as it evokes natural harmony, moon, and sun, calling on various abstractions: "aspiring Fancy," which wanders "sublime thro' visionary vales" (84, 85); Contemplation, imagined as sitting high on the same rock that the speaker has fancied as her own site (117); and Memory, which retraces ancient history (119 ff.). All further the sense of remoteness from the everyday and the atmosphere of exaltation.

The pleasure of less grandiose memory also plays an important part in *Beachy Head*. A short passage on "Haunts of my youth" (297) repeats the word *pleasant* and conveys, again without explicit statement, the emotion of pleasure. Vivid specific detail, such as the tufts of wool from wandering lambs held on the spiny branches of thorn trees, convince the reader of the speaker's claim, "I behold ye yet!" (298). The act of memory itself generates pleasure, the poet suggests, and individual memories set forth in the poem sketch a pleasant past.

Past and present frequently mingle. A rural cottage, its garden lovingly described, recalls earlier delight in such gardens. Memory of the gardens calls up other memories, of nature in wilder forms, wildflowers, brooks, and woodland. Here the verb *loved* occurs twice: "I loved [Nature's] rudest scenes" (347); "I loved to trace the brooks" (354). Again, repetition signals emotion: love for the landscape, past and present, in all its manifestations.

For all the stress on pleasant memories, the plaintive note of the sonnets recurs here as well.

> *I* once was happy, when while yet a child,
> I learn'd to love these upland solitudes,
> And, when elastic as the mountain air,
> To my light spirit, care was yet unknown
> And evil unforeseen: – Early it came,
> And childhood scarcely passed, I was condemned,
> A guiltless exile, silently to sigh,
> While Memory, with faithful pencil, drew
> The contrast.
>
> (282–90)

Wedded to her melancholy persona, Smith cannot forego reminders of her unhappy lot – an important part of her poetic stock.

Although her novels proved more profitable than her poetry, Smith found a consistent and enthusiastic audience for her verse. The pleasure of reading melancholy poetry of feeling, readily available toward the end of the eighteenth century, depends partly on identification – readers unhappy themselves can escape into the unhappiness of another – and partly on a kind of cost-free pity. No matter how close the identification between a poet and her persona, the speaker of a poem functions essentially as a fictional character. To pity such a character neither demands nor allows action. The reader, therefore, can enjoy the release of real or metaphorical tears with no accompanying obligation and no attendant shame. To mourn the distresses of others testifies to one's delicacy of feeling and capacity for sympathy.

As the idea of mourning for a character's situation suggests, explicit or suppressed narrative underlies much poetry of painful feeling. *Beachy Head* alludes to a sketchy story about a child suddenly separated from the countryside she loves and forced to live in the city as an adult. The *Elegiac Sonnets* hint a story of loss and betrayal, which Smith elaborates with increasing specificity in her prefaces to successive editions. Published between 1784 and 1797, the *Sonnets* originally appeared with a brief preface expressing the writer's hope to find readers with "sensibility of heart." Not until the preface to the sixth edition, dated 1792, does Smith explicitly declare the nature of her sorrows. She records a dialogue between herself and a friend who delicately suggests "a more cheerful style of composition." Originally, Smith replies, she "struck the chords of the melancholy lyre" not for the sake of the public but for herself: "I wrote mournfully because I was unhappy." Nine years have passed, she continues, and she remains unhappy, because the "Honourable Men" who promised to procure for her children their rightful inheritance have not done so. She does not describe her further sorrows, "of a domestic and painful nature," but insists that while they continue, a more cheerful style will remain unavailable to her. In the 1797 preface to Volume II, she adds to allusions to her financial misfortunes the news that a son has been maimed in battle; her most beloved daughter has died; and her youngest son has been deprived of education.

References to the lost daughter recur in the sonnets, as do comments about the men who have betrayed her financially. The back story of a woman heroically struggling against personal misfortune of various kinds lends imaginative substance to the poetry's melancholy tone. Readers thus can identify with or pity a half-imaginary, half-real person situated in a complex narrative texture. Smith's successive elaborations of her own story underline the new place of the personal in poetry. The standards of decorum that had governed poets early in the century were shifting. Within a few years, Wordsworth would begin work on a quasi-epic for the nineteenth century: *The Prelude*, a history of his own mind containing, like *Beachy Head*, many nostalgic sequences about a childhood in nature. Over the course of the eighteenth century, an enlarged sense of the grounds of public interest had developed.

The next chapter will consider more fully the place of narrative in late eighteenth-century poetry, but its connection to the elevation of feeling as primary subject for verse makes it part, too, of this chapter's material. Narrative concerns underlie another important sonnet sequence of the late century, a sequence also primarily committed to the celebration of feeling. Mary Robinson, notorious as one-time mistress of the Prince of Wales, in 1796 published *Sappho and Phaon*, a series of forty-four sonnets, most of them in the voice of Sappho, that reflected on the legendary love affair in which Phaon ultimately abandoned and betrayed his mistress. The sonnets do not actually tell the story, although they suggest its salient aspects. They tell instead of Sappho's reactions before, during, and after her liaison with Phaon.

In an "Account of Sappho" prefixed to the poems, Robinson makes clear the reason for her interest in the Greek poet. She cites Addison in praise of the "vivid glow of sensibility" that marked Sappho's poems and adds, about the poems, "They possessed none of the artificial decorations of a feigned passion; they were the genuine effusions of a supremely enlightened soul, labouring to subdue a fatal enchantment;

and vainly opposing the conscious pride of illustrious fame, against the warm susceptibility of a generous bosom." Her own poems' project focused on conveying and implicitly justifying Sappho's "warm susceptibility" and on dramatizing her conflict. Sappho's enlightened soul, in Robinson's version, comes to equate moral excellence with vulnerability to feeling.

Not, however, at the beginning of the sonnet sequence. Early poems in the group depict the temple of chastity and the bower of pleasure, with apparent ambivalence about the value of commitment to either. Sonnet IV records conflicting commitments to love and to art. By Sonnet V, however, the speaker appears to have made a clear choice. The sonnet begins, "O! How can LOVE exulting Reason quell!" It declares the "wretch" lost who "Wastes the short Summer of delicious days" (6) in love, and it warns those who dwell with "holy Innocence" (9) to "Tempt not the path where pleasure's flow'ry wile / In sweet, but pois'nous fetters, holds the mind" (13–14). The lover must relinquish reason, fame, and innocence – all in order to dwell "In passion's thorny wild, forlorn" (8). Unmistakably, a bad choice.

Yet despite the clear negative import assigned to the choice of love, the sonnet, like Smith's on the churchyard, conveys the speaker's attraction to the negative side. The exclamatory first line, declaring Love's power over "exulting Reason," sounds exultant itself. With power to subdue also "each nobler passion" (2), Love seems an irresistible force, with all passion's energy. Those committed, in contrast, to Innocence have "Each thought compos'd, and ev'ry wish resign'd" (12). They seem in comparison to the devotees of Love a pallid lot. As the speaker warns them not to attempt the flowery path of pleasure, on which their minds would be fettered, she implicitly raises the question of whether thought or feeling, mind or emotion, has more importance. That question had been raised at the beginning of the century, when the answer seemed self-evident: as Pope put it, reason was the mariners' card by which one steered, passion the gale that provided the energy for motion. In Robinson's treatment, nothing is self-evident. If the choice of love is unmistakably bad from a rational standpoint, one must remember that other standpoints remain conceivable.

And other standpoints duly show up. The clear narrative pattern supporting the sonnet sequence makes it possible to see and ponder connections among individual poems and to perceive the emotional paradoxes and inconsistencies that mark the course of the love affair.

Sonnet XI begins, also in exclamatory fashion, "O! Reason! vaunted Sov'reign of the mind! / Thou pompous vision with a sounding name!" No longer is Reason capable of binding and subduing:

> Can'st thou, the soul's rebellious passions tame?
> Can'st thou in spells the vagrant fancy bind?
> Ah, no! capricious as the wav'ring wind
> Are sighs of Love that dim thy boasted flame.
>
> (3–6)

The operative forces – Reason, Love, Pleasure, fame – remain the same as in the earlier poem, with the addition of Folly, Fate, Frenzy, and hope, but the dynamic among them has shifted.

We do not customarily read sonnet sequences in an effort to ascertain the proper place of reason in the human psyche, nor is the proper place of reason finally the central issue of Robinson's work. The conflicting views of reason's place and power belong to the individual psychic drama at the poetry's center. Sonnet sequences detailing the travails of love appeared frequently during the Renaissance, Shakespeare's being the best-known among them, but such a series of poems, intensely focused on the varying responses of a single consciousness, would have been inconceivable earlier in the eighteenth century. Robinson's bold enterprise avoids taking for granted the period's moral truisms. Her investigation of the wild vagaries of consciousness uses love as its pretext rather than its subject. The poems explore the full meaning of that vivid glow of sensibility that Addison attributed to Sappho. They arguably justify Robinson's claim that Sappho – the Sappho she imagines – possesses a supremely enlightened soul.

Individual poems, as well as the entire sequence, gather lyrical intensity.

> Love steals unheeded o'er the tranquil mind,
> As Summer breezes fan the sleeping main.
> (Sonnet XVII, 1–2)

> My tresses all unbound, nor gems display,
> Nor scents Arabian! on my path no flow'rs
> Imbibe the morn's resuscitating pow'rs,
> For one blank sorrow, saddens all my way!
> (Sonnet XXI, 5–8)

O THOU! meek Orb! that stealing o'er the dale
   Cheer'st with thy modest beams the moon of night!
   On the smooth lake diffusing silv'ry light,
Sublimely still, and beautifully pale!
What can thy cool and placid eye avail,
   Where fierce despair absorbs the mental sight . . . ?
                    (Sonnet XXIV, 1–6)

Robinson imagines the consciousness ravaged by love to be vividly aware of the natural world outside as well as of the passions within. She writes of both with exactitude and grace.

One of the most affecting sonnets (Sonnet XXVIII) concerns the painful pleasure of memory. At the outset, the speaker rejects the "sophistry" (1) of those who recommend reflection and hope as remedies against care. Neither is relevant, she says, to the situation of the deserted lover who wishes to linger in the spot associated with earlier joys.

He never lov'd, who could not muse and sigh,
   Spangling the sacred turf with frequent tears,
   Where the small rivulet, that ripples by,
   Recalls the scenes of past and happier years,
   When, on its banks he watch'd the speaking eye,
And one sweet smile o'erpaid an age of fears!
                    (9–14)

The quiet tone, the exactitude of *Spangling*, the lack of emphasis on self: all contribute to a resonant evocation of the psyche's longing to preserve even the source of amorous pain.

The sequence culminates, as does the legend of Sappho's life, in the protagonist's suicidal leap from a cliff. Sonnet XLIII has her standing on the cliff, reflecting on what will follow her plunge. She reacts to the immediate beauty of the sinking sun and the moon, then compares Reason to the moon, imagining its power as calming "rebellious Fancy's fev'rish dream" (11) – presumably after her death. Mysteriously, she appears to imagine herself as composing new poetry after her death: "Then shall my Lyre disdain love's dread control, / And loftier passions, prompt the loftier theme!" (13–14). Only in an imagined state is it possible for the poet to "disdain" the love that always exercises control when it appears. Passion energizes poetry, but "loftier passions" have a hard time surviving in competition with erotic love.

The final sonnet (XLIV), spoken in the voice of the poet who has composed this record of Sappho and who has previously ventriloquized her predecessor's voice, claims "Sympathy" as her inspiration, celebrates "Sky-born VIRTUE" (9), and promises for Virtue "more than mortal raptures" (13) in heaven. This startling retreat from the unconventionality of the preceding poems protects the poet from accusations of immorality: she has only tried to convey a sympathetic understanding of Sappho's ways of thinking and feeling; her real commitment is to virtue. It also underlines the point suggested by Sappho's pre-suicide meditation: no hope exists in this world for stable reconciliation of the claims of reason and passion, thrilling tumult and restorative calm. One can only alternate, not resolve their contradictory demands and possibilities.

Another popular late-century series of sonnets, by William Lisle Bowles, likewise displayed a panoply of feeling. Love does not here serve as ruling passion, nor does Bowles, like Charlotte Smith, insist on the pain of his own experience. A gentle melancholy prevails in many of the poems – melancholy often more enjoyable than not. *Sonnet: Written at Tinemouth, Northumberland, after a Tempestuous Voyage* begins with the speaker musing about the fearful aspects of the voyage just past, in contrast with the tranquility of the ocean he now contemplates and the smiling sun that beams on the scene. The sestet quite gratuitously brings in a vaguely personified figure of "sorrow":

> Sooth'd by the scene, ev'n thus on sorrow's breast
> A kindred stillness steals, and bids her rest;
> Whilst sad airs stilly sigh along the deep,
> Like melodies which mourn upon the lyre,
> Wak'd by the breeze, and as they mourn, expire.
>
> (10–14)

The sad airs and mourning melodies, like the scene of quiet sun-touched ocean, have a soothing effect. Sorrow becomes aestheticized, a kind of emotional beauty.

Similarly, in *Sonnet: To the River Wensbeck* Bowles imagines the "plaintive song" (3) of the river. That imagining enables him to listen to the wind "And think I hear meek sorrow's plaint, reclin'd / O'er the forsaken tomb of one she lov'd!" (6–7). Again, sorrow provides a decorative accessory. The sonnet continues to reiterate the pleasure that the scene of river and woods provides the weary passer-by – who thanks the river with a tear. That tear of thanks epitomizes the way in which Bowles transforms conventional signs of suffering into gratifying moments. Phrases like "melancholy musick" and "mournful magic" (*Written at Ostend, July 22, 1787*, 7, 11) express the intimate relation between pleasure and pain that provides the foundation for many of the sonnets.

A longer poem that pays homage to Gray's churchyard elegy, Bowles's *Elegy Written at the Hot-Wells, Bristol*, makes more complicated use of the pleasure–pain motif. Bristol Hot-Wells was a spa where the ill came in search of healing. The elegy dwells on the contrast between the "gladsome ray" (18) of early sun and the sick folk who droop and sigh and imagine themselves in the tomb. Then the poet goes on to imagine other possible denizens of the scene:

> Some beauteous maid, deceiv'd in early youth,
>     Pale o'er yon spring may hang in mute distress;
> Who dreamt of faith, of happiness, and truth,
>     Of love – that virtue would protect and bless.
>                                         (53–56)

There is also a "musing youth" (57), stricken too young with sorrow for a lost friend. Youth and maid alike, imaginary though they are, provide objects of contemplation for the poet and for his readers, sufficiently distanced for aesthetic effect, but offering also the satisfaction of benevolent sympathy. The speaker goes on to mourn his dead friend Thomas Russell, then to generalize about how many friends of his (and, presumably, the reader's) youth have already died. He survives, pondering his past, marked alike by pleasure and by tears. The poem ends on a positive note: the speaker declares himself thankful for landscape and sun and leaves the scene for "the crouded world, where fortune guides" (99).

Bowles's verse suggests with particular clarity the importance and the appeal of late eighteenth-century poetry of feeling. In its stress on the vagaries of personal consciousness, it speaks to and for a period of increasing individualism. What an individual human being felt could now be imagined as of interest to others. If one's own emotions seemed fascinating, the interior life of others might hold comparable fascination: what had once been assumed as private became stuff for public consumption.

The power of this poetry, however, did not depend only on valuing the individual. On the contrary: the "sensibility" to which it was designed to appeal was understood as involving high responsiveness to the needs and feelings of others. When Bowles invokes the sick and imagines the disappointed, he solicits the sympathy of his readers – even as Charlotte Smith invites sympathy for the wrongs she has suffered and Robinson asks our sympathy for Sappho's complex emotional life. The feelings represented in the poetry include sentiments responding to the distress of others. Moreover, poems often provide hinted or narrated stimuli for the reader to react in comparable fashion. They thus both model and provoke the forms of sensibility that many in this period admired most.

They do not, of course, provide the same satisfactions as those offered by such earlier works as *The Dunciad*. The satiric energies poetically active in the first half of the eighteenth century generated verse that issued from and solicited powerful emotion – emotion such as contempt and loathing, or possibly fear. By the century's end, love poetry, epitomized by Robinson's sonnet sequence, assumed a more conspicuous place. Such poetry had never altogether disappeared, but most post-seventeenth-century love poems had assumed highly conventionalized forms; they did not inhabit the poetic mainstream. Now the kind of emotion that seemed appropriate to poetry had changed. No longer was the welfare of the community dominant as impetus or subject for verse. The workings of the individual consciousness had become more engaging.

# 13

# Narrative and Reflection

Even as openly lyric utterance became more common in eighteenth-century poetry, emphasis on narrative also increased. Robinson published an entire volume of *Lyrical Tales* right at the turn of the century (1800); Charlotte Smith both composed and translated fables. Two of the late century's most popular short poems, William Cowper's tale of John Gilpin and Robert Burns's *Tam o'Shanter*, relied on narrative frameworks. Both strikingly demonstrate how the metrics and movement of a poem can intensify – even create – its narrative interest.

*The Diverting History of John Gilpin, Showing How He Went Farther Than He Intended, and Came Safe Home Again* summarizes its entire action in its title. The story could hardly be more trivial: a man and his wife plan to celebrate their wedding anniversary at dinner in a neighboring town; because the "chaise and pair" have room for only the wife, her children, her sister, and the sister's child, John must ride horseback; the horse, borrowed from a friend, runs away with him; after losing two hats, two wigs, his cloak, and two bottles of wine, he finally arrives safely at the inn. Yet this ridiculous narrative holds the reader's interest for 53 quatrains because of the rollicking verse in which it is embodied. That verse, couched in idiomatic language and moving fast, constantly reassures us that we are not required to ponder anything and that no disaster will ensue.

Even more striking is the effect of language and meter in *Tam o'Shanter*. The story told here might easily be imagined as bearing far different import. It tells of a drunken Scotsman who, after an evening of pleasure with friends in a tavern, rides homeward on a stormy night, only to find himself confronted with a coven of witches, vigorously dancing to music played by a large black dog, with Satan presiding over the scene. Although most of the witches are hags, they include one comely young girl in a short petticoat, who dances so wildly that Tam, forgetting himself, cheers her on. The scene dissolves; then the entire horde pursue the interloper, whose horse, Maggie, runs so valiantly that she just escapes, at the cost of her tail. Like John Gilpin, Tam arrives safely home.

It's not hard to imagine this story told in another key: a frightening campfire tale, perhaps. Witches are scary. Satan is not to be laughed at. But Burns's tetrameter couplets, racing cheerfully on, remove all potential terror, even when they prophesy the worst:

> Ah, *Tam*! Ah, *Tam*! thou'll get thy fairin!
> In hell they'll roast thee like a herrin!
> In vain thy *Kate* awaits thy comin!
> *Kate* soon will be a woefu' woman!
> (201–04)

The atmosphere of comedy comes partly from the earthy simile – being roasted in hell like a herring – and partly from the plethora of exclamation points, but mostly from the sheer speed with which the poem foretells multiplied disasters. That speed never varies, whether Burns reports drinking bouts or journeys home or horrid spectacles. It's all a romp, the meter tells us, and the appended moral underlines the point, warning against the joys of drink and of thinking about short petticoats.

Both poems accomplish more than joking. *John Gilpin* implicitly reflects on the relations between husbands and wives, suggesting that henpecked husbands may yet love their wives, who in turn care profoundly for them, and pointing out also that spectators often see little of the truth. Those who watch John's headlong career think him racing or consider him a highwayman. The reader who considers him merely a fool is comparably misguided, missing the genuine good humor that characterizes him throughout. *Tam o'Shanter* considers the relations of men to one another, as well as to women, evoking the warmth and fellowship of the tavern evening – and the extreme irritation of the deserted wife. Just before Tam leaves for home, the narrator summarizes:

> Kings may be blest, but *Tam* was glorious,
> O'er a' the ills o' life victorious!
> (56–57)

His sense of triumph sustains him through the storm, but his native lasciviousness gets him into trouble: punishment for drunkenness and for repeatedly abandoning his wife, but hardly serious punishment after all. The poem purveys a large tolerance for human weakness, and an apparent willingness to accept even the diabolic.

Such playful works as these call attention to the fact that narrative poetry could function in different keys and for different purposes. Earlier in the century, such poets as Pope had incorporated short stories in long reflective poems, usually to provide positive or negative examples in the service of satire. As the century neared its close, embedded narratives continued to appear, elucidating feeling and judgment in diverse contexts. They proved useful to intensify lyric as well as satiric response. Poets showed increasing awareness of how the incorporation of stories might help in the pursuit of a moral or emotional project.

*The Deserted Village* once more epitomizes in some respects the period's methods. Goldsmith's vision of a lost idyllic past includes various nameless figures whose histories and practices represent the rural virtues threatened by modern encroachments. The most extensive vignette concerns the village preacher, whose described activities center on alleviating the cares of others.

> He watched and wept, he prayed and felt, for all.
> And, as a bird each fond endearment tries,
> To tempt its new fledged offspring to the skies;
> He tried each art, reproved each dull delay,
> Allured to brighter worlds, and led the way.
>
> (178–82)

Weeping, praying, and feeling, central in the clergyman's fulfilling of his Christian functions, are valued activities throughout the poem, which attempts to arouse emotion in response to public policy and national change. The analogy to the bird both stresses the preacher's tender feelings and allies him with the natural order that recent changes have threatened.

Considered as a story, the account of the preacher (as of the schoolteacher and of the "wretched matron" [133] forced to pick her firewood from thorn trees) has a beginning and end but no dramatic middle. The beginning, in each case, depends on a specific locality, a lost edifice of the village or the sight of the matron bending in labor. The end consists in a reminder that the past is past. The middle includes numerous details of daily activity but deliberately refrains from dramatic emphasis, as it refrains from sharply individualized characterization. Although the stories contain moments of specificity and immediacy – children running after the preacher at the end of his sermon, plucking his gown, "to share the good man's smile" (186); the list of the schoolmaster's intellectual skills (210–12) – their place in the poem depends on their characters' claim to typicality. Clergymen were like this in the old, good villages, they suggest; schoolmasters behaved in this fashion.

Despite lacking the drama and the particularity that we may expect to mark effective narrative, the little stories serve important purposes in *The Deserted Village*. They root the speaker's complaints firmly in the human. We feel sufficiently acquainted with the schoolmaster to smile over his pride in his knowledge – and to regret the loss of his vocation. The good preacher who soothes the wandering beggar impresses by his charity; the prospect for the villagers seems the more dismal because it presumably does not include his presence. At the very least, these tales provide signposts for the kinds of feeling the poet wishes to generate.

Crabbe, setting out to refute Goldsmith in *The Village*, explores narrative possibilities in ways that foreshadow his accomplishment in the nineteenth century, which would center more firmly on narrative. Goldsmith had provided a sentimental vignette of a "poor houseless shivering female" (329), who once "wept at tales of innocence distrest" (330) but now has lost her virtue and her friends. Beset by cold and rain, she lies down near her betrayer's door, with heavy heart deploring her decision to leave the lovely village. Crabbe turns this figure into material for a simile, comparing the look of the betrayed maiden to that of the blooming weeds that substitute for useful crops.

> So looks the nymph whom wretched arts adorn,
> Betray'd by man, then left for man to scorn;
> Whose cheek in vain assumes the mimic rose,
> While her sad eyes the troubled breast disclose.
> (*The Village* 1: 79–82)

The economical couplets tell a familiar story. The poet both takes its familiarity for granted and invites new attention to it by his stress on emotion – the man's scorn, the woman's troubled breast. Although the simile depends on appearances, the garishness of the woman's cosmetics and apparel analogous to the misleading splendor of the weeds, the poem remains vague about the betrayed nymph's appearance, aside from the "mimic rose" of her cheek and the sad eyes that suggest a meaning quite different from that of the weeds. Weeds presumably do not have feelings. The woman treated as a weed does. The story implied by Crabbe's two couplets comments on destructive social assumptions as well as makes a rather facile visual comparison. It arouses feeling in order to make its comment.

True to his debunking purpose, Crabbe tells stories of consistently negative import. When he promises to "paint the cot, As truth will paint it, and as bards will not" (1: 52–53), he declares himself taught by the examples around him; his little narratives transmit those examples to the reader. Thus we learn of the village athletes who have turned into smugglers; of the unusually accomplished worker who, weak with age, now finds himself disdained by rich and poor alike; of the doctor, "A potent quack, long vers'd in human ills, / Who first insults the victim whom he kills" (284–85); and of the youthful clergyman who prefers hunting to attending his parishioners. All exemplify a corrupted rural society. All, like the characters of *The Deserted Village*, inhabit narratives of generalized import and enforce by feeling the significance of Crabbe's passionate description.

Charlotte Smith, whose numerous melancholy sonnets might lead one to think that her interests focus entirely on feeling, in fact makes extensive use of embedded narratives, which play important parts in her two longest poems, *The Emigrants* and *Beachy Head*. A shorter piece, rather misleadingly entitled *Elegy*, demonstrates her skill at implying a story not fully narrated. She apparently lacked confidence in her success at this exercise, since she included in an appendix to the fifth edition of *Elegiac Sonnets* (1789) a summary of the implicit story, but *Elegy* in fact makes its story quite clear and gains power by its indirection.

Smith's elegy imitates Gray's in its stanzaic form, but the quatrains work to very different effect in the later poem, as even a single example will show:

> Part, raging waters part, and shew beneath,
> In your dread caves, his pale and mangled form;

> Now, while the demons of despair and death
> Ride on the blast, and urge the howling storm!
>
> (37–40)

The soothing melody of Gray's metrical patterns here gives way to a more spasmodic movement, appropriate to the disturbed consciousness of the young woman who speaks all but the concluding stanza. The lurid imagery of mangled corpse, demons, and storm reinforce the uneasiness of the uneven rhythms.

The speaker, a woman suffering from the loss of her lover, who has been torn away from her by an avaricious father and has subsequently drowned, stands by the tomb of the lover's father, on whom she invokes vengeance. As in Smith's sonnet written in the churchyard, the angry sea overwhelms the land and bears away the father's bones, as well as the despairing woman herself, who has expressed her longing for death. The sufferer is represented as totally absorbed in her grief, unconcerned to communicate her misery or her story, addressing the wind and waves and her dead lover. She speaks, in other words, only to those who cannot hear.

Yet her words appear to have mysterious power. At the beginning of the final stanza, when, suddenly, "The ocean hears" (65), the waves come and tear away "the proud agressor's tomb" (67); and the woman is granted the peace of death, which she has sought. The event is by no means implausible: a woman who stands on the shore in the midst of a violent storm may well suffer injury or death as a result. Yet Smith's poem leaves a small residue of mystery. Has the ocean indeed "heard"? What can that conceivably mean? As metaphorical or as literal possibility, the ocean's responsiveness insists on the power of female passion. Letting her story emerge entirely by means of the feelings of a participant in it, the poet finds a new way to emphasize emotion's importance, suggesting feeling as the source of action and of meaning. Story matters less than the emotion that generates and explains it, yet narrative also lends new authority to feeling as poetic subject.

*The Emigrants* employs a loose narrative framework for a politicized topic. Set in 1792 and 1793 (each of the two books is assigned a different date), the poem contemplates the French Revolution by pondering the situation of the Catholic clergy who fled the country when the revolutionaries abolished religion. English readers of the time might be expected both to deplore the horrors of the Revolution and to retain considerable distrust for Catholicism in all its manifestations. Smith, however, invites sympathy for the exiles, even while she suggests that they have engaged in misguided practices in the past.

The poem's intricate plan depends on the interweaving of three stories, none of them fully told. The story of the exiles, narrated from the point of view of an English Protestant observer, yields frequently to hints about the life story of the poem's speaker, a negative progression from childhood pleasure to adult suffering. The third story, also one of negative progression, tells of England's political decay. The mingling of the three implies an argument about the inevitable implication of the political in the personal. The narrator's misery in adulthood derives from the injustice of the legal system; the exiles' misery reflects political developments in their native country.

Before the emigrants designated by the title make an appearance in the poem, we learn about the narrator's unhappiness. *The Emigrants* sets its scene elaborately, first with a "stage direction" designating location and time, then with a description of early morning sunlight on the sea. The description yields to reflection – a recurrent pattern here – on the unhappiness of multitudes who awaken from happy dreams to harsh reality. God surely means well to His creation, the narrator reflects, yet she herself suffers so much that she yearns to live in solitude, amidst natural beauty that would protect her from awareness of widespread human woe and enable her better to bear "Those that injustice, and duplicity / And faithlessness and folly, fix on me" (1: 59–60). Knowledge of the suffering of others only makes her situation worse. She cannot find peace; she only labors like the wave, constantly baffled by the barrier of the beach, struggling over and over in vain to attain its goal. Then she reproaches herself: no physical situation will protect her from pain; the human condition inevitably involves suffering. At this moment, the band of emigrants appears in order to exemplify the point.

Despite her emphatic assertions of pain, the speaker's account of her suffering seems oddly devoid of affect – partly as a result of frequent interruptions in the form of self-reproach and contemplation of the human situation at large. The curious remoteness of feeling suggests that this woman's self-revelation has the status of exemplary story rather than heartfelt lamentation. One is more likely to feel conscious of its function in the poem than to respond to it as imaginative reality. Perhaps the difficulty of responding comes from the fact that, as readers of Smith's sonnets, we have heard this story too often before: the narrator's voice often resembles that of the sonnets. But in fact similar remoteness, caused by the technique of external observation, marks the initial account of the exiles, whose "dejected looks" (1: 95) indicate that they too serve as representatives of misery. The narrator applies various abstract nouns – Freedom, Anarchy, Bigotry – to their situation before proclaiming that she laments their fate.

> And, as disconsolate and sad ye hang
> Upon the barrier of the rock, and seem
> To murmur your despondence, waiting long
> Some fortunate reverse that never comes;
> Methinks in each expressive face, I see
> Discriminated anguish.
>
> (1: 108–13)

The verbs *seems* and *Methinks* emphasize the extent to which the observer creates meaning in what she sees. As she goes on to generate mini-narratives about individuals within the group, we may realize how insistently the stories she perceives, remembers, and invents create as well as corroborate the melancholy mood that dominates the poem.

More than two decades separate *The Emigrants* from *The Deserted Village*. Smith's reliance on blank verse rather than couplets and her frequent excursions into more or less rhapsodic natural description suggest that she inhabits a different poetic universe from Goldsmith's. Her generalizing narrative technique, however, resembles that of her predecessor. Here is a representative account of one of the emigrants:

> There droops one,
> Who in a moping cloister long consum'd
> This life inactive, to obtain a better,
> And thought that meagre abstinence, to wake
> From his hard pallet with the midnight bell,
> To live on eleemosynary bread,
> And to renounce God's works, would please that God.
> And now the poor pale wretch receives, amaz'd,
> The pity, strangers give to his distress,
> Because these strangers are, by his dark creed,
> Condemn'd as Heretics – and with sick heart
> Regrets his pious prison, and his beads. –
>
> (1: 113–24)

Like Goldsmith's good schoolmaster, this figure is assigned a sketchy history, a number of activities, and various thoughts and feelings. The speaker suggests her pity for him in such phrases as "poor pale wretch." Yet she remains remote, and her interest in him, like Goldsmith's in the schoolmaster, focuses on how he functions within a community. The emigrants are a human species worth examining. They have unknowable individual stories, but general narratives about them can plausibly be invented. Such stories serve, as in *The Deserted Village*, to suggest histories larger than personal and to indicate meanings. They may engage the reader by their relative specificity and by their hints (never fully realized) of drama, but their designs on the reader derive from a large polemic purpose.

The speaker's remoteness from the victims of revolution diminishes when she sees them as like herself: "I too have known / Involuntary exile" (1: 155–56). She sketches a devoted pastor, the counterpart of Goldsmith's village preacher. Then she breaks off to provide a more specific and detailed narrative than she has heretofore offered, of an exiled woman sitting on the cliffs while her children play around her. Again, the narrative palpably belongs to the speaker's imagination. She imagines the woman's inner life as well as her circumstances, articulating images assigned to the exile's fancy. The sitter's husband comes to summon her away. His aristocratic air rouses the speaker to rebuke: he should learn that the common man is as good as he. Even in England, though, citizens reject this truth: another hint of domestic political concerns that underlie this poem's argument.

At this point, Smith moves to rather Thomsonian expansion of her point about the equal worth of all human beings. One who has lived under the control of "Despotism," when despotism disguises itself with luxury, resembles the dweller in a city who has forgotten the beauty of nature. The victim of despotism does not recognize the slavery that binds him. As such reflections continue, the story of the French victims first of despotism, then of Revolution merges with an even more shadowy narrative of English victims. The "Poor wand'ring wretches" (1: 296) who roam the downs somehow become equated with "Fortune's worthless favourites! / Who feed on England's vitals" (1: 314–15): those who have risen by corruption, who now condescend to dependents once equal to them in fortune and still superior in worth. The account of their careers quickly turns to diatribe, with a panoply of personifications: fair Order sinking her decent head, lawless Anarchy overturning celestial Freedom's throne, Confusion, Patriot Virtue, Vengeance, Avarice, and so on. The poem's first book concludes in adjurations to England to commit itself to "acts of pure humanity" (1: 368) rather than of war.

The turn to personifications constitutes a shift from the narrative to the pictorial. Fair Order's decent head, celestial Freedom's radiant throne: such phrases would remind eighteenth-century readers of a long tradition of allegorical painting. Tableaus like the one Smith evokes would have been generically familiar and easy to interpret. Coming as it does at a moment of potential drama – a brief vision of the wronged triumphing over their oppressors in a "resistless torrent" (1: 338) of revolution – the scene of personifications marks the poet's transition to a kind of didacticism familiar in earlier poetry. The subject of that didacticism, though, the recommendation of humanitarian commitment, sounds less familiar. We have encountered in the late eighteenth century much poetry celebrating or invoking the emotion of "sympathy," the capacity to feel with and for others, and particularly to share their suffering. To convert this emotion to a political virtue, however, is something new. Smith forthrightly condemns war, mocking the roar of victory that tells "with what success wide-wasting War / Has by our brave Compatriots thinned the world" (1: 381–82). She implicitly contrasts the thinning of the world through war with the kind of moral thickening she advocates, national action to help humankind rather than to promote conflict. Imaginatively converting an individual sentiment to a form of national action, she appropriately concludes a book that has mingled the personal and the political throughout.

Book 1 of *The Emigrants* is dated November, 1792. Book 2 belongs to April, 1793, after the execution of Louis XVI and the declaration of war between England and France. It too begins with scene-setting, much briefer than in the previous book, and with evocation of the speaker's "own wayward destiny," "Hard as it is, and difficult to bear!" (2: 7, 8). Her concern about the exiles intensifies her despondency, she says, and she yearns for "an interval from Care, / That weighs my wearied spirit down to earth" (2: 19–20). An affecting evocation of the springtime scene briefly interrupts her self-dramatizing proclamations of suffering, only to yield to direct statement that nature no longer brings joy to her soul, which dwells only "On human follies, and on human woes" (2: 42). That subject leads her inevitably to reflections on France, both generalizations about corruption and vice and recurrent allusions to the fates of the king, queen, and prince of France. As she watches a shepherd boy on the hill and constructs a tiny story of his life, she imagines the young prince in a similar pastoral role, therefore happier than he can be at present. She compares herself to Marie Antoinette. Then she tells a longer story, of an imaginary laborer who becomes ill and needs the bounty of the vanished owner of a nearby mansion, who once provided the crumbs from his table as nourishment for the needy.

The emigrants then become tale-tellers and picture-drawers, reporting what they have seen and known in France. The poem's speaker duly passes on two lurid tales: one of a mother fleeing battle, who dies with her infant, "overwhelm'd / Beneath accumulated horror" (2: 279–80); the other about a "feudal Chief" (2: 292), returning home from distant lands, only to find his entire family murdered in his castle. He, as a result, becomes floridly insane. Memory then leads the speaker to tell of her own idyllic childhood and of her subsequent awakening "to never-ending toil, / To terror and to tears!" (2: 350–51). After another story of childhood bliss, the second book concludes in a long prayer for an end to war, the return of the exiles to their native land, and a universal "reign of Reason, Liberty, and Peace!" (2: 444).

The reminiscences of childhood, although manifestly idealized, convey immediacy and conviction, impressions intensified by Smith's reliance on simple, direct diction in the passages reporting her memories. The stories of dying mothers and shocked feudal lords, for all the ostensible intensity of their emotional claims, sound like set pieces. Although each concerns a specific, if unnamed, individual person, a specific, horrifying situation, and a set of specific events, the vignettes seem as generalized as Goldsmith's account of schoolmaster and pastor.

The poet who could write "When bickering arrows of electric fire / Flash on the evening sky" (2: 400–01), sharply evoking the play of summer lightning, presumably had her reasons for resorting to cliché in lines like "Guessing but too well / The fatal truth, he shudders as he goes" (2: 298–99). We might speculate that the reasons had something to do with the evolving emphasis on a poetry of feeling. As we have seen, poets of Smith's period – indeed, Smith herself, especially in the sonnets – often made strong claims on their readers' emotions. The project of *The Emigrants*, however, involves reason as well as feeling. The mingling of the personal and the political, the intertwined telling of stories of self, emigrants, and nation: these devices help to construct an argument inviting reasoned assent. As Goldsmith in *The Deserted Village* tells stories with larger than individual resonance, so Smith asks her readers to grasp that even a lurid tale of a dying mother matters as a statement about war, not simply as an appeal to sympathetic feeling. Sympathy is by no means irrelevant, but the poem endeavors to translate individual responses into the kind of national humanitarianism advocated at the end of its first book. It's not enough, then, to evoke a reader's shudders or tears. The stories in effect provide a kind of outline of emotional stimulus rather than a full panorama. They gesture toward emotion while insisting that the audience should not allow itself to be distracted from the meaning of individual stories in a larger pattern. Hence, perhaps, the poem's refusal ever to dwell on a story in detail. It sketches rather than develops its stories: its argument matters more.

*Beachy Head*, left incomplete at the time of its author's death, also draws on narrative as well as description. Two embedded stories figure importantly in the poem, the tale of the "stranger" on the hill, a tale apparently provoked by contemplation of the landscape, and the story of the hermit with which the unfinished poem concludes. The mysterious figure on the hill appears about two-thirds of the way through *Beachy Head*, after the speaker has rhapsodically described a rural scene she loves. That scene includes a ruined castle dating from the twelfth century. Toward the beginning of the poem, Smith has offered a brief retrospect of English history, with emphasis on its battles, and has described herself as retreating with pleasure from contemplation of wars to the immediate delights of the countryside. The ruined castle, too, is associated with battles, having been "rais'd what time / The Conqueror's successors fiercely fought, / Tearing with civil feuds the desolate land" (497–99). Again, though, the subject of battles quickly vanishes: a tiller of the soil lives there now.

The story of the stranger, associated with the castle, does not, however, belong to it; the castle only reminds the speaker of someone who lived "once" in a similar "castellated mansion" (506), not because he was born to the aristocracy but because he has taken refuge in the ruins. He spends his days wandering around the surrounding country. The country people contemplate him with some suspicion, though the maidens have constructed a story about him: he has gone mad as a result of unrequited love. The song he sings, in which he seems to allude to himself as "The Shepherd of the Hill" (555), a song that the maidens continue to sing, indeed speaks of love. He does not seem unhappy: he enjoys his quiet life in communion with nature. Yet he writes poetry, "rhapsodies" sometimes found by the country folk, that indeed suggests unreciprocated love. We are not told what becomes of him. Instead, the poem converts him into an emblem of hope, a "visionary" (655) who lives in a dream of "ideal bliss" (667) that keeps him happy:

> For what is life, when Hope has ceas'd to strew
> Her fragile flowers along its thorny way?
> And sad and gloomy are his days, who lives
> Of Hope abandon'd!
>
> (668–71)

In its meditation on and dramatization of the workings of fantasy, this little narrative serves as centerpiece for the poem. The speaker's explicit comment glorifies fantasy as a form of hope, but the story itself suggests a more complex view. After all, the interpretation of the stranger's fantasy as hope constitutes a fantasy of its own. Nothing in the story tells us that the isolate actually suffers from unrequited love. Indeed, this notion emerges first as the reading of local girls, by implication romanticizing an unknown man's condition. The evidence for his state as lover is the "rhapsody" he composes, about living in an idealized natural setting with the lost Amanda. The narrator apparently takes that rhapsody as conveying the truth of his situation, but it may be pure fiction, serving needs that we know not of. Nor do we know what needs the narrator fills by imagining that the romanticized figure of a mysterious stranger, articulating the dreams of a man deprived of his beloved, speaks for himself.

In suggesting the uses of fantasy, the degree to which false or idealized versions of reality can serve mysterious personal purposes, *Beachy Head* implicitly acknowledges the degree to which the portrayals of childhood in nature, purporting to be memories, that compose much of the poem may themselves constitute fantasies. The poem is largely constructed on the basis of dreams of the past: of the national past, first and briefly; then of a personal past colored by nostalgia and presumably by the present grief to which the speaker alludes. The self-awareness hinted by the story of the dweller in castle ruins adds an extra dimension to the loving descriptions that largely create the texture of *Beachy Head*.

The story of the hermit of the rock immediately follows that of the stranger on the hill. The hermit's story simpler and less mediated, yet contains the same mystery of past life as the other tale. Nothing is known of the hermit's past, except that he has been "long disgusted with the world / And all its ways" (674–75). He too lives happily in nature, but he focuses outward,

> for his heart
> Was feelingly alive to all that breath'd;
> And outraged as he was, in sanguine youth,
> By human crimes, he still acutely felt
> For human misery.
>
> (687–91)

He manifests this feeling repeatedly by rescuing sailors from their wrecked ships. If he cannot rescue them, he buries their bodies in the chalk of the cliffs and prays for them. Finally, he himself drowns in a storm, to be buried by the mountain shepherds. At this point the poem breaks off. Its final lines assert that "dying in the cause of charity / His spirit, from its earthly bondage freed, / Had to some better region fled for ever" (729–31).

The cause of charity and the capacity to feel for human misery provide alternatives to the life of fantasy. All three characters of the poem – the speaker herself, the castle-dweller, and the hermit – live harmoniously in a natural world and appreciate its beauty and serenity. Smith brilliantly manages to have it two ways at once. On the one hand, she evokes the wonder of nature in its details and the appeal of waking dreams – of love and of harmony. On the other, she asserts by concrete example the importance of that ideal of human responsibility that she suggests also in *The Emigrants*. In no sustained way does *Beachy Head* elevate one of these visions over the other. It illustrates, it enacts, the power of both.

The intricate purposes narrative serves in Smith's longer poems help to define the ways in which she belongs to the eighteenth rather than the nineteenth century. Often claimed as a Romantic poet, Charlotte Smith in many respects indeed foretells the poetry that would come immediately after her. Her larger purposes, however, which centered on notions of community and responsibility, speak more of the past than of the future. Indeed, part of the interest her poetry holds depends on the tension between her self-absorption – her conviction that no one else ever suffered as she has suffered – and her belief in the urgency of affirming the ties that bind human beings together. Inasmuch as she articulates a belief in that "social love," the counterpart of self-love, which eighteenth-century thinkers often affirmed as an innate principle of human action, she looks backward. Yet the eighteenth-century view of social harmony remained firmly hierarchical. Smith, in her reactions to the French Revolution, strongly suggests her faith in the equality of human beings, insisting on the superficiality of rank distinctions. She thus foretells the future.

Novelists and poets alike, toward the end of the eighteenth century, show themselves poised between opposed assumptions and poetic procedures. Like Smith, Mary Robinson relied sometimes on lavish personification, likely to strike a modern reader as "artificial"; at other times, her poetry proclaims itself a direct, passionate outpouring. Like Smith too, she draws on the resources of narrative. The sonnet sequence of *Sappho and Phaon* tells a story of emotional development but also, more indirectly, of a love relationship. The narrative of a faithless man and a helplessly devoted woman accumulates a powerful sense of inevitability, so that Sappho's suicide, both triumph and defeat, comes to seem the only possible resolution for the story. In celebrating love – a deplorable subject for a writer, according to literary critics and moralists earlier in the eighteenth century – and assigning the highest value to individual feelings, Robinson parts company with her predecessors. Similarly, the narrative poems of *Lyrical Tales*, published in 1800 but presumably written in the final years of the eighteenth century, show the strong influence of *Lyrical Ballads* (1798), innovative works by Wordsworth and Coleridge that celebrated ordinary people and emotion of many kinds. Wordsworth and Coleridge too, though, built on the emotion-infused narratives constructed by those who came before. Ann Yearsley, in *Clifton Hill*, complains about those "Who hear, unheeding, Misery's bitter tale" (96). She wishes to make the general point, the familiar eighteenth-century point, that people should feel for one another. Wordsworth and Coleridge would take for granted the capacity of humans to sympathize with their fellows, but their sense of the value of Misery's bitter tale corresponded closely to Yearsley's.

# 14

# Poetic Languages: Diction Old and New

Wordsworth's preface to the second edition of *Lyrical Ballads* (1800), one of the best-known critical utterances of all time, asserts a new view of the language of poetry, claiming that no essential difference divides the language of prose from that of poetry. Much of the eighteenth-century poetry that we have considered draws heavily on kinds of diction that belong peculiarly to verse. Wordsworth disapproved. Analyzing Thomas Gray's poignant sonnet on the death of Richard West, Wordsworth insists that only the lines that use solely the diction of ordinary prose have any value, thus categorically dismissing most of the poem. He explains that he himself has eschewed terminology that belongs primarily to poetic tradition, partly because so many bad poets have employed it, but partly because the "poetic" seems to him inherently false.

Wordsworth's view, articulated strongly and clearly, has had a profound effect on subsequent critical opinion. Many share the notion that language more evocative of previous poetry than of direct experience must be inferior to "fresh" and "original" diction. Yet originality is not necessarily or always a mark of poetic excellence. Eighteenth-century poets employed different kinds of language for different purposes. Often they deliberately drew on well-worn words and phrases to declare their own relation to poetic tradition, to invite comparison with past achievements, and to enrich the suggestions conveyed by their lines.

Wordsworth thought his judgments of Gray's diction self-evident, expecting that his readers would readily perceive that only the four lines he singles out have value. Perceptions, however, vary. The lines Wordsworth declares valueless include "To warm their little loves the birds complain": direct enough in diction, but presumably unacceptable because based on "pathetic fallacy," which, attributing human emotion to the inanimate or lower animal world, thus constitutes a kind of artifice. Wordsworth fails to recognize the poignancy of such a line or to acknowledge how the sonnet deliberately plays two kinds of diction against one another: on the one hand, "reddening Phoebus lifts his golden fire," alluding to mythological tradition and the decorative kind of poetry it had often fostered; on the other, "[I] weep the more because I weep in vain," the bare statement of a kind of personal feeling that decorative allusion cannot reach or express, the inadequacy of such allusion supplying part of the poem's subject. The later poet takes little pleasure in his predecessor's verse. He wants something new.

The eighteenth century began with Dryden's dismissal of the age just past in favor of the imagined newness ahead. The nineteenth century opens with Wordsworth's rejection of most poetry from the immediately past epoch. In both instances, rejection depends on perception: thus on interpretation. Dryden reads the wars and loves that have preceded him as unworthy; Wordsworth finds Gray's poetry likewise unworthy. Perhaps an inability to read with pleasure what has come just before must always precede the innovations that create dramatic literary shifts. Wordsworth in fact drew heavily on his eighteenth-century predecessors, but his sense of absolute newness was crucial to his enterprise.

Wordsworth is not the subject of our story. His expression of the need for a new kind of diction, though, may remind us of the variety that already infused the poetry of the late eighteenth century. If it was important to Wordsworth to reject the immediate past, it is also important that we, with more historical perspective, can again grasp the values of that past, can learn how to read its poetry with pleasure, and can understand the large scope of that poetry, in language as well as subject.

To the very end of the century (and after), many poets – including, in his early work, Wordsworth himself – indeed relied on forms of poetic diction, although they often turned it to new purposes. Anna Laetitia Barbauld, for instance, often makes rather ostentatious use of mythological reference and well-worn poetic diction, as if to reassure her readers about her propriety. Thus, toward the beginning of *A Summer Evening's Meditation*, she writes of skies that

> With mild maiden beams
> Of temper'd light, invite the cherish'd eye

> To wander o'er their sphere; where hung aloft
> DIAN's bright crescent, like a silver bow
> New strung in heaven, lifts high its beamy horns
> Impatient for the night, and seems to push
> Her brother down the sky.
>
> (4–10)

"The cherish'd eye" and "beamy horns" sound like Thomson; the moon as a "bright crescent" seems very familiar indeed; the reference to Diana and to the sun as brother of the moon recall the past. In subsequent lines, the planet Venus, Evening, and Contemplation are personified in conventional terms. The poet appears deliberately to emphasize her participation in a long poetic tradition.

The poem that follows this introduction, however, proves less predictable than we might anticipate. As we would expect, Contemplation leads the speaker to wander through the evening woods, observing the landscape and reflecting on the nature of things. The reflections quickly move beyond the immediate scene, although not before they transform that scene's meaning:

> Nature's self is hush'd,
> And, but a scatter'd leaf, which rustles thro'
> The thick-wove foliage, not a sound is heard
> To break the midnight air; tho' the rais'd ear,
> Intensely listening, drinks in every breath.
> How deep the silence, yet how loud the praise!
> But are they silent all? or is there not
> A tongue in every star that talks with man,
> And wooes him to be wise; nor wooes in vain:
> This dead of midnight is the noon of thought,
> And wisdom mounts her zenith with the stars.
>
> (41–51)

The absence of aural stimuli, except for the single rustling leaf, becomes the woodland's salient feature. Then silence turns into sound: loud praise resides within it, the stars perhaps have tongues. Midnight transforms itself to noon. The universe seems suddenly full of paradoxes. Meaning depends on perception, and the poem reveals itself as a meditation on kinds of perception that do not derive from the senses alone. Barbauld's language remains conventional. The fact emphasizes the daring of her departure from established ways of understanding the natural world. The world she imagines is suffused with divinity.

More than forty years before Barbauld, James Thomson wrote a visionary *Hymn* to stand as a conclusion to *The Seasons*. Like Barbauld's, his is a powerful poem. The differences between the two works may suggest to what different purposes language might be used in the later years of the eighteenth century.

Like Barbauld, Thomson understood divine presence as infused throughout its works.

> Mysterious Round! what Skill, what Force divine,
> Deep-felt, in These appear! a simple Train,
> Yet so delightful mix'd, with such kind Art,
> Such Beauty and Beneficence combin'd;
> Shade, unperceiv'd, so softening into Shade;
> And all so forming an harmonious Whole;
> That, as they still succeed, they ravish still.
> But, wandering oft, with brute unconscious Gaze,
> Man marks not Thee, marks not the mighty Hand
> That, ever-busy, wheels the silent Spheres.
>
> (21–30)

As so often in the poetry of Thomson's period, adjectives here carry much of the meaning. The adjectives – *Mysterious, simple, delightful, kind, harmonious,* and so on – delineate emotional or moral qualities. A few – *Deep-felt, unperceived, unconscious* – suggest the effect of the panoply of seasons on a human observer, but the presence of that observer is most fully imagined negatively, in the final suggestions about Man who "marks not" what happens all about him. Physical reality is altogether irrelevant. The poet relies largely on abstractions to emphasize, rather, the qualities and achievements of the divine force manifested in and through the physical.

Thomson's diction is not exactly that of common men: Wordsworth would presumably have disapproved of words like *Beneficence* and phrases like *brute unconscious Gaze*, to say nothing of the exclamation points and the circuitous sentence structure. Yet the poet's language is direct and communicative and his enthusiasm palpable, although derived from what one might call an abstract perception, a deduction from available evidence.

Barbauld's diction, sentence structure, and dependence on adjectives resemble Thomson's, and she too contemplates the wonders of creation as manifestations of God's work, although she uses a good deal of concrete detail. She is adventurous in quite a different way from Thomson's. "At this hour," she writes, "the self-collected soul / Turns inward, and beholds a stranger there" (52–53). The "stranger" proves to be "a spark of fire divine" (56), evidence of God's presence within the human soul: nothing adventurous in that idea. The phrasing, though; the notion of finding a stranger within the self – such aspects of the verse point to Barbauld's willingness to entertain the unexpected. Her discovery of God in the universe depends on an imaginative voyage among the planets.

> Seiz'd in thought
> On fancy's wild and roving wing I sail,
> From the green borders of the peopled earth,
> And the pale moon, her duteous fair attendant;
> From solitary Mars; from the vast orb
> Of Jupiter, whose huge gigantic bulk
> Dances in ether like the lightest leaf;
> To the dim verge, the suburbs of the system,
> Where cheerless Saturn 'midst her watry moons
> Girt with a lucid zone, majestic sits
> In gloomy grandeur; like an exil'd queen
> Amongst her weeping handmaids: fearless thence
> I launch into the trackless deeps of space. . . .
>                         (71–83)

The flight of fancy, in Barbauld's treatment, becomes an end in itself. Thomson and Barbauld alike employ fancy in the service of testimonies to divinity, but Barbauld takes manifest pleasure in the details that fancy finds: the gigantism of Jupiter and the planet's paradoxical lightness, the idea of the very edge of the universe ("the suburbs of the system"), the watery moons of Saturn, the simile of the exiled queen to define Saturn's position, and especially the idea of her own imaginative capacity to "launch into the trackless deeps of space." Delighting in the fanciful, she asserts her individual consciousness in the very act of declaring the universal presence of God. Yet her language and her allusions reassuringly affirm the conventional. The peopled earth, its green borders, even fancy's wing: all belong to established tradition, as do the lucid zone and the queen among her handmaids. If Barbauld draws both on science and on soaring imagination, with far more stress on the specific than Thomson provides, she still presents herself as working in familiar poetic terms.

Toward the very end of the century, Anna Seward demonstrated yet more emphatically how conventional diction could serve fresh purposes. In *Colebrooke Dale* she deplores the destruction of rural beauty by industrial ugliness, responding directly and openly to aesthetic and moral effects of the growing emphasis on manufacture and trade. For the purpose she relies heavily on poetic diction, including the kind of Latinate terminology that had been popular much earlier in the century. Thus the workmen employed in the new factories become "Tribes" (7), recalling the finny or winged tribes of earlier verse, with "fuliginous" [sooty] cheeks (8). It is unsurprising that Seward evokes "pearly-wristed Naiads" (12) to suggest the beauty of the earlier, uncontaminated river; more surprising that she describes the ugliness of the present by relying on the same kind of formal language employed by nature poets much earlier in the eighteenth century.

> dim where she stands,
> Circled by lofty Mountains, that condense
> Her dark, and spiral wreaths to drizzling rains,
> Frequent, and sullied; as the neighboring Wilds
> Ope their swart veins, and feed her cavern'd flames;
> While to her dusky Sister sullen yields
> Long desolated Ketley's livid breast
> The ponderous metal.
>
> (87–94)

Seward does not paint a pretty picture, but her language and her insistent personification recall poetry of an earlier time. The recollection may help to remind the reader of past values as well, values that, according to Seward, the pattern of industrialization violates. By the time the poem, in its concluding lines, commands, "Albion, blush!" (97), its use of a semi-archaic term for England can evoke a bygone time and a bygone set of assumptions.

Seward does not always sound so reactionary in her deployment of standard rhetoric. When she contemplates Goethe's wildly popular *Sorrows of Young Werther*, a romantic work that precipitated a wave of youthful suicides throughout Europe, as young men in particular imitated Goethe's protagonist, she writes in couplets; she relies heavily on adjective–noun constructions; she employs a well-worn vocabulary. But *Written in the Blank Page of the Sorrows of Werther* defends rather than deplores Goethe's achievement. Although it emphasizes the value of "generous sympathy" (23), it dwells almost lasciviously on the novel's lurid details:

> The wretched victim of a baneful flame,
> Where ill-starr'd Love its deadliest lightning shed
> On the pale Suicide's devoted [doomed] head,
> And woes, that would no holier thought allow,
> Threw ghastly shadows on the bleeding brow. –
>
> (12–16)

Sympathy, the poem declares, should lead the reader to compassionate the frailties of the Goethe's protagonist. Seward's lines, though, suggest more strongly the dubious pleasures of contemplating human misery at a safe distance. She offers such hints, however, within a context established by value terms heavily used by her poetic predecessors (as well as by eighteenth-century moralists): *sympathetic, mercy, glowing heart, prudence, virtuous, compassion, generous, noble*. A structure of moralistic abstract diction provides a strategy of concealment, obscuring the true emotional thrust of Seward's poem.

William Lisle Bowles, who may provide a final example of a late-eighteenth-century poet whose language recalled the past, lived, like Wordsworth, to the middle of the nineteenth century but drew heavily on the earlier eighteenth century in his writing. Samuel Taylor Coleridge, Wordsworth's close associate, admired Bowles's early verse, which often expresses what we would now call a Romantic sensibility, despite its reliance on conventional language. For him, as for Seward, poetic diction constitutes a strategy. More precisely, it enables a series of strategies.

On occasion, Bowles deliberately ventriloquizes an earlier poet, as in a sonnet that imagines John Milton in old age by means of language recalling specific passages in Milton's work. We may hear echoes of his predecessors, though, even in poems with no specific literary reference: Sonnet XXI, for instance, which devotes its octave to reporting the promises of "the voice of Hope" (5), foretelling "long days of bliss sincere!" (2). The voice speaks not of erotic love but of "social scenes, . . . / Of truth, of friendship, of affection meek" (6–7) – terminology recalling the earlier eighteenth-century stress on community and community values. The sestet, in contrast, reports the ringing of a deathbell, as a result of which "Chill darkness wrapt the pleasurable bow'rs" (12). The sonnet concludes with a suggestion of death's horror, as Hope, mysteriously, takes a new role: "pointing to yon breathless clay, / She cried, 'No peace be thine, away, away!'" (13–14). The situation of the dead person is not at issue: only that of the listener, the poem's speaker. The calm and conventional language of "social scenes" and "pleasurable bowers" contrasts sharply with the frenzied tone of those final words, addressed to the onlooker and assuming his situation as the poem's most compelling issue. The disparity between the octave, evoking an atmosphere of communal peace, and the sestet, focused on the emotional situation of one horrified man, challenges the assumption of continuity contained in locutions like "bliss secure" and "affection meek." The final exclamation, despite its archaic form ("No peace be thine") undercuts the reassurance implied by "poetic" language and sentence structure ("whispering sweet" rather than "sweetly," "bliss sincere" rather than "sincere bliss," and so on), which speak of continuity and tradition. Bowles thus appears to use the poetic diction that Wordsworth deplored with full awareness both of its power and of its limitations.

In one of his best-known poems, *Elegy Written at the Hot-Wells, Bristol*, Bowles makes purposeful and protracted allusion to Thomas Gray's *Elegy Written in a Country Church Yard*. His diction, his rhythms, and his sequence of thought all resemble those of his predecessor. Inviting comparison to the earlier poem, Bowles, like Gray before him, allows himself to imagine inhabitants for the scene he contemplates, a spa where the ill come to take the waters in hope of finding cures. Gray's imagined beings are villagers who have died; Bowles's may yet be alive. The more significant contrast between the two poems involves their attitudes toward society. Gray uses his meditations on village graves as the basis for reflecting on differences between the lots of the rich and the poor; Bowles interests himself entirely in individual situations, including his own. Whereas Gray sees the village as a community and himself as an isolate, included only after his imagined death, Bowles celebrates personal friendships and comments on the sadness of loss without reference to a larger social context.

The insistent allusions to Gray, however, provide that reference for him. He implicitly provides a historical setting for his personal reflections, inviting his readers to ruminate about present and past, about simple village life as opposed to sophisticated spa life, about the possible range of attitudes toward death. Bowles can safely assume that everyone will have read Gray. His echoes of the past, through reminiscences of Gray's diction, substitute for extended exegesis.

Not all poets who preceded Wordsworth, however, relied – self-consciously or naively – on poetic diction. Robert Burns might be seen as following a Wordsworthian program before the fact, exploring the possibilities of a language of common folk. His particular version of the common folk inhabited Scotland, where he himself worked at the plough – not, as he was immediately imagined to be, a self-educated laborer like Stephen Duck before him, but one who had nonetheless faced real financial as well as social difficulties. The language he adopted was a rural Scots dialect. He interspersed it cannily with more orthodox diction, but his poetry's effects depend heavily on an unexpected idiom that suggested a new view of how poetry should work on the reader.

In one early poem, *The Vision*, he explicitly ponders the poet's situation. He imagines himself sitting alone by the hearth when suddenly a beautiful young woman appears. She eventually identifies herself as the Muse of his native place, offers a recapitulation of his past, prophesies his future, and urges him not to repine at his humble sphere: the role of *"rustic Bard"* (216), she assures him, holds great bliss.

This Scottish Muse turns out to speak standard English. Thus, the conclusion of her advice:

> To give my counsels all in one,
> Thy *tuneful flame* still careful fan;
> Preserve the *dignity of Man*,
>     With Soul erect;
> And trust, the UNIVERSAL PLAN
>     Will all protect.
>             (217–22)

In substance, in syntax, and in language, this harks back to the century's early years. Pope celebrated the "universal plan" and assumed the dignity of man; Thomson might have written about a "tuneful flame." The late-century poet is advised to behave and to believe like his predecessors.

The Muse's advice, however, inhabits a poem dominated by a different tone, a different kind of diction, and apparently different assumptions. Here is the poet meditating about his situation, before the Muse's appearance:

> Had I to guid advice but harket,
> I might, by this [time], hae led a market,
> Or strutted in a Bank and clarket
>     My *Cash-Account*;
> While here, half-mad, half-fed, half-sarket [clothed],
>     Is a' th' amount.
>
>                         (25–30)

Although self-castigation provides the explicit theme, the sheer energy of the verse undercuts it, as do the ironic implications of strutting in a bank or "clarking" [clerking, or writing up] one's cash account. Despite the fact that he acknowledges as good advice the counsel that would have led him to bank or market, despite the desperation of his half-mad, half-fed, half-clothed situation, he makes the reader respond to his resilience and his vigor.

The use of dialect does much to convey those qualities. Those not born to this way of speaking – most of Burns's current readers – may need to sound out the words on the page and to rely on footnotes for translations, yet the energetic rhymes of *harket*, *market*, *clarket*, and *sarket*, regardless of their meanings, carry their own message. Active refusal to accept the values that we now call capitalistic appropriately defines the poet's alienated status, but the liveliness of Burns's rhyming as he ironically suggests his alienation betrays pleasure in his position – ability to zestfully ruminate over his difference.

The Muse speaks more or less standard English; the poet she inspires employs Scots dialect. Not Scots dialect alone, though: he proves capable of writing in as orthodox fashion as the Muse herself. Thus, describing the vision of Ayrshire embodied in the Muse's mantle, he writes,

> Here, rivers in the sea were lost;
> There, mountains to the skies were tost:
> Here, tumbling billows mark'd the coast,
>     With surging foam;
> There, distant shone, *Art*'s lofty boast,
>     The lordly dome.
>
>                         (73–78)

Four successive stanzas in this vein conclude with the allegation that Ayr can boast a race "To ev'ry nobler virtue bred, / And polish'd grace" (89–90). In personifying Art, in praising "The lordly dome," in celebrating noble virtue and polished grace, Burns both demonstrates his control of English and his capacity to incorporate familiar poetic subjects and familiar behavioral standards.

The poem as a whole, however, betrays an uneasy tension between the two modes of diction – a tension that in fact expresses the central meaning of *The Vision*. On the one hand, the use of Scots diction both supplies and conveys Burns's poetic energy. On the other, it keeps him – or so he feels – from being altogether respectable. Toward the end of the poem, the Muse explains that he cannot hope to equal such poets as Thomson (a fellow Scot who eschewed dialect and native material), Shenstone (who strategically employed Spenserian diction), and Gray. He must shine alone in a *"humble sphere"* (212), content with the pleasure that arises from the act of producing poetry. Instead of the laurel wreath of fame, the Muse supplies him with a wreath of native holly, decorative but not hallowed by literary tradition. The contest between Scots and English diction implies a conflict of poetic assumptions and values.

On the whole, as his best-known poems attest, Burns opted for the voice of the *"rustic Bard"* that the Muse labeled him (216). His familiar lyrics and narratives provide persuasive demonstrations of dialect's power to create a strangeness that yet embodies singular directness. *To a Mouse, On turning her up in her Nest with the Plough, November, 1785* offers a case in point. The first stanza contains only a few words of standard English, yet it communicates readily:

> Wee, sleeket, cowran, tim'rous *beastie*,
> O, what a panic's in thy breastie!
> Thou need na start awa sae hasty,
>> Wi' bickering brattle!
> I wad be laith to rin an' chase thee,
>> Wi' murd'ring *pattle*!
>> (1–6)

In the same stanzaic form as *The Vision*, this evokes a sharply different tone, sounding like the immediate reflections of a man in the situation sketched by the title. We need no glossary to get the point. A glossary will tell us that a pattle is an implement for scraping off mud and that "bickering brattle" means "scurrying haste," but the sound of the words and their context conveys the general meaning. From the first line – indeed, the first word – we know of the speaker's sympathy for his inadvertent victim.

That sympathy, as the poem spells it out, involves intimate knowledge of a field mouse's way of life: how the little animal builds its nest, how laboriously it works to protect itself from the cold, how it must suffer, given the coming of winter, with no new sources of greenery to rebuild its dwelling. Despite his farmer's knowledge of animals' ways, despite his immediate occupation as ploughman, despite his use of Scots vernacular, the poem's speaker proves also to have a sophisticated awareness of an eighteenth-century vocabulary of moral thought:

> I'm truly sorry Man's dominion
> Has broken Nature's social union,
> An' justifies that ill opinion,
> > Which makes thee startle,
> At me, thy poor, earth-born companion,
> > An' *fellow-mortal*!
>
> > > (7–12)

Aside from the repeated contraction of *and*, nothing in this second stanza betrays the countryman. The first two stanzas thus establish the speaker as a man of dual nature, or at least dual allegiance: to a concrete, immediate form of responsiveness and to a more abstract reflectiveness. Although *To a Mouse* devotes more space to the man's immediate awareness of the mouse's situation, it depends for its effect on the duality early conveyed.

It turns out that the speaker, for all his sympathy, feels concerned with himself above all. The mouse, dispossessed, may be imagined as worried solely about the urgencies of shelter. The man, reflecting on the mouse, finds a pretext for declaring his own desperate situation, worse than that of any small rodent:

> Still, thou art blest, compar'd wi' *me*!
> The *present* only toucheth thee:
> But Och! I *backward* cast my e'e,
> > On prospects drear!

An' *forward*, tho' I canna *see*,
   I *guess* an' *fear*!

(43–9)

Touches of Scots dialect continue to enliven the verse, but the impulse behind it now belongs more closely to the second, meditative aspect of the speaker. As he ponders the relation between man and mouse, he perceives that a conventional sign of human superiority to lower species, the capacity to remember and to reflect, in fact marks a heightened capacity for suffering.

The moments of dialect in this final stanza remind us of what we might call the narrative elements in the poem, which in fact contains two tiny stories: that of turning up the mouse's nest, and the imagined episode of the mouse trying in vain to rebuild its nest. Both stories belong to the dialect speaker, the country man. *To a Mouse*, however, is also an emotional meditation on an apparently insignificant event. The speaker's other language, for meditation, reminds us that he belongs not only to a specific rural environment but also to the human community of thinkers and feelers and to a tradition, both literary and philosophical, of thought and feeling. Burns's capacity to manipulate two opposed modes of diction within a single poem created some of his most brilliant effects.

One of his best-known works, however, exemplifies his skill within a single poetic register. *A Red, Red Rose*, a small love poem, employs a ballad stanza, a repetitive structure, and surpassingly simple diction, abundantly supporting, before the fact, Wordsworth's assertion that poetry should be written in the language of common men. The four-stanza poem contains a single three-syllable word and six words of two syllables; all the rest are monosyllabic. Its allusions to rose, song, sea, and sun evoke universally familiar experience. It employs simple sentence structure and uses simple repetition for emphasis. Transparent in meaning – I love you very much, it says: nothing more – it presents itself as the uncomplicated utterance of an uncomplicated person.

The poem's central term is the dialect form *luve*, used in three different senses: to designate the woman loved by the speaker, to declare a feeling, and to serve as an active verb. Inserted twice into an opening sentence otherwise written in ordinary English, the dialect locution has a startling effect. Its slight strangeness slows down the reading of the first stanza: the modern reader inevitably pauses over the word, thus giving it the emphasis it emotionally demands. Both the word's difference from the stanza's otherwise plain English vocabulary and its faint suggestion of a social class issue (would an educated man use such a term?) generate a slight sense of distance, intensified by the odd syntax of the next stanza and by such locutions as "my bonie lass."

Despite its ostensible simplicity, the poem has its own complexities, playing as it does with paradoxes of permanence and evanescence. The first stanza, comparing the beloved object to a newly sprung rose and to a beautifully played melody, suggests an equation between the loved one and brief experiences of aesthetic perfection. The next stanza, however, insists on permanence beyond all imagining – "Till a' the seas gang dry" (8) – for the emotion lavished on the beloved. Her physical beauty, her existence in the state of aesthetic perfection, may not endure; the feeling her beauty has helped to arouse will. Only in the final stanza do we learn that the poem's occasion is a parting. Despite the emphasized endurance of the love delineated, the physical conjunction of the lovers is at a temporary end. The speaker cannot say, "I will be with you forever"; he can only say, "I will always return." And of course the shadow of death looms over this as over all partings: the reader knows that, like the rose and the melody, every person will die and the assertion of eternal love will be nullified. The lyric thus exists as a defiant assertion of love against mortality.

The suggestions of Scots dialect add an extra note of pathos to such defiance. Hinting that the speaker lacks the worldly resources of wealth, status, and education, such language raises the possibility that his assertions of eternal devotion defy probable earthly contingencies as well as the vicissitudes of mortality. The insistence on personal integrity and on the power of emotional connection develops power from its bareness, its lack of pretension, its evocations of the universal. Anyone, everyone, the poem implicitly proclaims, can claim the same power.

In Burns's hands, a kind of diction often associated with broad jokes takes on serious poetic purpose. On occasion – on frequent occasion – the poet himself used it for comic effects, as in *To a Louse On Seeing one on a Lady's Bonnet at Church*, where the development of comic perspective creates an unexpected context for a serious moral perception, and in *Tam o'Shanter*, that energetic narrative of broad emotional range. Burns's demonstration of the resources of Scots vernacular not only made a nationalist statement. It also contributed to the growing realization that poetry could communicate a vast variety of thought and feeling in new ways, ways not sanctioned by tradition. Burns, to be sure, by no means abandoned tradition. In *A Red, Red Rose*, he not only relies on ballad rhythms and forms; he also addresses his beloved as thou, and he uses a flower simile hallowed by ancient usage. But his use of vernacular was intimately linked to the freshness of thought and expression that he brought to lyric, moral, and narrative verse.

# 15

# Mary Robinson and William Cowper

Like the other pairings we have examined, Mary Robinson and William Cowper have little obviously in common beyond the period in which they flourished. Robinson lived a dramatic life: a disastrous early marriage, appearances on stage, a time as mistress of a prince, a prolonged unhappy love affair with a man who finally married another, a tell-all memoir that received wide attention. Cowper, in contrast, retired early from any semblance of public life, had several mental breakdowns, and lived reclusively, never marrying. They shared, however, great poetic productivity in various modes. In different ways, both foretell developments of the Romantic Period in the early nineteenth century, the period of Wordsworth, Keats, and Shelley, while they also recapitulate literary patterns of the century now nearing its end.

Robinson published her first volume of poetry at the age of seventeen. Heavily derivative, it reveals influences from Theocritus to Pope and Prior, demonstrating a young woman's skill at versification but suggesting that she had as yet little to say. Sixteen years later, a second book, still heavily reliant on eighteenth-century convention, shows signs of a poet seeking a voice of her own. When she addresses the Muse (*Ode to the Muse*), she asks at length for the power to depict emotion and to render the beauties of nature. The poem, however, ends rather surprisingly:

> But, if thy magic pow'rs impart
> One sad sensation to the heart,
> If thy warm precepts can dispense
> One thrilling transport o'er my sense;
> Oh! keep thy gifts, and let me fly,
> In APATHY's cold arms to die.
>
> (129–34)

Begging for the capacity to render emotion, the poet yet expresses herself as rejecting experienced emotion (like Collins in *Ode to Fear*), dreading intensity of feeling. Poetic power, in the ode's version of it, belongs to the voyeur: it is the prerogative of an onlooker at life.

The problem suggested by *Ode to the Muse*, of the poet's relation to feeling, in a sense dominates virtually all of Robinson's work. The 1791 volume also contains an *Ode to Della Crusca* (Robert Merry, leader of a group of poets with whom Robinson associated herself: the Della Cruscans, noted for the emotionalism of their verse), in which the speaker praises Merry for poetry that affects the heart so strongly that "ev'ry nerve, with quiv'ring throb divine, / In madd'ning tumults, owns thy wond'rous pow'r" (5–6). In rhapsodic verse, Robinson declares both her intention constantly to recite Merry's compositions and her determination to imitate his achievement, finally asserting that this ode itself, constituting such an imitation, offers a "wild, untutor'd picture of the heart" (77). In other poems in the volume, she writes to and about her lover, ever more insistent on the strength and the significance of her own feelings. The feeling self has become her subject.

More compelling to a twenty-first-century reader are some of Robinson's later solutions to the dilemma of how to express intense emotion persuasively in verse. One recourse, which she would explore more fully in the 1800 volume called *Lyrical Tales*, produces *The Maniac* in Robinson's 1793 *Poems*. The turn toward subjects beyond herself, and ultimately toward narrative, provides a rationale for strong feeling and allows Robinson guilt-free indulgence. *The Maniac* focuses on an old man who manifests unmistakable insanity. Formulated mainly as a series of questions – "Why does that agonizing shriek / The mind's unpitied anguish speak?" (4–5), etc. – the poem explores a series of narrative possibilities, all derived from the speaker's imagination rather than her knowledge. The man himself, Robinson's *Memoir* tells us, really existed, and the poem issued, almost unconsciously, from a laudanum-induced stupor. Whatever the circumstances of its composition, *The Maniac* makes apparent Robinson's search for emotional pretexts. Beginning with questions about the perceived circumstances of the madman's situation, the poem becomes increasingly fanciful, moving to questions about imagined circumstances – the maniac climbing the crags and howling to the waves, drinking the midnight dew, stretched on "sepulchral stone" (33). Then it goes on to speculations about the possible causes for the victim's madness: unrequited or betrayed love, ungrateful friends, loss of fortune, avarice, ambition, his own seduction of a maiden.

Early in the poem, in a peculiarly telling formulation, Robinson refers to her subject as "thing forlorn!" (6), thus briefly depriving him of humanity. The phrase occurs in a line that begs the maniac to tell her of himself and "let me share thy woe" (6), but it suggests that the suffering human being has indeed become an object: an object for poetic speculation. *The Maniac* concludes by recurring to the idea of sharing the madman's woes:

> Oh! tell me, tell me all thy pain;
> Pour to mine ear thy frenzied strain,
> And I will share thy pangs, and soothe thy woes!
>    Poor MANIAC! I will dry thy tears,
>    And bathe thy wounds, and calm thy fears,
> And with soft Pity's balm enchant thee to repose.
>
> (115–20)

The sentiments would have sounded familiar from the middle of the eighteenth century on, as would the stress on aspects of the maniac's situation calculated to arouse the reader's pity and sympathy. Yet there is something new here as well: the emphasis on the onlooker's position – the importance of the "I," tacit throughout, as that "I" imagines possibilities, and explicit at the end. The poem's speaker sees herself as powerful, capable of calming the madman's fears and enchanting him to sleep. She also understands the maniac as an imaginative stimulus, an aspect of his appearance that might not in an earlier period have been apparent. Reaching for emotional intensity, the poet invokes not only pity, as a predecessor earlier in the century might have done, but also fear, fascination, horror, and moral distaste, as well as pity for miscellaneous other human objects along the way: seduced maidens, bilked creditors, widows and orphans. Intense emotion is the poem's aim and method.

It is no accident that the 1793 volume includes an *Ode to Rapture*, imagined as a power so thrilling as to be half frightening even to its creator, Nature herself. The purpose of rapture, the ode indicates, is to generate a "magic THRILL" (31). The poem's epigraph, from Frances Greville's eighteenth-century *Ode to Indifference*, asserts that bliss beyond a certain bound turns to agony, and Robinson's ode hints the same thing

– and hints the thrill of the conjunction. When she writes a long characterization of herself, in *Stanzas to a Friend Who Desired to Have My Portrait*, she claims the intensity and the nobility of her feelings:

> I'm jealous, for I fondly love;
> No feeble flame my heart can prove;
>     Caprice ne'er dimm'd its fires:
> I blush to see the human mind,
> For nobler, prouder claims design'd,
>     The slave of low desires.
>
> (73–78)

The rollicking metrical movement may suggest less than serious intent, but the substance of the verse corroborates the implication of various experiments in Robinson's other poems.

In *Sappho and Phaon* (1796), on which we have already touched, Robinson largely solved the problem of finding a persuasive method to communicate intense emotion. By adopting a consistent persona linked to a historical figure marked, or so tradition held, by passionate intensity, she created a plausible justification for the exploration of erotic feeling and its consequences. She could investigate extended possibilities of a single voice, imagining a range of situations. She could put emotions under a microscope without risking the charge of self-obsession. If she used her own experience and feelings as guides, she transformed them into plausible material for her semi-historical protagonist.

A look at two sonnets will illustrate how closely Robinson focused on the vagaries of emotional experience. Sonnet 27 begins like a conventional eighteenth-century nature poem:

> Oh! ye bright Stars! That on the Ebon fields
>     Of Heav'n's vast empire, trembling seem to stand;
>     'Till rosy morn unlocks her portal bland,
> Where the proud Sun his fiery banner wields!
>
> (1–4)

The word most likely to attract attention here is *bland*, unlike the other adjectives an unexpected modifier. Morning's gates are "bland" – soft, mild, gentle, balmy, soothing – in contrast with the fieriness of Sun's banner, the flaming force to which the stars, the next quatrain tells us, must yield. The gentleness of these gates has no effect in the sonnet: it exists only for the moment, to be overwhelmed by the energies outside it.

The second quatrain not only establishes the stars' yielding; it also sets up the poem's central analogy.

> To flames, less fierce than mine, your luster yields,
> And pow'rs more strong my countless tears command;
> Love strikes the feeling heart with ruthless hand,
> And only spares the breast which dullness shields.
>
> (5–8)

The speaker claims emotional force greater than the sun's fire. The powers that dictate her tears exceed those of the sun. She delineates herself both as powerful, the source of amazing energy, and as victimized, forced to weep by other powers over which she has no control. Love exists as a force within – origin of her "flames" – and without, striking her heart destructively. Yet her victimization testifies to her capacity: the alternative is "dullness."

Elaborating the point in the third quatrain, the lover asserts directly that nature only bestows "The fine affections of the soul, to prove / A keener sense of desolating woes" (10–11). She will then, she claims, not boast her fine feelings:

> If bliss from coldness, pain from passion flows,
> Ah! who would wish to feel, or learn to love?
>
> (13–14)

This resolution, however, carries little conviction. Formulated as a question, it does not even offer a direct assertion. Yet the poem's rational structure has led to an inevitable conclusion. Stars shine in a dark sky, only to give way to the sun's superior strength; the female lover burns more fiercely than the sun but must yield to the ruthless power of passion; only dullness prevents passion's pain. It might seem to follow that one would prefer coldness and dullness to passion, since coldness creates "bliss" and passion only pain. Although the final question invites a negative answer – "no one" – the sonnet's emotional logic insists on another possibility. The reader feels little doubt that the poem's speaker would in fact choose passion over dullness, however strongly she declares that reason must lead to another decision.

One implicit justification for the choice of passion depends on the sonnet's imagery, its association of individual female feeling with the powers of the cosmos. Moreover, the poet employs language with positive associations – "the feeling heart," "the fine affections of the soul," even "a keener sense" – in connection with love, and the traditionally negative nouns, "coldness" and "dullness," for the alternative. The sonnet demonstrates that pain flows from passion; it does not at all show that bliss derives from coldness. The alternative to feeling is lack of feeling: impossible to imagine as a source of bliss. In short, the sonnet implies two contradictory arguments: one that celebrates, another that denigrates love. In the guise of recommending coldness over passion, it eloquently conveys the divided feelings that constitute a central source of Sappho's suffering.

A final example of Robinson's capacity to convey paradoxical complexities of feeling is Sonnet 37, in which the speaker imagines her death. The opening quatrain in its physical specificity convincingly suggests at least a half-longing for death, as Sappho contemplates her suffering and the alternative of peace:

> When, in the gloomy mansion of the dead,
>> This with'ring heart, this faded form shall sleep:
>> When these fond eyes, at length shall cease to weep,
> And earth's cold lap receive this fev'rish head . . .
>
> (1–4)

The sonnet continues, however, in a more fanciful mode, imagining other poets weeping for the dead woman and Envy himself shedding a tear. Then the speaker dreams of her ghost as happy, smiling at her freedom from mortal care. "My breast shall bathe in endless rapture" in the afterlife, she writes (12), because she will no longer be doomed as a victim of love. The concluding couplet, however, abruptly reverses the poem's logic: "Ah! no! my restless shade would still deplore, / Nor taste that bliss, which Phaon did not share" (13–14).

In the light of those final lines, the import of the twelve lines preceding them changes sharply. The sonnet's language is formal, traditional, and distanced; until the last couplet, the poem may impress one as primarily a rhetorical exercise. The exclamatory conclusion, however, reveals that exercise as an effort to distance intolerable feeling. Its new suggestion about the nature of Sappho's imagined ghost defines the

intolerable pain of a love equally desperate in the beloved's presence
or absence. Like the other sonnets in the sequence, this one insists that
emotion is never simple or single.

Robinson's final volume, *Lyrical Tales*, published in the year of her
death and containing verse presumably written in the century's
concluding years, conveys the same message by multiple narrative
and lyrical devices. Varied in form, subject, and technique, the tales
venture far afield. Sometimes, as in *The Horrors of Anarchy*, they rely
on the elaborate personifications characteristic of verse from much
earlier in the century. Often, they make every effort to arouse the
reader's pity, occasionally for members of groups not often accorded
sympathy in earlier times: a poor soldier from India, say, or a monk.
On occasion, Robinson works in complicated ways to generate complicated emotions.

*The Fugitive* is a case in point. "Oft have I seen yon solitary man," it
begins (1), introducing a detailed description from the point of view
of an onlooker trying to fathom the man's situation from his appearance. "What is He?" that onlooker asks (30), and why does he appear
to have nothing to do, acting "like a truant boy" (33) as he loiters near
the glen. Predictably, the observer moves on to speculation: the tear
in the solitary man's eye seems to say that the world is to him a desert.
"Is it so?" the speaker inquires, continuing,

> Poor traveller! Oh tell me, tell me all –
> For I, like thee, am but a Fugitive
> An alien from delight, in this dark scene!
> (34–36)

The speaker's identification with the solitary, unhappy man may
recall poetic moves by Robinson's contemporary, Charlotte Smith, but
Robinson goes beyond the moment of self-pity to reflect more pene-
tratingly on the man's situation and its implications.

She does not, however, go beyond the implications of "Oh tell me,
tell me all." The need to have those encountered reveal, by language
or by interpreted experience, the gist of their stories animates all the
lyrical tales. The poet tacitly disclaims invention in her narratives. Instead
of inventing, she interprets, and she believes that everything is
interpretable. She speaks of "The fever, throbbing in the tyrant's veins
/ In quick, strong language" (66–67): even the fever tells a story (of

mortality). She looks more closely at the features of the solitary man and understands all:

> And, now I mark thy features, I behold
> The cause of thy complaining. Thou art here
> A persecuted exile!
>
> (37–39)

Moreover, she knows – from looking at him – what kind of exile: a priest, torn from his kindred, and those kindred massacred.

Unlike Charlotte Smith reflecting on the situation of exiled priests, Robinson does not comment at all on the fugitive's religious position or its relation to English tradition. Instead, in an unexpected move, she declares the priest just like everyone else. God is always with him. Moreover, everyone suffers; the most successful, the poem's examples suggest, are likely to suffer most. The poem concludes with religious uplift:

> Exiled Man!
> Be cheerful! Thou art not a fugitive!
> All are thy kindred – all thy brothers, here –
> The hoping – trembling Creatures – of one GOD!
>
> (74–77)

The dashes, presumably intended to render the discontinuities of intense feeling, emphasize the emotional importance of this resolution. A poem that has begun with the exiled man as object of an observer's gaze and interpretation has moved toward an orthodox eighteenth-century kind of sympathy – imaginative identification with the victim's feeling – but then beyond that to a deeper realization: that labels, categories of separation (fugitive, exile, priest) only cut off awareness of common humanity. The adjectives of the final line have special weight, implying that common humanity means common vulnerability, not only to the vicissitudes of fortune specified earlier, but also to the uncertainties inherent in the mortal condition.

In the tales Robinson experiments with a variety of tones, meters, and themes. She tells comic stories and sad ones, long drawn-out narratives and economical vignettes, even a ghost story (*The Haunted Beach*) that makes skillful use of repetition to generate a haunting atmosphere.

Like Wordsworth, she interests herself in the lives of the poor. Like Collins, although by different means, she explores emotional possibility. Like Gray, she draws on the ballad tradition, though her retellings of ballad sound very different from Gray's. She freely employs familiar eighteenth-century diction and artificial syntactical patterns, while reaching for new subject matter. In short, she establishes herself as a transitional figure of impressive range.

Her younger contemporary, William Cowper, likewise looks before and after and writes of many subjects in many literary modes. In an earlier chapter, we glimpsed the complexity of his moral prohibitions and recommendations in *The Task*, his great long poem. That poem comprises a compendium of eighteenth-century attitudes and poetic techniques – as well as a prophecy of what lay ahead. Moreover, Cowper wrote many shorter works in which he also explored varying poetic possibilities. Like Robinson, he exemplifies his period's imaginative fertility.

The religious and moral purpose of *The Task* informs the poem's many didactic sequences, which often suggest an attitude toward poetry's function more commonplace earlier in the century. A powerful sense of that purpose does not, however, prevent Cowper from paying close attention to the world around him. His sensitivity to detail makes him a brilliant painter of landscape and of botanical minutiae, notably in the poem's well-known sequences about flowers and trees. It also emerges in frequent accounts of animals.

> Drawn from his refuge in some lonely elm
> That age or injury has hollow'd deep,
> Where, on his bed of wool and matted leaves,
> He has outslept the winter, ventures forth
> To frisk awhile, and bask in the warm sun,
> The squirrel, flippant, pert, and full of play:
> He sees me, and at once, swift as a bird,
> Ascends the neighb'ring beech; there whisks his brush,
> And perks his ears, and stamps and cries aloud,
> With all the prettiness of feign'd alarm,
> And anger insignificantly fierce.
>
> (6: 310–20)

The elaborate syntactical inversion, suspending the revelation of the sentence's subject for six lines, is not unusual for Cowper, who often uses it as a device to focus attention on action rather than actor. Indeed, he shows himself vividly aware of all a squirrel's actions: his immediate playfulness, his alternative basking in the warm sun, and his seeking of refuge in the carefully described nest within a hollow tree. The watcher, conscious of his own effect on what he sees, reveals his affection for the objects of his observation – not only the squirrel but also, in the same sequence, a hare and a stock-dove.

The detail itself provides pleasure, partly because of the palpable pleasure the poet takes in recalling and recording it. Wordsworth admired Cowper's rendition of the natural world, as have many others before and after him: Cowper was widely read throughout the nineteenth century. He conveys a sense of wonder at the riches of nature and the riches of language available to describe them:

> Laburnum, rich
> In streaming gold; syringa, iv'ry pure;
> The scentless and the scented rose; this red
> And of an humbler growth, the other tall,
> And throwing up into the darkest gloom
> Of neighb'ring cypress, or more sable yew,
> Her silver globes, light as the foamy surf
> That the wind severs from the broken wave . . .
>
> (6: 149–56)

The poet constructs an elaborate sequence of contrasts, even within eight lines: linguistic contrasts, between the sonorousness of *Laburnum* and *syringa* and the simplicity of *rose*; contrast between the scented and the scentless rose, between the heaviness of cypress or yew and the lightness of the rose's "silver globes," between the tall flower and the short one, between the red and the white. He thus evokes nature's order even in a scene of wild profusion, flower after flower for thirty lines.

Neither the account of the squirrel nor that of the flowers lacks moral weight. The speaker concludes, after describing the squirrel, that anyone "not pleas'd / With sight of animals enjoying life" (6: 324–25) has a hard heart, devoid of sympathy, and is unfit for human fellowship. About the flowers, he observes that the sequence from winter to spring, with its lavish floral display, comprises nature's lecture to man on "heav'nly truth" (6: 183), her demonstration that a soul lives and works in all things, "and that soul is God" (184). In other words, Cowper sanctions the pleasure of nature: to enjoy the spectacle before us testifies to our sympathy and our faith.

The poet's concept of the human task (discussed briefly in Chapter 11) involves self-awareness. His most inclusive formulation of the nature of that task specifies it as "the service of mankind" (3: 372). Such service, however, demands self-knowledge first of all:

> He that attends to his interior self,
> That has a heart, and keeps it; has a mind
> That hungers, and supplies it; and who seeks
> A social, not a dissipated life;
> Has business; feels himself engag'd t' achieve
> No unimportant, though a silent, task.
>
> (3: 373–78)

*The Task* serves as a demonstration of how the mind can be supplied, the heart kept pure, and the social life constructed so as to avoid corruption. It testifies to the wonder of the world and to the mind's capacity for discrimination.

Among Cowper's other works, the *Olney Hymns* have probably achieved the highest level of consistent popularity. Perhaps most familiar among them is number 35, *Light Shining Out of Darkness*:

> God moves in a mysterious way,
>   His wonders to perform;
> He plants his footsteps in the sea,
>   And rides upon the storm.
>
>   (1–4)

With a series of images drawn from nature – sea and storm, mines, clouds, flowers – Cowper develops his theme: God is both good and unfathomable. Human beings experience the wrong emotions. They are not in a position to judge or to predict. Moreover, the final stanza points out, they are certain to be wrong if they try to figure out God's purposes from contemplating His work: "GOD is his own interpreter, / And he will make it plain" (23–24). The facts of the poet's biography lend special poignancy to the hymn, with its insistence that interpretation will ultimately come without human effort. Cowper's bouts of insanity were marked by his conviction of his own damnation – based on his elaborate interpretation of unlikely clues. In this, as in other hymns, he seems to talk to himself. That impression contributes to the immediacy and energy that one feels in his verse.

In a hymn written in the first-person singular, *Self-Acquaintance* (number 63), Cowper speaks openly of his internal struggles:

> DEAR LORD, accept a sinful heart,
> 　Which of itself complains
> And mourns, with much and frequent smart,
> 　The evil it contains.
>
> 　　　　　　　　　　(1–4)

Although the dominant diction, here as in the other hymns, relies on a familiar, undemanding vocabulary, the hymn turns on a series of personifications. Legality, discontent, unbelief, and presumption, all imagined as independent entities, work against the sinner's simple acceptance of God. Finally, his thoughts too are conceived as powers independent of himself, eager to roam "In quest of what they love" (18). The poem appears to have set up an impossible dilemma: forces outside the speaker's control dictate his responses. Yet the final stanza resolves all impossibilities:

> Oh, cleanse me in a Saviour's blood,
> 　Transform me by thy pow'r,
> And make me thy belov'd abode,
> 　And let me rove no more.
>
> 　　　　　　　　　　(21–24)

Now the speaker takes responsibility for himself. *Me*, iterated in every line, declares that he no longer sees himself as a concatenation of warring forces. Once he remembers the promise of salvation, he can acknowledge that he himself – "me" – has been roving: he has previously attributed the wandering to those disconnected thoughts. He can now conceive of himself as inhabited by Christ, a stable lodging rather than a waverer.

The emotional power of this, as of most great hymns, derives from its dwelling on common human experience – a quality we saw earlier in Watts's hymn. To feel out of control of our thoughts, unable to do what we think we want to do – surely everyone has gone through such a state. Cowper characteristically uses ordinary aspects of the human condition as a way to contemplate the necessity, by his way of thinking, of God. Ordinary experience and ordinary language help to make faith acceptable and after a fashion comprehensible. In many of the hymns, though, he also introduces the personal, using himself as a type of the human condition, and thus lending extra immediacy to his voice.

Personal or not, the voice of the hymns does not much resemble the characteristic voice of *The Task*, where the poet often thunders his denunciations of individual and national corruption, where he expresses his faith in more complicated terms, and where his elaborated nature descriptions declare his status as an unusually exact and articulate observer. Closer to the tone of *The Task* is another famous, though much shorter, poem, *Yardley Oak*, also written in blank verse and also involving reflection on the natural – which is to say, the divine – order. Yet Cowper strikes a more intimate note here, addressing the ancient oak as a friend, and using contemplation of its great age as a way to think about the mystery of time, which turns a tiny acorn into a giant tree. The poet allows himself to fancy that a deer's hoof softened the earth enough to make it a welcoming receptacle for the acorn. He imagines in detail the process of growth that brought the tree into being. He realizes that people pay attention to the tree only while it is strong and useful, sheltering people and animals from storm. Now, though,

> Thou hast outliv'd
> Thy popularity and art become
> (Unless verse rescue thee awhile) a thing
> Forgotten, as the foliage of thy youth.
> (56–59)

In 184 lines about an ancient, hollowed out tree (the poem remained unfinished), Cowper moves through different moods and tones – melancholy to faintly comic ("I will perform / Myself the oracle, and will discourse / In my own ear such matter as I may"; 141–43). His verse indeed "rescues" the tree to attention, although his parenthetical formulation of that possibility makes it seem doubtful. The kind of attention he demands for the tree is sensuous, reflective, imaginative, philosophic. He sees metaphoric possibilities in the great structure with hollow core and "sincere" (116) root: the tree resembles a kingdom with foundations laid in virtue and wisdom but with a superstructure hollowed out by venality. Less abstractly, he sees the hollow tree as "An huge

throat calling to the clouds for drink" (112). He imagines the past –
the tree's glorious maturity, when its substance might have provided
the sides or deck of an admiral's flagship. That past was happier
than the present: men did not then fell thousands of oaks "to supply
/ The bottomless demands of contest wag'd / For senatorial honours"
(101–03). Spared by the ax, the poet reflects, the tree was left to be
whittled away by time.

Time, the poem insists, is always relative. No matter how short or
how long a lifespan – tree's or man's – it seems short in retrospect. Yet
time endured can be miserable in the passing: "mental and corporeal
ill" (164) afflict humankind. That realization leads Cowper to a
reimagining of Christ as blessed in being spared the arduous process
of mental growth that mortals experience. Yet Christ belonged to history, and changed it: the incomplete poem appears to be on the verge
of discussing the relation between time and history.

Cowper's extraordinary accomplishment here is to discuss matters
of weight in an intimate and often informal tone. He succeeds in developing (in *The Task* as well as in many of the shorter poems) a personal
voice that does not demand personal revelation. Unlike Robinson in
Sappho's voice, and often in her own, he rarely claims intense emotion,
although he often conveys it. Even in his poems of intense despair, he
preserves a dignity of reticence. Thus *The Cast-away*, written the year
before his death, spends most of its sixty-six lines describing in
painful detail the drowning of a sailor who has fallen overboard. The
opening stanza establishes an analogy between the sailor and the
speaker, describing the castaway as "such a destin'd wretch as I" (3),
but the poem does not until line fifty-nine return to the analogy.
Instead, it conveys the speaker's sympathy for the victim, whose ship-
mates attempt to throw him lifesaving materials but know their own
lives depend on their flight, who fights against his destiny, but who
finally, inevitably, sinks.

The last two stanzas recur to the speaker's situation:

> misery still delights to trace
> Its 'semblance in another's case.

> No voice divine the storm allay'd,
>   No light propitious shone;
> When snatch'd from all effectual aid,

> We perish'd, each alone;
> But I beneath a rougher sea,
> And whelm'd in deeper gulphs than he.
>
> (59–66)

Although the statement of the speaker's desperate circumstances could hardly be more emphatic, he acknowledges no affect. The simple factual statement suggests a kind of competition in misery but hints also the numbness of despair. The voice of easy intimacy that marks so many of Cowper's poems gives way at last (he would die during the next year) to the voice of a man locked within himself. For him, no hope is conceivable.

Dryden, in the final year of his life, greeted the new century with hope, even as he assessed the failures of the time immediately past. Cowper, in his psychotic depression, can hardly be taken as representative of his historical moment. But it seems at least symbolically appropriate that instead of, like Dryden, talking about the old age and the new one, he speaks of himself. Poetry openly about the self would become increasingly ubiquitous and increasingly various during the early years of the nineteenth century. The poetic accomplishments of the eighteenth century had opened new possibilities, suggesting directions for lyric as well as for narrative and satiric verse.

William Wordsworth considered himself, and has been considered by many later critics, the spokesman for a new poetic era. *Lyrical Ballads*, published in 1798, a collection of poems by Wordsworth and by his friend Samuel Taylor Coleridge, announced a new attention to the concerns and the language of simple people as well as new modes of imaginative exploration. Only five years earlier, Wordsworth had published a poem entitled *An Evening Walk*. Here are its opening lines:

> Far from my dearest Friend, 'tis mine to rove
> Through bare grey dell, high wood, and pastoral cove;
> Where Derwent rests, and listens to the roar
> That stuns the tremulous cliffs of high Lodore;
> Where peace to Grasmere's lonely island leads,
> To willowy hedge-rows, and to emerald meads . . .
>
> (1–6)

The couplet form, inverted syntax, invocation of resounding proper nouns, adjective–noun combinations, and such locutions as "emerald meads" and "pastoral cove": all have many precedents in the poems we have considered. Wordsworth wrote as an eighteenth-century poet before he wrote as a nineteenth-century one. He was, after all, an eighteenth-century man (born 1770) before he was a nineteenth-century one.

By 1800, he had published *Nutting*. Here is part of its evocation of a human being in nature:

> I saw the sparkling foam,
> And – with my cheek on one of those green stones
> That, fleeced with moss, under the shady trees,
> Lay round me, scattered like a flock of sheep –
> I heard the murmur and the murmuring sound,
> In that sweet mood when pleasure loves to pay
> Tribute to ease; and, of its joy secure,
> The heart luxuriates with indifferent things,
> Wasting its kindliness on stocks and stones,
> And on the vacant air.
>
> (34–43)

Normal sentence structure, relaxed meter, ordinary language: this sounds very different. Wordsworth now interests himself in intricate psychological responses. Immediately after enjoying the described sense of communion with nature, the speaker reports, he violated the scene by pulling down a bough. He exults in the nuts he has gathered, then feels pain, rebuked by the natural world. The freshness of his vision and the precision with which he articulates it mark the beginning of a new kind of nature poetry, informed by the writing of such poets as Cowper and Charlotte Smith, but moving often in unexpected directions.

Wordsworth both drew on and rebelled against his poetic predecessors – as Pope drew on and rebelled against his. The continuum of poetry persists across the centuries, its survivals and its shifts alike compelling.

# Bibliography

## Suggestions for Further Reading

A number of valuable works survey the body of eighteenth-century poetry with special emphasis on its diversity. Margaret Anne Doody, *The Daring Muse: Augustan Poetry Reconsidered* (Cambridge: Cambridge UP, 1985) examines verse from the Restoration to the end of the eighteenth century, repudiating the traditional view that the period's poetry was disciplined to the point of tedium and insisting on the energy and variety of the century's poetic production. Both accessible and wide-ranging, David Fairer, *English Poetry of the Eighteenth Century, 1700–1789* (New York: Longman, 2003) emphasizes his subject's variety and makes a point of integrating little-known poets both into their historical context and into the literary scene. Blanford Parker, *The Triumph of Augustan Poetics* (Cambridge: Cambridge UP, 1998) concentrates on the first half of the century, offering a cogent explanation of the movement from satire to natural description in poetry and examining the hostile reaction to the new mode by Samuel Johnson and others. Eric Rothstein, *Restoration and Eighteenth-Century Poetry, 1660–1780* (Boston: Routledge, 1981) provides an authoritative survey of the period, marked by due skepticism about the false neatness of claims that works of a given time span necessarily have much in common, and marked also by provocative readings of individual texts.

Two collections of essays by multiple contributors provide varied points of view on eighteenth-century literature. Christine Gerrard, ed., *A Companion to Eighteenth-Century Poetry* (Oxford: Blackwell, 2006) includes discussions both of context and of substance, considering poetry's relation to politics and to aesthetic movements as well as to social phenomena, and offering close readings of individual works.

John Sitter, ed., *The Cambridge Companion to Eighteenth-Century Poetry* (Cambridge: Cambridge UP, 2001) contains essays about formal issues, about such matters as the relation of poetry and politics and the nature of publication, and about poetic sub-genres – among other things.

A work of importance is Paula R. Backscheider, *Eighteenth-Century Women Poets and Their Poetry: Inventing Agency, Inventing Genre* (Baltimore: Johns Hopkins UP, 2005), which examines the verse of more than forty female poets and shows in detail how women both utilized and transformed traditional forms. Backscheider's demonstration of women's poetic contributions covers new ground, and her claims implicitly demand rethinking of much received opinion about eighteenth-century poetry.

More specialized in scope are works that consider a single aspect of the period's poetry or a single category of poems. Dustin H. Griffin, *Patriotism and Poetry in Eighteenth-Century Britain* (Cambridge: Cambridge UP, 2002) argues that even poetry often considered to exemplify a retreat into privacy may participate in the lively debate over patriotism that, as this study demonstrates, throve throughout the century in Great Britain. A different perspective on a similar subject emerges in Suvir Kaul, *Poems of Nation, Anthems of Empire: English Verse in the Long Eighteenth Century* (Charlottesville: UP of Virginia, 2000). Kaul focuses on nationalism rather than patriotism, arguing that much English poetry of the late seventeenth and the eighteenth century concerns itself with such matters as the expansion of trade and the control of colonies. Like Griffin, he considers the poetry a form of intervention in public discussion. With a very different perspective, Shaun Irlam, *Elations: The Poetics of Enthusiasm in Eighteenth-Century Britain* (Stanford: Stanford UP, 1999) shows how the religious enthusiasm of the seventeenth century led to increasing emphasis on emotion in the poetry of the eighteenth century. The book considers eighteenth-century aesthetic theory as well as poetic practice. Donna Landry, *The Muses of Resistance: Laboring-Class Women's Poetry in Britain, 1739–1796* (Cambridge: Cambridge UP, 1990), as the title indicates, investigates a previously ignored body of verse, claiming its literary as well as social significance. Patricia Meyer Spacks, *The Poetry of Vision: Five Eighteenth-Century Poets* (Cambridge: Harvard UP, 1967), provides critical readings of Thomson, Collins, Gray, Smart, and Cowper.

Focus on specific poetic sub-genres allows some critics to direct their attention to important aesthetic and social issues. Donald Davie, *The*

*Eighteenth-Century Hymn in England* (Cambridge: Cambridge UP, 1993) treats a variety of hymns, examining them primarily in their poetic rather than their spiritual or social aspects. Two works on the verse epistle show contrasting approaches. William C. Dowling, *The Epistolary Moment: The Poetics of the Eighteenth-Century Verse Epistle* (Princeton: Princeton UP, 1991) concentrates on formal and philosophic problems, calling attention to the "internal audience" of epistles and to the relation between the popularity of this mode and the development of solipsism in the period. Bill Overton, *The Eighteenth-Century British Verse Epistle* (Basingstoke: Palgrave Macmillan, 2007) emphasizes the great variety of the form and the range of poets who employed it, stressing the epistle's popularity among working-class as well as elite writers. Claiming the strong influence of Milton's *Il Penseroso* on eighteenth-century poets, Anne Williams, *Prophetic Strain: The Greater Lyric in the Eighteenth Century* (Chicago: U Chicago P, 1984) argues for according major importance to the lyric mode during the period.

Separate volumes examine many, but not all, of the individual poets considered in the present study. A selective list follows, with critical and biographical works suggested in sequence as their subjects first appear in the present text.

## Chapter 1: How to live: the moral and the social

Among the vast number of critical studies devoted to Alexander Pope, a particularly valuable one is *The Cambridge Companion to Alexander Pope*, ed. Pat Rogers (Cambridge: Cambridge UP, 2007), which contains essays by various scholars covering the full range of Pope's work and locating the poet and his production in historical and cultural context. I. R. F. Gordon, *A Preface to Pope*, 2nd ed. (London: Longman, 1993) provides a valuable overview, as, with fuller literary analysis, does David Fairer, *The Poetry of Alexander Pope* (Harmondsworth: Penguin, 1989). Brean Hammond, *Pope Amongst the Satirists* (Tavistock: Northcote, 2003), intended for the general reader as well as for scholars, deals with some of Pope's important contemporaries as well as with Pope himself. A reprint of a 1955 study, Rebecca P. Parkin, *The Poetic Workmanship of Alexander Pope* (Temecula, CA: Textbook Publishers, 2003) focuses on formal aspects of the poet's verse. The authoritative biography, which also contains critical commentary, is Maynard Mack, *Alexander Pope: A Life* (New York: Norton, 1986).

Although Anne Finch has not yet attracted a great deal of critical attention, she is the subject of one twentieth-century biography. Barbara McGovern, *Anne Finch and Her Poetry: A Critical Biography* (Athens: U Georgia P, 1992) offers analytic accounts of the poet's work as well as a narrative of her life. Ann Messenger, ed., *Gender at Work: Four Women Writers of the Eighteenth Century* (Detroit: Wayne State UP, 1992) includes a useful essay on Finch.

## Chapter 2: Matters of feeling: poetry of emotion

Isaac Watts has been the subject of much commentary, but most work about him focuses on his theological rather than his poetic accomplishment. Donald Davie, in the work on hymns cited above (p. 268), provides a splendid exception to this generalization. A general introduction to Watts is Arthur Paul Davis, *Isaac Watts: His Life and Works* (New York: Dryden Press, 1943).

Jonathan Swift is famous for his prose as well as his poetry, and critical accounts of him characteristically deal with both. A useful introductory volume is R. Jay Stubblefield and Paul J. Degategno, *Critical Companion to Jonathan Swift: A Literary Reference to His Life and Works* (New York: Facts on File, 2006), which includes a capsule biography, an account of influences, and commentary on some specific works. *The Cambridge Companion to Jonathan Swift*, ed. Christopher Fox (Cambridge: Cambridge UP, 2004) contains thirteen essays by various hands that deal with aspects of Swift's work in its immediate social, political, and literary contexts. An earlier collection of essays by several authors is also useful: *Jonathan Swift: A Collection of Critical Essays*, ed. Claude Rawson (Englewood Cliffs, NJ: Prentice-Hall, 1995). The standard biography remains Irvin Ehrenpreis, *Swift: The Man, His Works and the Age* (London: Methuen, 1962), which offers astute literary analysis as well as commanding grasp of Swift in his world.

## Chapter 3: The power of detail: description in verse

The single book-length study of John Dyer is a biography: Ralph M. Williams, *Poet, Painter, and Parson: The Life of John Dyer* (New York: Bookman Associates, 1956). Less neglected is James Thomson, the subject of an excellent critical biography, James Sambrook, *James Thomson (1700–1748): A Life* (Oxford: Clarendon, 1991), which provides critical

readings of the poetry as well as biographical and historical information. *James Thomson: Essays for the Tercentenary*, ed. Richard Terry (Liverpool: Liverpool UP, 2000) offers up-to-date interpretations of Thomson's
work by several essayists.

John Gay has been the subject of more abundant critical attention.
Particularly useful for its placing of the poet in his immediate literary
context is *John Gay and the Scriblerians*, eds. Peter Lewis and Nigel Wood
(London: Vision, 1989), with essays by various hands. Patricia Meyer
Spacks, *John Gay* (New York: Twayne, 1965) offers a critical introduc-
tion to Gay's writing. Two biographies also include critical discussion:
William Henry Irving, *John Gay, Favorite of the Wits* (Durham, NC: Duke
UP, 1940) and David Nokes, *John Gay, A Profession of Friendship* (Oxford:
Oxford UP, 1995).

## Chapter 4: High language and low: the diction of poetry

All except one of the poets treated in this chapter – John Gay, Alexander
Pope, John Philips, and Anne Finch – provided subjects also for previous
chapters and have therefore received earlier bibliographical entries.
The exception, Philips, has not been the subject of any recent critical
or biographical attention.

## Chapter 5: Alexander Pope and Lady Mary Wortley Montagu

Two twentieth-century biographies focus on Lady Mary Wortley
Montagu. Robert Halsband, *The Life of Lady Mary Wortley Montagu*
(Oxford: Clarendon, 1956), emphasized Lady Mary's life rather than
her works. More recently, Isobel Grundy, *Lady Mary Wortley Montagu*
(Oxford: Oxford UP, 1999), supplied critical as well as biographical
insight, with full awareness of the poet's historical context. Marlon Bryan
Ross, *The Contours of Masculine Desire: Romanticism and the Rise of Women's
Poetry* (Oxford: Oxford UP, 1989), considers Lady Mary's poetry in the
context of verse by other women in the eighteenth century.

## Chapter 6: How to live: the place of work

Neither Stephen Duck nor Mary Collier has attracted much commentary since their own time. Duck figures in William J. Christmas, *The
Lab'ring Muses: Work, Writing, and the Social Order in English Plebeian*

*Poetry, 1730–1830* (Newark, DE: U of Delaware P, 2001); Collier has a place in a forthcoming study, Anne Milne, *"Lactilla Tends Her Fav'rite Cow": Ecocritical Readings of Animals and Women in Eighteenth-Century British Labouring-Class Women's Poetry* (Cranbury, NJ: Bucknell UP, 2008).

## Chapter 7: Matters of feeling: forms of the personal

Morris Golden provides a useful introduction to Thomas Gray in *Thomas Gray* (Boston: Twayne, 1988), which contains both biographical information and critical assessment. B. Eugene McCarthy, *Thomas Gray: The Progress of a Poet* (Madison, NJ: Fairleigh Dickinson UP, 1997) likewise provides both biography and criticism. W. B. Hutchings and William Ruddick, ed., *Thomas Gray: Contemporary Essays* (Liverpool: Liverpool UP, 1993) offers multiple points of view on the poet. More specialized are Robert F. Gleckner, *Gray Agonistes: Thomas Gray and Masculine Friendship* (Baltimore: Johns Hopkins UP, 1997) and Suvir Kaul, *Thomas Gray and Literary Authority: A Study in Ideology and Poetics* (Stanford: Stanford UP, 1992), which investigates both the poet's relation to contemporary poetic theory and his ideological commitments. Howard D. Weinbrot and Martin Price, *Context, Influence, and Mid-Eighteenth-Century Poetry: Papers Presented at a Clark Library Seminar* (Los Angeles: W.A. Clark Memorial Library, 1990), contains brief but illuminating essays on Collins as well as Gray.

Works on William Collins alone include Paul S. Sherwin, *Precious Bane: Collins and the Miltonic Legacy* (Austin: U of Texas P, 1977) and Richard Wendorf, *William Collins and Eighteenth-Century English Poetry* (Minneapolis: U of Minnesota P, 1981), which places Collins in the context of his contemporaries.

Edward Young has not attracted recent critical attention. Isabel St. John Bliss, *Edward Young* (Boston: Twayne, 1969), an introduction to the poet and his work; remains a useful general guide. Cecil Vivian Wicker, *Edward Young and the Fear of Death: A Study in Romantic Melancholy* (Albuquerque: U of New Mexico P, 1952), offers a more specialized perspective.

Joseph Warton and Thomas Warton have typically been treated together, as in Edmund Gosse, *Two Pioneers of Romanticism: Joseph and Thomas Warton* (London: British Academy, 1919) and Joan Pittock, *The Ascendancy of Taste: The Achievement of Joseph and Thomas Warton* (London:

Routledge and Kegan Paul, 1973). John A. Vance, *Joseph and Thomas Warton* (Boston: Twayne, 1983), provides a valuable introduction.

Samuel Johnson, even more renowned for his prose than for his poetry, has attracted generations of critics. One of his best twentieth-century interpreters was Donald Johnson Greene, author of an introductory volume in the Twayne series, *Samuel Johnson* (Boston: Twayne, 1989), and editor of *Samuel Johnson: A Collection of Critical Essays* (Englewood Cliffs, NJ: Prentice-Hall, 1965). Both these works (the second including essays of varied authorship) treat many aspects of Johnson, not only his poetry, as does the more recent *Cambridge Companion to Samuel Johnson*, ed. Greg Clingham (Cambridge: Cambridge UP, 1997). Focused specifically on Johnson's poetry are J. P. Hardy, *Reinterpretations: Essays on Poems by Milton, Pope and Johnson* (London: Routledge and Kegan Paul, 1971), and David F. Venturo, *Johnson the Poet: The Poetic Career of Samuel Johnson* (Newark, DE: U of Delaware P, 1999).

Peter Dixon, *Oliver Goldsmith Revisited* (Boston: Twayne, 1991), supplies both biographical and critical insight. For more extensive biographical and historical information, John Ginger, *The Notable Man: The Life and Times of Oliver Goldsmith* (London: Hamilton, 1977), provides a valuable resource. An important study, predominantly critical, is Robert Hazen Hopkins, *The True Genius of Oliver Goldsmith* (Baltimore: Johns Hopkins UP, 1969). Two valuable collections of critical essays by various authors are Harold Bloom, ed., *Oliver Goldsmith* (New York: Chelsea, 1987), and Andrew Swarbrick, ed., *The Art of Oliver Goldsmith* (London: Vision, 1984).

## Chapter 8: Structures of energy, structures of leisure: ode and blank verse

Works on Collins, Gray, and the Wartons appear in the listing for Chapter 7. On the subject of the ode, an important work is Paul H. Fry, *The Poet's Calling in the English Ode* (New Haven: Yale UP, 1980), which treats Gray and Collins among others. On blank verse, see Robert B. Shaw, *Blank Verse: A Guide to its History and Use* (Athens: Ohio UP, 2007).

## Chapter 9: Old poetry, old language: imitation and fraud

Bertram Hylton Davis, *Thomas Percy* (Boston: Twayne, 1981), provides the best introduction to Percy's life and accomplishment. Far more specialized is a detailed account of the preparation of Percy's *Reliques of Ancient English Poetry*: Nick Groom, *The Making of Percy's Reliques* (Oxford: Clarendon, 1999).

William Shenstone has been neglected in recent years. A. R. Humphreys wrote an excellent biography: *William Shenstone: An Eighteenth-Century Portrait* (Cambridge: Cambridge UP, 1937). More critically oriented is Marjorie Williams, *William Shenstone: A Chapter in Eighteenth-Century Taste* (Birmingham: Cornish Brothers, 1935).

The Twayne volume on Macpherson, Paul J. DeGategno, *James Macpherson* (Boston: Twayne, 1989), provides a good starting point for investigation of the poet. Fiona J. Stafford, *The Sublime Savage: A Study of James Macpherson and the Poems of Ossian* (Edinburgh: Edinburgh UP, 1988), offers detailed analysis of Macpherson's poetic accomplishment. Ian Haywood, *The Making of History: A Study of the Literary Forgeries of James Macpherson and Thomas Chatterton* (London: Associated University Presses, 1986), places two poets in useful conjunction with one another.

For Chatterton alone, one must go back to the early twentieth century for a biography: Edward Harry William Meyerstein, *A Life of Thomas Chatterton* (London: Ingpen and Grant, 1930). Donald S. Taylor, *Thomas Chatterton's Art: Experiments in Imagined History* (Princeton: Princeton UP, 1978), is a valuable critical study. Nick Groom, *Thomas Chatterton and Romantic Culture* (London: Macmillan, 1999), contains excellent critical essays.

## Chapter 10: Outliers: Mary Leapor and Christopher Smart

Mary Leapor has been the subject of one full-length study and of two important essays in recent books. Richard Greene, *Mary Leapor: A Study in Eighteenth-Century Women's Poetry* (Oxford: Clarendon, 1993), places Leapor in her immediate and broad social contexts and examines her both as a working-class poet and as a woman poet. Ann Messenger, *Pastoral Tradition and the Female Talent: Studies in Augustan Poetry* (New York: AMS, 2001), cited earlier, includes a long essay on Leapor (as well as one on Anne Finch). Sarah Prescott and David Shuttleton, eds., *Women and Poetry, 1660–1750* (Basingstoke: Palgrave Macmillan, 2003), a collection of essays by various writers, contains essays on Leapor, Finch, and Lady Mary Wortley Montagu, among others. It also includes several essays on more general topics, including one on working-class poetry.

The most recent biography of Christopher Smart, which also provides critical analysis of his work, with emphasis on his religious feeling, is Chris Mounsey, *Christopher Smart: Clown of God* (Lewisburg, PA: Bucknell UP, 2001). Critical studies include Neil Curry, *Christopher Smart* (Tavistock: Northcote House in association with the British Council, 2005), a brief analysis; and Harriet Guest, *A Form of Sound Words: The Religious Poetry of Christopher Smart* (Oxford: Clarendon, 1989). A collection of essays of varied authorship that stress the poet's relation to important intellectual currents of his period is Clement Hawes, ed., *Christopher Smart and the Enlightenment* (New York: St. Martin's, 1999).

## Chapter 11: How to live: poetry and politics

Neil Powell, *George Crabbe: An English Life, 1754–1832* (London: Pimlico, 2004) provides a full life of the poet. Shorter, and combined with critical assessment, is Terence Bareham, *George Crabbe* (New York: Barnes & Noble, 1977). Frank S. Whitehead, *George Crabbe: A Reappraisal* (London: Associated University Presses, 1995) offers a more recent critical view of Crabbe. Also useful is Oliver F. Sigworth, *Nature's Sternest Painter: Five Essays on the Poetry of George Crabbe* (Tucson: U of Arizona P, 1965).

William N. Free, *William Cowper* (New York: Twayne, 1970), offers valuable perspective on Cowper's life and poetry. Critical studies of the poetry include Bill Hutchings, *The Poetry of William Cowper* (London: Croom Helm, 1982); Vincent Newey, *Cowper's Poetry: A Critical Study and Reassessment* (Liverpool, Liverpool UP, 1982); and Conrad Brunström, *William Cowper: Religion, Satire, Society* (Lewisburg, PA: Bucknell UP, 2004).

Individual studies of the late-century woman poets include Dick Wakefield, *Anna Laetitia Barbauld* (London: Centaur, 2001); Betsy Aikin-Sneath Rodgers, *Georgian Chronicle: Mrs. Barbauld and Her Family* (London: Methuen, 1958); Deborah Kennedy, *Helen Maria Williams and the Age of Revolution* (London: Associated University Presses, 2002); and Paul Byrne, *Perdita: The Life of Mary Robinson* (London: HarperCollins, 2004). Judith Pascoe, *Romantic Theatricality: Gender, Poetry, and Spectatorship* (Ithaca, NY: Cornell UP, 1997), uses Mary Robinson, along with William Wordsworth, as a central example in an argument about Romanticism. Also focused on Romanticism is Anne Janowitz, *Women Romantic Poets: Anna Barbauld and Mary Robinson* (Tavistock: Northcote House in association with the British Council, 2004).

## Chapter 12: Matters of feeling: emotion celebrated

Charlotte Smith has attracted more critical attention than have many of her contemporaries. She is the subject of a short biography and critical study: Carrol L. Fry, *Charlotte Smith* (New York: Twayne, 1996), as well as a fuller biography: Loraine Fletcher, *Charlotte Smith: A Critical Biography* (Basingstoke: Macmillan, 1998). Amy Christine Billone, *Little Songs: Women, Silence, and the Nineteenth-Century Sonnet* (Columbus: Ohio State UP, 2007), treats Smith's sonnets in conjunction with those of later woman writers.

Ann Yearsley is discussed in Gary Lenhart, *The Stamp of Class: Reflections on Poetry and Social Class* (Ann Arbor; U of Michigan P, 2006), which also examines the work of Stephen Duck; and in Moira Ferguson, *Eighteenth-Century Women Poets: Nation, Class, and Gender* (Albany: State U of New York P, 1995).

William Lisle Bowles has received no biographical attention or significant critical appraisal in the twentieth or twenty-first century.

## Chapter 13: Narrative and reflection

Goldsmith, Charlotte Smith, and Robinson, the three poets treated in this chapter, have figured also earlier. Bibliographical suggestions for them therefore appear in previous sections.

## Chapter 14: Poetic languages: diction old and new

Robert Burns attracted a great deal of twentieth-century commentary. Among the many books devoted to him, useful biographies include David Daiches, *Robert Burns: The Poet* (Edinburgh: Saltire Society, 1994), and Maurice Lindsay, *Robert Burns: The Man, His Work, the Legend* (London: Hale, 1994). Both biographies also contain discussion of the poetry.

Intended for the beginning reader, George Scott Wilkie, *Understanding Robert Burns: Verse, Explanation and Glossary* (Glasgow: Neil Wilson, 2002) supplies a great deal of useful information. Two multi-authored collections of essays offer varied perspectives on the poet's achievement. Carol McGuirk, ed., *Critical Essays on Robert Burns* (London: Prentice-Hall, 1998) and Kenneth Simpson, ed., *Burns Now* (Edinburgh; Canongate Academic, 1994), both exemplify a range of modern views on a poet who has retained appeal for recent readers.

More specialized are two studies whose titles suggest their orientation: Liam McIlvanney, *Burns the Radical: Poetry and Politics in Late Eighteenth-Century Scotland* (East Linton: Tuckwell, 2002); and Carol McGuirk, *Robert Burns and the Sentimental Era* (Athens: U of Georgia P, 1985), which locates Burns firmly in an important poetic tradition of his period.

## Chapter 15: Mary Robinson and William Cowper

Since both Robinson and Cowper have been treated earlier, suggestions for further reading are likewise in earlier sections.

## Textual Sources

For every poem cited that appears in *Eighteenth-Century Poetry: An Annotated Anthology*, eds. David Fairer and Christine Gerrard (Oxford: Blackwell, 1999), I have used the text printed in that anthology. Other textual sources appear in alphabetical order below.

Blair, Robert. *The Grave. A Poem*. London, 1753.
Bowles, William Lisle. *Sonnets, with Other Poems*. Bath, 1794.
Butler, Samuel. *Hudibras, The First Part*. London, 1664.
Collins, William. *Odes on Several Descriptive and Allegoric Subjects*. London, 1747.
Cowper, William. *Poems*. 2 vols. London, 1786.
Cowper, William. *The Task, A Poem*. London, 1785.
Crabbe, George. *The Village: A Poem*. London, 1783.
Dryden, John. *The Works*. Vol. 16. Ed. Vinton A. Dearing. Berkeley: U of California P, 1996.
Gay, John. *The Shepherd's Week. In Six Pastorals*. London, 1714.
Gay, John. *Trivia: or, The Art of Walking the Streets of London*. 2nd ed. London, 1716.
Gray, Thomas. *Poems*. London, 1768.
Jones, Mary. *Miscellanies in Prose and Verse*. Oxford, 1750.
Jonson, Ben. *Works*. Eds. C. H. Herford, Percy and Evelyn Simpson. Vol. 8. Oxford: Clarendon, 1947.
Leapor, Mary. *Poems Upon Several Occasions*. 2 vols. London, 1751.
Macpherson, James. *Fingal, An Ancient Epic Poem*. London, 1762.
Montagu, Lady Mary Wortley. *Essays and Poems and Simplicity, a Comedy*. Eds. Robert Halsband and Isobel Grundy. Oxford: Clarendon, 1977.

Montagu, Lady Mary Wortley. *Letters of the Right Honourable Lady M—y W—y M—e: Written, During her Travels in Europe, Asia and Africa.* London, 1763.

Pope, Alexander. *Of the Use of Riches. An Epistle to the Right Honorable Allen Lord Bathurst.* London, 1732.

Pope, Alexander. *The Dunciad, in Four Books.* London, 1744.

Pope, Alexander. *The Second Epistle of the Second Book of Horace.* London, 1737.

Pope, Alexander. *The Works of Mr. Alexander Pope.* London, 1717.

Robinson, Mary. *Sappho and Phaon. In a Series of Legitimate Sonnets.* London, 1796.

Robinson, Mary. *The Poetical Works.* 3 vols. London, 1806.

Seward, Anna. *The Poetical Works.* Ed. Walter Scott. 3 vols. Edinburgh, 1810.

Shenstone, William. *Poetical Works.* Vol. 1. London, 1764.

Smart, Christopher. *Hymns for the Amusement of Children.* Philadelphia, 1791.

Smart, Christopher. *The Poetical Works.* Ed. Karina Williamson. Vol. 1. Oxford: Clarendon, 1980.

Smith, Charlotte. *Beachy Head: With Other Poems.* London, 1807.

Smith, Charlotte. *Elegiac Sonnets, and Other Poems.* 8th ed. 2 vols. London, 1797.

Smith, Charlotte. *The Emigrants, A Poem, in Two Books.* London, 1793.

Thomson, James. *The Seasons.* London, 1746.

Thomson, James. *The Works of James Thomson.* Vol. 2. London, 1750.

Warton, Joseph. *Odes on Various Subjects.* London, 1746.

Warton, Thomas. *Poems on Several Occasions.* London, 1748.

Watts, Isaac. *The Psalms of David, Imitated in the Language of the New Testament.* 2nd ed. London, 1719.

Winchilsea, Anne, Countess of. *The Poems.* Ed. Myra Reynolds. Chicago: U of Chicago P, 1903.

Winchilsea, Anne, Countess of. *Miscellany Poems, on Several Occasions.* London, 1713.

Wordsworth, William. *The Poetical Works.* Ed. Thomas Hutchinson. Int. and notes George McLean Harper. New York: Oxford UP, 1933.

Young, Edward. *The Complaint: Or, Night-Thoughts on Life, Death, & Immortality.* London, 1742.

# Index